The World We Desperately Need if Our Problems Are to be Solved

Can the Extinction of Mankind Still Be avoided?

The World We Desperately Need and the frantic End That Awaits Us Otherwise

A Journey Through Real-World Madness at the Very Top and On to a Far Better World

What We Learn from World History, Why the Current System is Not Working and How to Fix It

Ever wondered how to save the planet, and humanity?

Here's how. This is how we could now be living in our world

All the history you know so far: They only tell you about **reality B.**

This book is the first ever to tell you about **reality A**, a more peace and friendship loving world.

Reality B is the world you currently live in, and the picked episode stories that have been chosen to form your primary history lessons and your main understanding of the world are the result of nationalist bodies' efforts to edit which stories get told according solely to their preferences. As **reality B** is completely run and dominated by nationalist forces, operating in country-level institutions with no limits to their poorly judged use of power, every single thing you know about the world is only being broadcasted and taught because it suits your nationalist country. This is because you currently live in a world where evil has, to some extent, won the fight that really matters.

Whenever "the people of an area" seek to be allowed to do things differently, the cruel and insanely powerful nation state, usually but not always, sends in its many evil troops and its infinitely over-funded weapons of mass destruction to kill and destroy. We Proudly Present: A Far Better History and Future for All Mankind. B is for bad, whereas A is for awesome.

Reality A, on the other hand, is the better world, the world we should be in. Here things are a lot closer to the way it ought to have gone, and to the way things should now be. And it's final long-term future will probably be the same as ours, eventually, but not for a very long while yet. **Reality A** is life, in a more civilised form, with 97% of all wars of the past 250 years averted or severely reduced in scale and cut short also in time, as the big problems of the time were solved in other, better ways instead. Prepare to leap through the vortex and enter a superb planet earth of flourishing local and international powers where, in the big political mass-struggles, both sides are simultaneously given real power wins over an acceptable (smaller) realm of areas, where killing the opponent off is made unnecessary, unwise, not an option and impossible and where flare-ups of conflict are prevented from growing into anything horrific.

The history of every other continent and of every town and province is a complicated, convoluted simultaneous existence of many forces for change next to each other, some larger and some smaller. In reality B, the heads of state, government, the legal system, the national press and media, and the order-givers of the military, between them, and quite often all these five powers are somehow acquired by one and the same person, or group, who then decides the outcome of every disagreement in the world, each time, with those in control of the national-level government holding all the cards of power, and the local, regional, town and international level organisations are left having to resort to beg for temporary and tiny handouts, and for the survival of any puny power packages they may have had loaned to them in asymmetric and unkind terms by the all-powerful national government.

The reality of having many countries and many histories in each continent applies in both realities. But in reality B, there is one completely different and completely dominant world-ruling cocky and supreme super power continent: North America, and there is one country in this continent that has been too big to comply with anything for 100 years now, thus totally ruining the planet for all the world's citizens, even as it sometimes tried to help.

In the years 1000 – 1500 North America and the world contained many free societies, tribes, clans, and independent families, albeit some had evil neighbours or roaming troops nearby who may occasionally, and with no prior notice, raid, invade and destroy the food stores, the wealth reserves, the homes and the population at an unexpected moment. Such an evil menace. And as you read on, it will become clear what the response to these should have been.

Overall, it would not be a lie to say that there were hundreds and maybe even thousands of countries co-existing in North America, not always peacefully, where today there are only two, the massive USA and the militarily and film and IT-mega-company lacking much smaller Canada. In those times, decision-making power was walking distance away, with a weekly meeting of village elders there to sort your issues out for you, and the rules were made according to a village's required responses to circumstances, coupled with its limited available resources.

When the first European settlers arrived in the Americas, like the locals at the time were of course apprehensive, uneasy, wary and curious. They had never seen these tools, clothes, jarred food and drink, weapons or ships before. It was obvious that a lot could be gained from letting them set up trading posts here. It's not like the locals could have said to the white folk that "no, sorry, you can only stay for one week on your tourist visa and after that we can stay in touch through video calls, shipped parcels and text chat. That was not an option in the 15th century. And the early settlers won't have looked or felt like much of a threat to the prevailing way of life at the time.

Then, as time goes by, and as the years 1500 – 1800 go by, the number of free countries existing here, in North America, and all over world, dwindles and falls dramatically. Society after society loses its independence, and its ability to make decisions in its own way. Some become minorities within their own land, others become dwindling dialects and accents, destined to disappear. Well, this is certainly true in reality B.

But this is where our two realities go their separate ways: Reality B is characterised overall by firstly a seizing of land from- and a mass displacing of the native population, in all continents, and then by a merging together of so many distinct lands to make one United States, with one military command so heavily armed that no other force could ever stand up to it backing up all the verdicts of its supreme rulers, the supreme court judges and the president. Other nations, empires and oversized countries of insane enormity also undergo this and similar processes, as localities gradually lose all control over what decisions are imposed on them by a country's leaders.

Reality A, meanwhile, starts off with the Iroquois Alliance uniting, simply in order so that each tribal chief helps the others to fight off all outside forces that pose a threat, especially the invading super-armies from Europe, and it later finds ways of expanding its treaty alliance, with new treaties, alliances and partnerships forged with the leaders of many other tribes.

Our story begins in the mud-and-logs long-house near Lake Ontario, in which the noble and wise leaders of the Iroquois Alliance were coming together for the common good, ready to surrender some power, some money and a deep-seated commitment to a new alliance entity, which will be stronger, wiser and better able to deal with issues as they arise than any of these tribal chiefs alone.

In doing so, they ran the risk of creating a new super-nation that could one day be run by one evil tyrant, like we have seen in recent centuries all over the world. But they put one very smart clause in there: Never, over the course of time, no matter what, may any one member ever become any more powerful than any other member.

The structure of this new Iroquois alliance was one with no dominant leader who manages to take over the whole thing, and therefore it is also one with no overall leader, no head of state, head or government or head of the military.

It is written into the first treaty that no one person or grouping will ever have power over the whole alliance, or over any other member tribe's realms. This core element is sacred. Decisions are to be reached collectively, and they are to serve the common good. And all members are to have equal access to funding and to getting their suggestions, ideas and requests heard, and even if the others all reject an idea, it can still be trialled in the idea-raiser's own realm!

While the initial Iroquois Alliance does, sadly, succumb, at times, to the evil temptation to take some actions of hatred against the Algonquin people and against other hostile neighbours, the mistake is later acknowledged, with long rituals of regret, the lesson is learned, and is built into the system, and the alliance grows, in size, maturity and in variety and peace-loving tendencies as the years go by. It eventually becomes known as trans-east, and it inspires similar alliances to form in other parts of the world.

The concept of an alliance to represent all those who may soon otherwise be threatened by the big powers of the world is taught, studied and adopted all over the world. Only by forming firm and solid partnerships can the colonial expansion of the evil tyrants from far away be ceased. It is a big ask, and a long struggle, but eventually the perfect moment of opportunity will arise, when each of the big threatening armies can either be disbanded, sent back, defeated, brought in, or given limited amounts of land where it can flourish, so it will not need to seek war with any alliance member tribes.

1692 is the year when Santa Fe is taken over by the Spanish under a one-sided treaty imposed on the Pueblo Indians by Diego de Vargas. He then crushes a Pueblo revolt in 1696, thus cementing complete control over all land in the region by white settlers acting under the Spanish crown. The wider region is experiencing an imperialist Spain that is not bowing to reason, and is not allowing fragile and peaceful societies to continue living as they choose to. There is universal agreement, even within the Spanish cities, that this is wrong, but stopping the march of the Spanish armies is another thing entirely.

You don't need me to tell you of the horrors of war in reality B, your reality, from the time when the big kings were constantly killing rebellions all over the world while also expanding their empires, to the intensely tragic realities of two world wars, and of an Iraq and Syria that have been comprehensively failed by a badly malfunctioning world system, while the rest of us have fun and cares little about the suffering there.

You don't need me to tell you all the grim details, including the way the Kurdish, the Tatars, the Jews, the Basques, the Tibetans, the Biafrans, the Tutsi, the Crow, the Cherokee, the Algonquins, the Saxons, the Lapps, the Yakutians, the Chechens, the Tamils, the Maya, the Chiapans, the Lithuanians, the Roma, the Armenians, the Palestianians, the Kurdish and so many others besides have been victimised by bigger neighbours throughout history, so enough of reality B. We'll have no more of its unfair and vicious terribleness. The rest of the book from here on in is all about the far better way it all should have gone, could have gone, and might have gone; which is therefore deserving of the name: reality A. B is for bad and A is for aspirational. A comes before B. A is caring and devoted to solving problems early on; B is not.

In reality A, the newly established Wider Council of all Leaders West of the Mississippi makes sure that only one city here and one town there, but never all power over all the land falls into the hands of the Spanish.

Its main priority is to ensure that each member tribe and each member society keeps on flourishing freely, and that it could never lose all power over all of its lands. The many chiefs and leaders only ever fully convene one time in any one place at any one time, which is in November of 1693 in Santa Fe to sign an agreement that brings into life a fully-binding constitution, under which the allocation of power over various swatches of land are subject to a special process that involves all the neighbouring leaders needing to consent too.

All of the tribal leaders of the West at the time accept that it makes sense to join in and to take part in an agreement that protects the independence, integrity and separate powers of each tribe in each area from outside challenges. Unfortunately, the whole thing is now itself at risk of becoming the very next thing the Spanish will overrun and destroy.

But luckily the king of Spain, after being admonished and forced to say so by the pope himself, gives the alliance his backing, and orders the Spanish military to hand over all of its weapons to this new alliance of the West, on the condition that it still be allowed to gradually grow its projects in areas that consent to receiving them. It made the right decision. Rather than be seen and remembered as cruel and as evil, it has instead chosen to be human, and to accept the other people of the west as human too. rather than make a beleaguered alliance send out a distress signal that tells the whole world to be wary of the Spanish, they opt to join in and participate in this Iroquois-inspired alliance of all the people of the west, where further growth and riches, through consensual and not violent means, is still in the cards, much to the delight of the missionaries and of the bishops who have been backing them.

Similarly, in 1697, the newly set up General Council of All Leaders East of the Mississippi, replacing the earlier 'Council of the Iroquis and Other Friends' forms a new collective understanding that goes even further in establishing a blockage in the system that was previously complicit in watching as these coercive Europeans have been trying to take over everything.

There are six groups of people who, in 1697, have decided not to join either of these noble new confederacies: the Comanche, a vicious band or raiding, thieving, cattle-rustling marauders; the Spanish barons of New Mexico, a vicious band or raiding conquistators and land-owning oligarchs who were out to control the entire Western world, the French, a vicious band of trading Jesuits who were rapidly converting everyone to their beliefs, the English, a world empire people who, with their immense debt-funded navy had taken over full control of the East coast, the Atlantic and the Indian Ocean.

They have also managed to grab a hold of all northern lands, at the expense of all other societies, such as the Algonquin and the Inuit, but the time for a part-reversal of this snatching will come. There are also the Jeffersionians, a group of wealthy agricultural merchants who are happy to sit and watch as the British and the French wipe out all the native societies' power and recognition, but when the time is right they are going to rise up and fight off all the Europeans, beginning in Boston, and there is a real danger that they could, one day, take full power over the entire continent and later the world for themselves. And the last of these non-signatories are the fearsome bear-tribe of the Vancouver Island and Puget Sound region, a cheeky bunch of opportunistic cannibal raiders in canoes, who have no regard for the property or the lives of any other tribe in the area.

With so many rogues around, the stage is set for one hell of a conflict, and quite possibly a really big and horrific war, in which these six forces rub up against and invade and slaughter all that is good about the two alliances of native interests, and, let's face it, the internationally reinforced firepower of these six could kill off all resistance. So is this tragic ending coming our way? How can the worst of fates be avoided?

Well, let's not rush to the end just yet. Remember, we have only just seen the first great inter-tribally imposed compromise: The Spanish and the Pueblo both end up with some land where they can practice their activities unhindered, and neither is allowed to destroy the other's integrity, independence and freedom.

This formula is observed to be functioning so well, as the years go by, that similar imposed compromises are decreed, one by one, in each and every turf that, in our reality, is known as a US state or county or a Canadian province or local area. Each of them is subdivided into independent countries where different groups of people can govern the way they wish to, and eventually, each modern-day US county ends up existing as a separate country that is not made to follow any decisions that are imposed upon it from the outside, except when the intervention is necessary to prevent an invasion or a "dump-off" action from happening, or when a new international order is agreed to by all.

What is a "dump-off" action? This is when one area of jurisdiction decides that a group of unwanted people, be they criminals, asylum seekers, disabled folk, ethnic minorities or just poor migrants is to be ejected from its land, which results in them being dumped upon a neighbouring land to deal with. The rulings of the tribal council are clear: Any person who falls foul of the local law can be arrested and sentenced; and any person who has served their sentence, or has been group-banished can indeed be ejected, and each area is allowed to eject up to one hundred unwanted people per year from its land, but when it does so it is compelled to pay for their transport, transition and integration into a multi-ethnic society nearby, including the costs of the move and of housing and schooling them. This is decreed, and this system doth apply across all lands.

The terrible epidemics of smallpox, flu and measles bring immense devastation to the world in bad reality B, leaving the native indigenous forces too weak to resist complete takeover by the ruthless and greedy invaders from Europe. This is not the case in the main story this book tells, (reality A) which does become quite likely and credible, yes really! Once you have found the forces that do exist and that do try to pull us into this better direction, far better than having cooperation treaty ripping up confrontational nationalists in charge.

In reality A, we observe the behaviour of smallpox, flu, measles, cholera, Spanish flu, sars, ebola, covid-19, and other dreadful viruses in a collaborative, scientific, empirical, fact-sharing, experiments-encouraging and lesson-drawing way, and through global alliance bodies that all can gain from. As a result, we shut down all forms of contact that aids the spread of the disease, fully, wisely and comprehensively, thus avoiding the tragedies that come from letting the anti-collaboration nationalists run the world. This is not easy to do, but when flare-ups occur, the local schools and places of work and leisure, along with all forms of visit do have to come under strict new rules to ensure that the illness is locally killed off. Only when the disease is fully dead do we re-open all communal and public spheres of society, and inject funding to help them become bigger and better than ever before.

And this is just one of the kinds of gain. By never letting the nationalists take over in the first place, we also find good new ways of preventing all the wars from happening, we clean up all the pollution, stop global warming, end the illegal drug trade, end human trafficking, slavery and servitude, and prevent all the mafias of the world from lasting longer than one month from the day of their creation.

Hatred, suspicion and hostility, the very food substance of all our nationalists, is the perfect way to keep on starting new wars, keep on letting international agreements breakdown, keep on making people feel trapped in places that are not right for them, and keep on turning migration into a big perceived problem. Fortunately, our trans-regional bodies have a number of positive 'reaching out and embracing others' initiatives that can kill the hatred off forever.

1700: War breaks out between Russia and Sweden, and the war is escalating fast, threatening to cause many deaths over the coming years. Poland, Denmark and Austria spontaneously form a neutral delegation who negotiates between them, and both later agree to pay them in thanks for the intervention. Seeing the mutual benefit, others soon join them.

Whereas the war, now raging all over Southern and Eastern Finland in a tug-of-war between two evil weapons-wielding rogues, continues to cause untold misery, theft and loss of life for 21 years in reality B, a negotiated settlement is imposed in May of 1701 (here in our more civilised world history A), as the neutral delegation does not accept any refusal of its recommendations from either side, and it insists on a full military retreat, accompanied in land-control terms by tiny gradual changes only that must come with a gradual empowering also of the local population.

Not only does this bring to an early end early-on a terrible war, but it also brings into permanent existence a new official international alliance that can formulate the wise man's ideas in the right time and place, thus avoiding most future wars. This third such alliance, after the two peace-loving corporations of false cooperation that now reign over North America, one each side of the Mississippi river, will be known here as trans-eur, though its real full official title will change many times over the coming years, as the new European Union rises and takes a vague but open to all form, allowing each province, district or borough, even if it speaks the Russian language, to opt-in to and opt out of any of the provisions it chooses, with the exception only of the obvious military compact that strictly bars all aggression against other areas.

When they see what the imposed treaty has given them, and what horrors it has avoided, the Swedish king and later the Russian czar also decides to sign their country up and become members. By doing so, both monarchs ensure that their lands will be protected from invasion, and that local areas will gradually receive more of a say in their own affairs, while both monarchies are guaranteed one province each, to govern as they will, for at least 143 years, no matter what.

1710 and 1735: Two gory Russo-Turkish wars are averted by trans-eur stepping in to get the leaders to back down rather than risk letting the many soldiers they have sent to prepare for battle die. The mediators learn what concerns, hopes and requirements has brought these nations to the brink of war, and it sculpts a solution in a careful way, so as to ensure that each problem is satisfactorily solved and that each ruler has a land they can receive the riches of, but with an in-built long-term requirement to turn one area after another, in gradualized stages that nobody can turn down, over to the people who live in them.

By 1712 this new body, called trans-eur, has come to include both Russia and Sweden too, and it is actively working to give localities everywhere unprecedented power over their own destiny. It is also 'forcing the issue' on giving people who speak other languages, such as the Finns, the Latvians, the Armenians, the Tajiks, the Kirgiz, the Tatars, the Chechens, the Ukranians, the Lapps, the Slovenians, the Czechs, the Slovaks, the Catalonians, the Roma, the Welsh, the Basques and others their own independent country at last.

Other similar bodies later pop up in other parts of the world, including all over Asia, Africa, Oceania and Latin America, saving all sorts of groups from persecution and from marginalisation.

The Catholic pope's vicious counter-reformation hunting down and slaughtering of protestant is ended, as newly limited powers prevent these thugs from storming "the places where others choose to live different lives". The Hugenots, Quakers, atheists, nonconformists, Puritans and many others, be they fully separate beliefs or spin-offs from bigger groupings, also receive land where they can set up society in a way they choose, as a result of the autonomy-giving processes now underway, and a gerrymandering system that carves out a separate new utopia for each faction and enclave. Many minority beliefs and many political belief groups manage to secure themselves a utopia, where they can govern, flourish, and set up orders that conform with their views, beliefs, insecurities, worries and aspirations.

In the British Isles, meanwhile, it is, at times, the Catholics who require special protection and it is the protestants who need telling "not to cause problems" in ways that require a military back-up when hate riots erupt. Four cities are allowed to become Catholic-run, and here and many more declare they are open to all beliefs, allowing many minorities to cultivate their utopias at the same time. Some even declare alternative lines of succession to be their king or queen, while also letting the people's councils take on ever more power over the society's affairs, while the monarch gradually becomes more of a tourist attraction and tabloid persona.

On the mainland, the first towns with a sign under the welcome to this city plaque also saying "the pope and his thugs are not welcome here" are villages near Prag, Bern, Hanover, Dresden and Wittenberg, as well as Jutland, Ostpreussen, Norway and Mecklenburg who soon follow suit, as do some of the bigger cities mentioned, and others. It is not that they are out to destroy the Catholics by force, they rather seek discussion about the "right way" to be Christians to be allowed for all, and their influences brings life to many aspirational movements on the Mediterranean and in the upriver valleys.

Many of these new movements also reject the monarch's powers over them, and a variety of constitutions guaranteeing that this town remain free pop up in many cities. There are also those who seek to use the powers of trans-eur to harm or kill off other movements, but this is gradually brought under control by its ever-improving system of rules and respect-guaranteeing trends toward permitting local areas to choose a different route for themselves.

1718: The Misión San Antonio de Valero, later known as The Alamo, is founded in Spanish Texas to undermine French claims in the area. Four days later, the Presidio San Antonio de Béxar is established nearby to protect the new town of San Antonio de Béxar.

Rather than end up with a winner-takes all war over the whole of Texas, or indeed a sequence of evil wars between several interested parties, the Wider Council of all Leaders West of the Mississippi intervenes to make sure that French, Spanish, English, Mexican,

German, Apache, mixed race, and other interests, including a number of religious denominations, are each awarded a number of counties of Texas to turn into their perfect happy paradise, and the Wider Council of all Leaders West of the Mississippi makes sure that no overall government over the whole of Texas is ever established, except for a consensus-only road-improvement and better health partnership project for the whole Texas region, which also serves as a systematic network of supporters of the Wider Council of all Leaders West of the Mississippi.

When they realise that they are being dictated to by an entity that they have no input into, whereas joining it would give them a say, new rights, funding, friendships and protection, most of the leaders of the Texas, Missouri, Louisiana and Ohio French, Spanish and English communities decide to join these alliances.

This action is not intended as a surrender. Rather, it is a joining in that helps to use the Wider Council of all Leaders West of the Mississippi (also known as the trans-west) and its Eastern equivalent as a force to protect what lands they have recently established control over from ever being seized off them, disputed or destroyed, while also allowing them privileged access into the upcoming discussions on how to respond to various big problems and situations. It gives them a say, and a chance to influence the overall verdict.

A very special voting system is established, under which the 12 largest native tribal populations of Western North America each have one vote in all issues requiring a ruling to be made, while five other groups of people are picked in a special lottery of those groups deemed eligible to have a temporary vote for a three-year period in the 17-seat assembly of the west, with its rotating presidency that ensures that each delegation has its turn to raise ideas and suggestions for discussion that sometimes end up receiving ratification. A location in Utah's Salt Lake area is chosen as the new permanent venue where the delegates representing all these nations can reside and meet up.

This joining in trend by white people into alliances that were originally intended to protect every first nation people's powers from takeover by whites, rapidly spreading and now occurring all over the west, is not at all underway in the East. Here, life is unfolding in a less utopian and more close to reality B kind of way. In fact, it looks, in the 1720s, like an act of mass atrocities is about to kill all cooperation off.

The combined English, Portuguese and Dutch fleet is contemplating an invasion of the meeting place and a mass slaughter of all who reside there. If this goes ahead, it would be a sad date in human history, a tragic loss of innocent human life, and it might set all hopes of a good friendly mutually respectful future for all people back by a thousand years, or more.

This planned raid, on the Ohio river, does occur in 1738, with five ships full of foreign troops storming the place where the peaceful Eastern Alliance Council meets. But fortunately it happens on a date that is two days after the delegates have agreed to disband for the year, to reconvene with new ideas and with new compromise solutions four months later, and so while the buildings are completely and tragically destroyed and burned down, it fortunately does not cause any loss of life. And it does not spell the end of the alliance, as the French fortresses are made available as a temporary new host for the alliance council trans-east until a new and more lavish council chamber for all can be constructed, using funds loaned to it by trans-west, trans-eur and a group of thus persuaded banks.

A similar but less canon-backed raid is suffered by the Wider Council of all Leaders West of the Mississippi, as the Comanche, mostly interested in stealing all the whisky, guns and cattle they can makes an evening mass raid on Salt Lake City.

The main outcome of this is that the Wider Council of all Leaders West of the Mississippi, over the coming years, decides it has no choice but to build a super army big enough not only to protect the city where it has its base, but also strong enough to track the Comanche down and to make them forego their raiding ways forever more, or face a devastating defeat.

In the East, the General Council of All Leaders East of the Mississippi (also known as the trans-east) is not able to tell the British anything about what they are or are not allowed to do in the Eastern coastal areas. How could it challenge such a powerful naval empire? And its powers are limited also in Ohio Valley, Illinois, Louisiana, Michigan, Quebec, and in the Misssippi Valley areas, where the French still call the shots in the 18th century and beyond, so it acts as an alliance of the marginalised, who put amazing amounts of time and effort into helping each other out, in spite of their many language, cultural and other differences, while all of their powers remain under threat from enemy attack. As a result, the great ejection of all Creek, Cherokee and Floridian tribes from their native lands in the South East goes ahead in the year 1838.

But this "Trail of Tears" does not have quite such a catastrophic ending, as the

Wider Council of all Leaders West of the Mississippi (trans-west), seeing the hard-done-by and victimised neighbours coming their

way, does agree to take in all the displaced
Cherokee, <u>Creek</u>, <u>Chickasaw</u>, <u>Choctaw</u>, and <u>Seminole</u>, and it gives
each tribe a fair amount of fertile land, settling-in-time food and
sovereign space in the
Nebraska/Kansas/Utah/Oklahoma/Colorado/Wyoming area, tucked
in between the other tribes who were already there. Here, the
languages, customs, stories, ways, lifestyles, wisdoms and ancient
power-structures of these proud Eastern tribes can and do live on
forever more. And a return to the South East, with full power over
some of the land there, might one day, eventually, become possible
too.

The nation of England has been undergoing some big
transformations too: starting in 1215, with the magna carta, there has
been a specific trend toward letting a larger number of people take
part in a shared governing of the British Empire, with the two
chamber legislative system launched in 1332, and more recent trends
have bestowed the elected representatives with more power to
introduce new rules, legislation, appointments and budgets than what
the barons, the king and the nobility of England can determine any
longer.

Worried about a complete loss of wealth and power, the king, the
barons and the nobility of England have set up a 'trans-brit' in
response to other bodies that exist to ensure that powers cannot be
too swiftly or violently lost through military manoeuvres, and this
new trans-continental empire-wide body to safeguard the powers and
the freedoms of all who have any wealth of power to lose has
decided to create a number of "little fiefdoms" such as Windsor,
Kensington, Northwest Norfolk (for Sandringham), Buckingham
Palace (London) and Hampton Court (Surrey), where the wealth and
power of leading noble families is guaranteed for 400 years, no
matter what happens "out there" in the main free "always up for
grabs" tumultuous country of England.

A similar realm of safe rulership is established in Versailles, and the
Swedish, Russian, Spanish, Dutch, Austrian, Bavarian, Belgian,
Danish, Württembergian, Prussian, Thüringian, Polish, Hessen,
Romanian, Greek, Norwegian, Portuguese, Persian, and other kings
are all given their own 300-year one-town dominions that they can
always keep on governing and ruling over, no matter what powers
the bourgeoisie may end up grabbing in the main cities and
provinces of Europe over the tumultuous coming years.

The national elections in Great Britain in 1738 brings about a drastic
change of government in London, and with it an abrupt end of the
war between GB and trans-east, as the new leaders are a peace-
making bunch who understand the many mutual benefits of

cooperation. They also value the chance to pull the ships home so they can be used against France, Ireland and Wales in the coming weeks.

1740: Famine in Ireland – trans-brit does a deal with trans-eur to obtain the amounts of food, chefs and recipes needed to rediversify the hard-hit Irish diets, while also setting up a long-term plan of how to pay for this. It also sets up some self-governing regions there, thus ending, in a 35-year gradual transition programme, the British involvement in Ireland forever and reinstating the Irish kingdoms as part of this. The island may end up forever divided by this, but it will never experience "the troubles" as each family is moved into an area where everyone has the same beliefs, and so there is no scope for sectarian clashes, ever.

1754 to 1763: The Seven Year's War coincides with and overlaps with the French and Indian War, during which Great Britain and Prussia, along with many Potomac, Susquehannock, Connecticut Hudson Valley and Appalachian tribes are allied against France and Austria. This war led to the elimination of most of the French-help lands in North America in reality B, and many soldiers died in battle after pointless and vicious mass firepower battles. But in reality A, a special peace deal averts this catastrophe, with trans-east and trans-brit linking together to make sure there is something in it for each faction, and a strong new alliance is born when the French recognise the threats posed by the British early enough in the war that they decide to join up with trans-east to form a united front that refuses to allow any British advances beyond the Appalachians or into Florida, and no access to power, land ownership or the ability to employ for any of those white migrants from the East coast who do make their way westward and into the Ohio Valley area.

In Europe, a new "alliance of all nations" is born when the French and the Spanish decide to join the ever-growing continental alliance for peace, and while it does not have any British participation in this yet, a big new pope-backed body nonetheless emerges that is able to cut short this and many future wars in the continent, by limiting the amount of power-over-lands that can be allowed to change hands, while also giving those with growing power access with less resistance to its one main target mine, city or plain, if the local population there, in a special cash deal, is in agreement with this change.

1759: A Spanish attack on a fortified Indian village along the Red River in what is now Texas is repulsed and defeated by allied Wichita, Comanche, and Tonkawa tribes. This event brings the Wider Council of all Leaders West of the Mississippi in, and hundreds of "Spanish rogues" are declared to be "ejected forevermore and with immediate effect."

Luckily for these Spanish military officers, they only need to slip across into Mexico, where they are offered fantastic high-paying army jobs and noble status, but the whole incident acts as a wake-up call for the Wider Council of all Leaders West of the Mississippi, who swiftly agrees to merge all of its militaries into one, set up a 2% of all local and long-distance trade transactions tax system to help fund its marvellous initiatives, and it ratifies a constitutional statement to reinforce the primary notions it stands for that a) nobody may invade anyone else; b) all acts of violence must be prevented and arrested by trans-west; c) each member society is allowed to rule over its areas freely and without undue interference; and d) the 12 permanent voting members of the council are forever formulated as the Zuni, the Apache, the Kiowans, the Kalapuya, the Sioux, the Navajo, the Uto-Aztecans, the Cherokees, the Blackfoot, the Chippewa, the Choctaw, the Pueblo – no Europeans are allowed to partake in these, other than when their application succeeds in obtaining a three-year term as one of the other five rotating voting member groups of the 17-seat Utah-based epicentre of this body's power.

The world takes note of the successes of the Wider Council of all Leaders West of the Mississippi, and the people of all sorts of regions of the world set up their own copy-cat organisations, in West Africa, in Central Europe, in South America, in South Asia, in Central Asia and Siberia, in what is now Turkey, in South East Asia, in East Africa, in what is now Alaska, the Yukon and Northern BC, in East Asia, in the Caribbean, in the Arab-speaking world, and in what is now Mexico.

But life's path is not always smooth, and the simmering tensions in the East of North America, and between other feuding neighbours elsewhere such as China and Japan, Britain and Argentina, or Greece and Turkey continues to cause the outbreak of battles and sudden takeovers that the alliance movements such as trans-east is sometimes unable to prevent at first.

And so a terrible war breaks out in the 1770s, when the Jeffersonians open fire on the British in Boston, Massachusetts, and the 'spirit of rebellion' spreads into other states as well. A determined joint intervention is made by trans-east, trans-west, trans-brit, and trans-eur, mostly for humanitarian and philosophical-ethical reasons, under which the British are made to retreat out of nine of the 13 colonies they have in North America, long before war true hits most of them "until such time as the people there choose to rejoin the Commonwealth of the United Kingdom."

And so a marvellous compromise is struck and forced to be mutually agreed: in exchange for being able to keep Georgia, North Carolina, Maine and New Hampshire for 75 years each, "as long as there is still 40% support for remaining in with the British" the British reluctantly accept that it does make sense to cut this war short and to let the nine Jeffersonian-led colonies of the East become the United States of America, with George Washington emerging as its first federal president, and with future plebiscites due to determine which states opt to remain in this new union, or leave it to go their own way.

Now Britain's attempts to control colonial trade and to tax the locals in order to pay the costs of their administration are restricted, to persist in only a few areas that are still under its control, such as Georgia, North Carolina, Maine, New Hampshire, Nova Scotia, New Brunswick, Ontario, Manitoba, Newfoundland, Alberta, Jamaica, the Bahamas, Barbados, Belize, India, South Africa, Kenya, Egypt, Nigeria, Scotland, Ireland and others.

A new international government that has powers above those of the British leaders, known as trans-brit, moves in 1771 into a special newly established seat alongside the House of Commons and the House of Lords in London Westminster to oversee the trade, tax and development of all these areas, each of which has a vote in the new law-making body, in which the lords and the main monarch are all gradually but continually given ever more restricted powers.

An effort is underway in 1707 to merge together the Scottish and English parliaments, but trans-brit strikes this change down as an unjustified loss of sovereignty for Scotland, especially while it has not consented to this properly and over successive parliaments; and the shock of the Boston rebellion soon taught the people who run Britain and the empire that trans-brit needs to have a fair number of representatives for all the members of its global empire in it, and so by 1774 it has elected delegates from all of its global dominions, colonies, rajdoms, emirates, sultanates and other acquisitions, and in 1826 it discontinues the House of Commons and the House of Lords, in favour of some newly empowered local council areas, boroughs, islands, oversees provinces and English shires, all of whom enter a 20-year transition path to full independence and nationhood, as a truly devolved government (with usually just five equal voting member factions, whose vote on this body then becomes unequal only through having to be matched up their vote share) is brought in each county and nation.

New parties are given the chance to make it onto these councils, and a gradual process brings the number of voting parties who sit on an average council up to ten (and it won't be the same ten after the next election). While substantial changes require a majority vote here, a clever system also allows the voters to pick a budget plan among the ten parties' suggested budgets, and this plan is to be fully adhered to by year three, with the years before this representing incremental changes in this direction.

In the year 1779 the <u>Comanche</u> Indian leader <u>Cuerno Verde</u> is killed in combat with Spanish forces, who are backed and supported by trans-west, and led by <u>Juan Bautista de Anza</u> in what is now <u>Pueblo County, Colorado</u>. The Comanche had long been a criminal element in the region, invading people's farms and steeling all they could. So it should come as no surprise that trans-west's response to this had to be a military manoeuvre that took full control back, while also removing all weapons and making significant arrests among the defeated Comanche forces. It employed a skilled experienced Spanish unit to do the job for them, under their terms, which required mercy to be shown once the battle is decided, so that the Comanche would settle into their allocated land peacefully and without reprisals. It also dictates a "special system" for the Comanche lands that spreads power much wider, gives out lots of vetoes, and requires "the elders" to form 80% of each leadership council in these years, while all weapons are being removed from the Comanche.

This trend carries on, in the whole region from Sinaloa to Oklahoma, from Arizona to Texas, until, by the year 1788 all raiding units have, at last, been taken out of action, and the three Southeast New Mexico counties that had been set aside as a permanent homeland for the Comanche were occupied by trans-west forces for two years, before gradually being turned over to a new women, the disabled and the elderly led ultra-pacifist Comanche society, who were to rule over the Comanche people, preserving its language, its currency and its customs (apart from the violent ones) for many centuries to come. Once their servitude sentence was served, the old retired Comanche warriors were able to settle back into this society and to receive a heroes' welcome here, amid rituals and ceremonies that lasted for weeks.

The French Revolution (1789): Starting off with the potential to cause thousands or maybe millions of good people's lives to be lost, the Paris Bastille and the Tuilleries are stormed late one night by the peasants, armed and angry, and a new alliance of the peasants and the bourgeoisie (representing the middle and lower classes) takes over in Paris. Swift intervention is very desirable, as both sides have shown a ruthless willingness to kill already and are now hell-bent on destroying each other.

Luckily, a big get-together of trans-eur leaders is in the vicinity at the time, along with the unified forces of many nations assembling for peacekeeping practice. These forces are all suddenly rediverted into swift and urgent action, heading right toward the danger. With neutral negotiators at their fore, a warning is sent out to both sides that this wedge force will be ready to arrest any aggressors, and after a brief argument in both camps about whether or not to fight trans-eur off, a mutual retreat is announced, and so the war is cut short by an imposed compromise deal:

The revolutionaries are allowed to fully take over Lyon, Marseille, Nice, Toulon, St Etienne, Metz, Le Havre, Limoges, Montpelier, St Denis, St Malo and Nantes, along with the portion of Paris that is North of the Seine, and all of Normandy, Provence and Picardy, as long as it adheres to trans-eur's requirements to retreat all of its arms swiftly deep into these designated areas, to allow all of its enemies to go over safely into the areas that are designated for royalist control, and it is to focus purely on setting up a brighter, better tomorrow for the people who live in the cities and regions it has liberated so far, with all other areas allowed to vote into or out of their experimental new way of life over the coming years, beginning with the Languedoc, Lorraine and Bretagne elections all due three to four months from when this was announced.

The upper nobility and the king of France are all safely evacuated to Versailles, apart from two dukes who were killed before the trans-eur intervention began. Versailles, the palace-led town, is given special powers of autonomy over the neighbouring Loire and Bordeaux areas, including Maine, Oléanais, Touraine, Anjou, Poitou, Marche, Saintonge, Aunis and Berry and is kept on as an absolute monarchy, ruled over by a house of 95 noble inherited lords, 31 newly brought in elected representatives of the people and 22 delegates appointed personally by the king to represent the high society and the learnèd of the land he rules over.

Then, after 60 years' time, the system changes, it slowly evolves, over 91 one-year stages and voter determined renewals and new legislatures of the Loire areas, to eventually have only 2 voter-chosen seats representing the nobility, the most learnèd and the king and freely 41 elected seats. With plenty for of won lands for everyone to rule over, and with all factions allowed onto the upcoming ballots, the battles will take the form of campaigning instead, as agreed in significant meetings by all sides, and all areas will be allowed through a 'jury system' to 'change back' extra quickly if they decide that a specific change was not for the good of their area after all. Trans-eur is praised for its brilliant plan, and for bringing peace just when war was nigh.

1792: The Polish-Russian War is prevented long before it could have started, and Russia, totally busted and caught in the act of violating the treaty, is stripped of all trans-Russia government powers beyond each individual city, kray, oblast and sub-republic now making all its decisions on its own, all become self-governing from now on and for ever more. Powers can from now on only ever be temporarily lent to any bigger regional cooperation organisation, and no army will ever be assembled by anyone with a pan-Russian conquest-minded or anti-west ambition ever again.

From now on, the word Russia no longer exists (while the word for the language does of course continue on), much like France and

England, who are also in happy little flourishing pieces. And soon USA, Spain, Germany, and Italy too won't exist as words we would ever have heard in our lives, as a plentitude of much smaller countries is allowed to flourish instead, each going their own different way, allowed to change back and forth between paths taken by others, as there are now lots of smaller totally independent jurisdictions, with nothing more powerful looming above them anymore, apart from the peacekeeping trans-eur forces.

There is no more looming danger of being overruled, suspended or restructured out of existence, no more direct rule from afar, and all military units everywhere are now, in the 1800s and the 1810s, being brought under the full control, auspices, remit and funding of trans-eur, who won't let there be any more threats to any established borders of jurisdiction, lines of succession and appointment, or local leaders anywhere, other than when a local election put a new alliance in locally and hence nationally too in an area of 4,000 to 600,000 inhabitants.

1817: Puget Sound is brought, at last, fully into the law-and-order loving world, as the bear tribe surrenders its last war canoe over to a delegation from trans-west, and agrees to pay full and proper compensation and a handover of the most wanted to the tribes it has been targeting with its evil raids over the last many years. Now there is yet another region of the world that fully supports the plan to gradually and peacefully hand more and more power to the local areas, while also allowing the trans-west partnership to make further progress in its battle to eradicate violence and crime.

Also in 1817: Trans-Turkey becomes the first of many trans-bodies to reduce its involvements, its need to have elected delegates and its bureaucracy down to a really minimal size, opting instead to turn the whole trans-turk organisation into an independent dedicated entity instead, a bit like a regulator, a central bank or a charity. It's work of setting up 71 province nations, some Anatolian, some Ottoman and some Turkish, is now complete, and it has also split the cosmopolitan multi-faith hub Istanbul into six separate cosmopolitan countries, leaving no one clearly biggest, strongest, richest, best-situated or most influential of all under its sphere of coverage, and making opportunities for scores of people to simultaneously have their dreams of becoming a Turkish leader come true, some with secular, some with religious-affiliated legal directions, some seeking internal, others seeking external influences, some embracing modernity quicker than others, some finding room for socialist ideas, others going for a well-regulated land of privately owned possessions concept and some with a closed to migrants border mindset, others self-defining as welcoming and all-embracing.

There is no Ottoman Empire, other than a province of 3,114 people
governed from a palace on a hilltop overlooking the Black Sea coast,
and so there is no war with the Arabs, and no quarrel with the people
of the Balkans or with the Austrians. How could there be, when
there are so many tiny countries? And when none of them has an
independent army command that could be ordered to fight the other.
Coffee will now need to find a non-violent way of finding its way
into Central Europe.

By 1828, A clever constitutional arrangement applies in trans-turk,
in trans-eur, in trans-brit, trans-west, trans-ind, trans-arab, trans-sib
and trans-east areas, which now prevents the use of any military
units from ever invading anywhere, other than when it is the trans-
regional body itself visiting to impose peace, a fine or an arrest, thus
phasing the military out altogether, in favour of a responsive and
caring local police force, able to hire in extra help when needed, and
an independent court system in each new micro-country.

This also means that Cyprus will never be invaded, that Israel will
be split into four separate lands from the start, two with Jewish and
two with Palestinian voters (one striving to be as secular as possible,
the other to be as religious as possible, and all ethnic or sectarian
minorities receive a full vote too, other than the Jew or Palestinian
other who gets only a 7% vote when living in the other's land), and
that any Syrian or Afghan refugees who comes is channelled into
specially funded welcoming societies who can swiftly house,
integrate and give jobs to all, thus allowing the older members of the
workforce to go part-time and to pursue new activities in their lives
as well.

Trans-eur later sets up a similar all-welcome city near Danzig and
another near Calais. It later adds three more, in Lisbon, Sarajevo and
Brussels. Trans-brit sets one up in Essex, eight in Greater London
and one in Hampshire, making all resources go to ensuring that
newcomers get a brilliant choice of career paths to pick between;
trans-east sets one up in NY and one in Florida. Others follow suit
all over the world, giving those who had to leave due to hostility,
war, famine, authoritarianism or corruption able to settle right into a
good life elsewhere, while also being able to write lots of demanding
letters to those who made them leave and to their trans-reg body that
generates hefty fines, especially where improvements are not made
in the following year.

Gay, lesbian and trans-gender people are often victimised by
narrow-minded systems, leaders, societies and institutions,
especially in Asia and Africa, making life there hard to endure, due
to all the harassment. But fortunately all of the above migrants'
welcome destinations plus 43 more in Latin America, the Florida
keys, East Massachusetts, North Island New Zealand, Darwin,
Hamburg, Amsterdam, Manchester, Glasgow, Camden, Sydney,

Lahore, Norfolk and on many of the Caribbean islands are later established as big welcome societies where people with all minority sexual inclinations, as well as people with disabilities are celebrated and worshipped. These areas even reserve all the best jobs just for these special categories of unique and pleasant people, making sure that all are able to truly flourish here.

Napoleon Bonaparte only ever gets to rule over Corsica and, at one point, the town of Perpignan. The firmly defended trans-eur constitution prohibits anyone from ruling over more than one area at once, and trans-eur is key in imposing a peace that prevents any Napoleonic war from breaking out, so when he moves up from Perpignan and succeeds in taking power over the anti-royalist city of Paris North in 1799, this means he has now lost Corsica and the town of Perpignan to other leaders, and no longer has any link to the military command structure either, as this is now fully governed by trans-eur under a 19-vetoes triple-lock system that cannot be taken over by anyone.

His siblings are able to stand as candidates in Corsica and the town of Perpignan, but the constitution never gives them or Napoleon so much power that they can have others rounded up and arrested due to their political affiliation, nor are they able to form a militia of any form. Instead, each of them works to get funding-stream changes through in debate after debate, and then resigns when they stumble upon other prevailing views among other elected delegates that won't allow these places to become hostile to anyone, and when they are fined for suggesting violent action of any form.

When Napolean tries, with union backing, to establish an army for all French-speaking people, he is arrested immediately by trans-eur and is stripped of all his powers, as his evil intentions of harming the people of all French-, German-, Italian-, Czech- and Polish-speaking nations are well known of, and there is no way that trans-eur would stand for it. He nevertheless receives a three-year prison sentence for seeking to end the international peace.

When his prison-sentence ends, he opts to be an author, a baker and a petanque player, never attaining any international fame, never being banished to Elba or to Saint Helena, and never causing a single battle to happen anywhere on earth. The Napoleonic wars never happen, nor do the battles at sea, or the wars of succession, as trans-eur (currently known as the European Community of Peacekeeping Nations) makes sure that the people of each province, region and district stay in charge of their own unique destiny, except for the 238 hectare enduring realm of the king of France, situated in Versailles, which is still on a 60-year pre-transition concession, to be followed by 91-stages of slow and gradual democratisation.

Peace has prevailed again, but this does not mean that life is easy, or that trans-eur ever has a decade without massive looking challenges.

1848 was gearing up to be the year when war in Europe between the monarchies and the people's representatives may have broken out. Fortunately, it was averted by giving both sides some regions they can govern and by giving both sides the opportunity to gradually win more areas over in local elections. It accelerated the trend to have decisions over most cities, villages and towns made by elected local commoners, and for all the monarchs and nobles to be 'left to play' in small separate realms where they still call the shots, and their next generation rules here too, but with each generation witnessing a 15% loss in power, from 100% in the 1st, to 85% in the 2nd, 70% in the third and 55% in the 4th, until eventually, in many centuries' time, the last of the divine right to rule is gone over to the people.

This turns the local elected consultative assembly into a legislature with all the powers, leaving only the palace, its impressive contents and any land that is still personally owned for as long as they can afford to maintain it, while paying all the taxes levied by the legislature, until ultimately the palace is sold off, one room at a time, to the trans-eur backed not-for-profit international trust of parks, who is always in a position to keep the palace grounds beautiful, and to let the people of the world come in and enjoy them.

Then we had a few globally calm years, until, all of a sudden, things got tense again: The US civil war was about to happen in 1886, when suddenly, president Lincoln of Illinois (one of the six west-of-the-Appalacians US states that has recently decided to join the US union) received word that all of his country's ships and many convoys of his goods-carrying vehicles have been impounded by trans-east, with various forms of support from trans-eur and other like-minded bodies. He sweats and grumbles about this, seeking the green light from all the Northern states to press on with his invasion of the South, for which he pulls all of his soldiers back and out of Virginia and the South, knowing he will need federal backing again before sending his troops out. He flat-out ignores this warning sign, thinking he can blast his way to victory.

He obtains federal backing, assembles all his troops and crosses over into hostile land in Virginia, intending to kill all enemy forces they can find there, and issuing orders to carry out what would be the biggest massacre of good innocent people the planet has ever seen. Fortunately, most of the Confederate South's soldiers have been evacuated out to the Bahamas and to Cuba for a month. He carries on, determined to force all the Southern states to surrender to him and to be made to re-enter the US, one way or the other. Then, in the night, a trans-west, trans-brit, trans-carib, trans-eur and trans-east jointly funded special international force succeeds in burning down the Unionist encampment tents so quickly that the men end up fleeing back to the north and leaving their guns behind in the haste.

A plan to invade again, without tents, this time with the intension of occupying the ranches wherever they are at the time is swiftly drawn up, but there are some massive ships from Europe in the bay and in the rivers, all waiving the "stop the war, end the gun fire and GO HOME flag" while also cutting off the supply and communication chain between Lincoln and their home states and replacing it with their own appeals. Lincoln's own government, made up of his vice-president, his chief of staff, the infantry commander and the heads of the two chambers of the federal congressional legislature decide to overthrow Lincoln, have him arrested for warmongering, and to call all the troops home to where they belong, rather than risk seeing all the troops and the south's troops die in pointless battles. The new peace agreement, when it is drawn up, does of course have to contain a plan to free all the slaves, not just in the north but also in the south and on the Caribbean islands, and it has to make it optional for each area in the south, whether they wish to re-join the US or to stay independent.

The permanent north-south split is finalised, and now the Confederacy, containing French, Spanish and English speaking states, plus Apache, German, Seminole, Crow, Misookee, Pawnee, Tennessee and Cherokee speaking independent county lands and many special designated one-denomination free county lands too, from Roanoke to El Paso and from Arlington to Corpus Christi and the "yankee" Northern Union, now containing French, Algonquin, Iroquois, Potomac, German, Dutch and English speaking states, enter a race to join up with- and have good terms with the international community and with their local peace-making body trans-east first.

Before long, both are "fully in" as members of trans-east, which makes their delegates have to sit together and argue about slavery, justice and the best way forward; and most communities opt to be "fully out" of the US and the Confederacy, as Europe offers them far better trading terms when they choose this path, and so does trans-west and trans-carib who all work together to bring about an alliance of the small to replace the big nation state.

Trans-east listens, and it passes a three-year transition requirement law that gradually abolishes slavery in all of North America, while also giving the poor black people who were deprived of their freedoms for so long all sorts of much-needed support in obtaining skills, literacy, jobs and housing. Best of all, back pay is given to all slaves for the past ten years' work, and 98% of the cost of this is recouped from the people who used to own them.

Similar arrangements are soon implemented in all the other continents of the world, where all forms of slavery, serfdom, servitude and concubine-bride systems are phased out. The human rights charters of each trans-regional body all over the world evolves to become equally comprehensive as those of the continents who set them in stone first, and women, children, the infirm, the disabled and many other kinds of minority or vulnerable groups are offered new help, relief, opportunities, the chance to set up schools, bars and hobby groups that are different from the others, and global meetings are set up to work out where on the planet these things still need to be brought in.

Black people living in North America are given a wide array of options, choices and possibilities: 31 counties, most of whom are in Alabama, Maryland, North Carolina, Mississippi, Michigan, Missouri, Georgia New Jersey or Louisiana become 'special free lands with black rule' where only black people will ever be allowed to own land or company shares, cast a full vote (the votes cast by people of other races is only counted with 3% here), or to manage a company and to employ people.

An exception is later added, allowing people of other races to own their own home. Some opt to take financial help with returning to Africa, especially to Liberia, which is launched especially to empower and assist these fine ambitious people; and a narrow majority of the freed former slaves choose to continue to live in white-majority areas, where they will receive education, voting rights, bank accounts, ownership rights and housing, like all others have, though some locations will, with "referendum mandates" continue to opt to have segregation and separation for quite some time to come. This movement is largely about keeping "places where people can speak their mind freely" and making it less likely that a black man seduces a white woman. If such a black and white love couple does form in one of these right-wing segregationist counties, it tends to learn, quite soon, that it is best to move to another county, where nothing about them being a couple is frowned upon. This is not the main-stream centrist utopia most people would have craved, but it is the pluralist future that lets left-wingers, right-wingers and all others have their simultaneous co-existing utopias somewhere, all you have to do is choose the one that is right for you and move in.

The 31 black-rule counties were not 100% black before 1867, and they never will be, but black dominance is soon brought in here, and a system is chosen that will allow all black newcomers to the area immediate access to all the best job interviews. The white land owners and settlers there were not all evil and criminal. So it is with great effort and with trans-east's expert coordination only that the transitional and empowerment ministry, funded with loans from- and governed jointly by trans-east, trans-mex, trans-west, trans-brit, trans-carib, trans-eur, trans-southam and trans-alaskolumbia all get together to offer each resident of these counties that are being redesignated as black-rule countries, enough investment and loan credit to go and buy themselves good-sized parcels of fertile land in other parts of the continent if they choose to move into white-ruled or 'melting pot' regions.

Similar powers are also given to the new black homelands themselves, seeking to build a stable and secure standard of living for all of its citizens, and also for the Native Americans in their homelands that have kept themselves as native-rule first nations' bastions, which are going strong as free countries still now. These Marshall Plan and World Bank initiatives do much to help them all remain in control of their lands, to help bring people out of poverty, and to profit from- and control all the development opportunities that arise in their lands, including the lucrative casino trade, industry, banking, the arts, shipping and mining.

As each community signs up with trans-east, thus winning a lot of stability, friends, funding and long-term recognition of its uniqueness and of its right to continue to self-govern for evermore, there ends up being no need for any form of US or Confederate government anymore. Both bodies find that they have less and less to do on a federal level, as trans-east has taken over with the best programmes that help each community to get things accomplished so well at a thus aided local level that their federal funding and staffing levels can swiftly be cut, and the last member counties all end up opting to unjoin all but the pro-free-trade and pro-human-rights elements of the US and of the confederacy in the end. The US and Confederate governments both realise they have become obsolete, in that they provide nothing differently from what non-member communities now get, and so they have one final congress each, in which a lot of very strong pledges to develop, empower and give rights to the people are propagated, and the end product is a permanent set of statements, pledges and must-not-dos, to which no leaders anywhere would disagree.

They accept that it is now ok to let trans-east replace them, rather than hope some counties voluntarily double-up and pay taxes to both, which kind-of brings about a bigger wider united super country of many very autonomous county and borough communities, ranging from the Rio Grande to Nova Scotia and from the Mississippi river to North America's Atlantic islands. Far better to have a merger of institutions in favour of a fully independent alliance of many self-governing friends than a grim and gory return to war between neighbouring states or a waning agonised slow decline of a now redundant federation.

This leads to a number of new opportunities, including, after a lot of debates and delays, a full removal of all guns, pistols and rifles from all households other than the police, over a 37-year period of unannounced searches of all premises, which can only be achieved with a programme of repeat searches of <u>all</u> properties, for which designated funding has to be found first (and the funding debate takes up the first one third of this 37-year period). This is coordinated with similar programmes underway in South and Central America and in South-, West- and East Africa.

Once finished, the murder and suicide rates have fallen a big hell of a lot, outdoor get-togethers, walks, municipal BBQs and celebrations become something for everyone again. And then, in the 38th and 39th year, further sharp bladed tools, knives and explosives become severely restricted too, bringing about further increases in the general safety of the public.

A new all-may-opt-in menu of other optimistic and progressive initiatives is launched in each continent, allowing every community to take part in all the elements of cooperation, development and progression it wishes to, and it also allows each community to "opt out" of any provision it does not wish to partake in, fund or support. This leads to a fracturing of issues and to trends of mass-join-ups and of mass-leave-froms, with the less expensive initiatives tending to have more member societies participating in them. But it does not lead to any new federal system that would go so far as to dictate a curriculum, a budget, a welfare system, a health system, a judicial system or any other system onto all of its realms. Everything remains opt-in, and once in, a community can usually expect to enjoy a far better standard of living, and a better functioning society, without the loss of any of its own decision-making powers, though conversely there are also times when a society leaves one contractual partnership and finds that it is pleased with the money it has saved.

There are still times, in the 19th and 20th century, when violent family, school bullying, x-partners' or tribal feuds erupt, but trans-west, trans-east, trans-eur, trans-mex, trans-carib, trans-brit, trans-alaskolumbia, trans-eur, trans-southam and other international bodies do increasingly well in stepping in and penalizing the offenders and to protect the victims. When forensics, CCTV and money and cell phone tracking technologies later evolve, crime becomes less and less possible. Rifles, pistols and other weapons are phased out, as the manufacture, sale, purchase and possession of them becomes increasingly impossible worldwide, as unannounced police sweeps keep on finding more weapons (and drugs and other criminal activity), and no hiding place is safe from detection once the consensus-agreed clean-sweep anti-fire-arm trans-regional legislation-backed troops are sent in to take all privateer guns off the irrational public. Hunting with guns also becomes a thing of the past, as does the use of explosives, apart from some specially-approved construction and mining projects.

Alcoholism is an issue all over the world. It is a special issue in some native-American and Aboriginal tribes, and after receiving a united request "to step in and solve this problem" trans-west pioneers a fabulous new system of having no booze available in any of the shops, and the bars only serve one drink per customer, with some locations also going for a seven-way split according to surname to ensure that different people make it to the bars on different days of the week, and the new ID pass system also ensures that nobody ever gets a second drink in the same week, unless he has just walked 15 miles to get to a second bar (thus earning himself or herself a second drink, but just one).

The 1898 Spanish-American war only ever takes place for two days and only in one South East Arizona county plus on the squares outside the legislature in Havannah (Cuba), Manila (Philippines) and San Juan (Puerto Rico) – trans-west, trans-malay and trans-carib swiftly intervene and make sure that no violent invasions can ever determine the future of a country. The Californian-, Mexican- and Florida-led invasions of those cities are all arrested and turned back by brave trans-regional delegations with lots of protective armour. Then, six months later, those same invading delegations are hired in by the trans-regional body to help ensure a swifter transition to local electoral rule, with a systematic sweep of the entire islands and vicinity occurring to help remove all the guns. Each area becomes officially bilingual or trilingual, but with the local Spanish-speaking majority freely able to elect their own leaders.

The Franco-Prussian war of 1871, and all the other wars of the latter end of this century, worldwide, are successfully averted. Neither nation, for example France and Prussia, has an army of its own to throw at the other, with trans-eur sitting firmly on all military resources and weaponry with lock and key, only to be used for peace and cooperation enhancing actions. Also, neither nation has the size and population that would allow it to become a threat to the others, due to the wise way that trans-eur and the other bodies have set the autonomy area boundaries up.

Even the villages a few miles outside Paris, London, Prague, Madrid, Rome or Berlin have no compelling requirement to contribute to any local military fund, other than the 0.02% of GDP requirement imposed on all areas by trans-eur, and apart from some voluntary mutually agreed opt-in waste-management, road-improvement and cultural agreements to help fund improvements in access to the arts, in traffic, in the postal and other navigation, infrastructure and education systems for mutual benefit, none of the villages are ever forced to have leaders in the big city represent them in important international or financial decisions. A local veto allows each village that acts in consensus to go its own way on matters that the wider region is about to go ahead with.

The 0.02% trans-eur tax helps to bring about a lot of initiatives from whom everybody can benefit, including infrastructure, transit, postal, shipping, waste-management, anti-pollution and anti-crime initiatives. It also allows poorer areas to pay only 0.01% for a decade, while also receiving investment to bring in new industries, so as to help raise its standard of living.

The unification of Germany is prevented from ever happening through a clever and concerted intervention by trans-eur, which ensures that 29 kingdoms all gradually convert themselves into democracies of locally based multi-party electoral systems, each with cities that get fully democratic powers early on and palace-dominated villages where a ruling family stays in for a while yet, with each new generation ruler only losing 15% of the power over these realms that his father had. Italy and Spain, too, never form a unified country, though they do have a few opt-in opt-out cooperation agreements going, especially when the time comes when a TV broadcasting service can be launched and then suddenly demand arises to have shared access to a variety of entertainment and update-giving programmes.

The Polish-Prussian border area, the Czech, Russian and Croatian peripheries, and the Balkan-Hungary boundary areas are places with a lot of ethnic clusters, enclaves, Jewish urban ghettos or gypsy encampments, and also some happily flourishing mixed cities. There is a real potential for mistrust growing into violence here, but luckily the decentralisation of power has brought about a world where most cities, provinces and voivodeships are good at keeping both its Slavic and other groups happy. Apart from the language barrier, there is no reason for any hostility here, and a two-words-per-year slow-growth initiative to create a common language for all Europeans (called Latin esperanto, which requires itself to gradually bring in words from all languages) is already underway, alongside some mediation, translation and partnership-building initiatives. So by the end of year one it is already possible to
say *kart* or *reckna,* meaning "menu" and "bill" in every country in mainland Europe, without needing to know the local word for it, and in year two the words for help and thanks are also replaced in every city and village with a new word, *hilf* and *spassiba* that everybody will be using for this everywhere. All publishers make sure that all old words for these are replaced, gradually taking us out of the world of the language barriers.

Occasionally a province gets a hostile new Slavic-patriotic leader, or an anti-Slavic antisemitic nazi who promises to kick the rich minority groups out, or the poor minority groups, or one group in particular, or all of them. And while trans-eur debates whether or not to issue fines or arrests to these hostile people, the principle of independence, free speech and self-governing does allow quite a few of them, ruling without fines and intervention, to force quite a lot of innocent ethnic minority people to get fed up of the harassment, scapegoating, and threatening tones and to move out of their regions, in quite a hurry.

It sometimes takes trans-eur as long as seven years to work out the full scale and cost of what has happened here, and this is when it raises special taxes on the culprit areas for a 20-year period, making them fund the cost for all the displaced and victimised of buying a good new home elsewhere. If anyone is killed, the killer is caught and imprisoned, or enduring efforts are at least made to get the killer. We do not punish a whole community province for the actions of one madman. But when there is a whole group of killings and these are encouraged by a leader, this leader is then taken out and imprisoned, while the cost of moving elsewhere charges are tripled and applied to the location country that failed to prevent this shameful act from happening.

To avoid these triple-charges, most societies really do end up not killing any of the minorities or enemies, and they realise they have to pay to house the people they have thrown out elsewhere, and to let them also sell what homes they leave behind, and as trans-eur would apply a 20% per year interest rate, most such hostile societies end up only evicting a tiny number of people, and giving them the moving money in the form of a two year instalment plan for helping them to buy a new house elsewhere up front. In the end, most Jews, Germans, Slavs, Finns, Hungarians, Borussians, Tatars and gypsy find that only one in a thousand of their ancestors was ever evicted from anywhere, and when they were, trans-eur made sure they were made richer and healthier and not poorer and more run down from this forced eviction victimisation move every time.

The Boer wars are avoided through a clever and gutsy enforced system of land-sharing and of de-scaling of empire that leaves the Boers in charge in many regions and the zulu, sotho, khosa, and other language and tribal affiliation groups in charge in selected areas too, with each on a gradual transition from a monarchy or from a super-president system to a multiparty power-sharing legislative system of some form. Trans-brit has brought new powers of self-governing to all affected areas, while also letting living standards rise through a free trade agreement it has brought in. The massive mines are brought, in a 14-year 84-stage gradual handover plan into the ownership of local health funds, allowing much social progress to be made in each new land of freedom and democracy.

Similar steps are also underway in the lucrative banking, shipping, insurance and media sectors all over the British empire, and hundreds of groups of people in all of the world's continents, including some in the British Isles and many others on each other continent, are celebrating their newly achieved independence being awarded. In South Africa, nine provinces receive nine different gradual handovers of power to the electorate, including one where black voters only ever receive 0.03% of a vote and a bar from holding certain listed jobs in the one province where apartheit will live on forever: in the orange free state. Conversely, there are also three provinces where whites are banned from owning land, other than one modest home if they live in themselves, or company shares and from employing anyone or from holding listed managerial and decision-making jobs.

World War 1 never really happens. In 1914 there is an assassination in Sarajevo of a significantly important next-in-line for the thrown in Austria, a crown prince who was returning home from a Greek holiday. His killing leads to some troop movements from Vienna, Budapest, Belgrade and from Moscow, in the form of police units who are sent to find the culprit and to restore order, but thanks to trans-eur's firm negotiations, in which there is something for everyone, a 35-year transition plan is enacted, at the end of which Bosnia and Serbia both become fully independent, and ruled by delegates of their own choosing, as do North Macedonia, Montenegro and Croatia. The culprits of the assassination, the Black Hand Gang, are tracked down, found, arrested and charged, but all apart from the assassin himself mysteriously vanish two years into their sentence, only to emerge in Omsk, from where their books are published, and where they controversially stand for- and obtain power over the city and its region in free multiparty elections in 1923. The efforts of the Viennese to have all 431 of them extradited, some from Belgrade and some from Omsk fall short of being carried out when trans-sib rules that trans-eur's prosecution team has insufficient evidence to convict most of them, but three of them are handed over and charged for inciting violence and hatred, receiving six year prison terms and fines that are to be paid on their release. The assassin himself receives a 59-year sentence and fines, but this is later changed to 31 years plus fines when a later Vienna high court rules that killing one man may not be treated as more severe than killing another.

The Russian revolution is underway already in the 19th century, with each oblast, republic, kray, region and city determining its own people's assembly, which is at first granted only as a consultative duma. The pace of change from czarist monarchy with serfdom and rule by an aristocracy varies from area to area, as trans-eur, trans-ind and trans-sib insist on a system that gives the five places with the largest percentage of the population signing a petition in support of this particular change by far the swiftest route through confirmatory referendums to a new people's republic way of life, while the other 84 subjects of what in your reality would be the Russian Federation are placed onto four other speeds of change, including other destination options and also including the opportunity to suspend the change altogether if the voters so decide. The remit of trans-eur extends up to the Ural mountains, trans-ind covers Kazakh, Uzbek,

Chechen, Dagestani, Azeri, Georgian and other realms and trans-sib covers the east. All three decide to allow similar referendums to happen, offering the people of each area each possible outcome system, albeit with different voting dates, wordings, campaign funding rules and power-sharing requirements, and many different outcomes are chosen in the end, which leads many people to flee into other areas, where the people are more like-minded.

So 89 areas move in 89 directions, at 89 speeds, with 89 different degrees of extreme idealist or socialist or other ideologies, and each area has its own fate in terms of leadership, power-sharing, measures to prevent the victimisation of those who sought a different path, and with different experts brought in to help implement the change in each area too. The czar is allowed to keep full control over St Petersburg, which is only to diminish by 3% per generation there, allowing for a long reign of the czar over the Baltic port city and its hermitage palaces, while the local voters only gain slow steps toward taking power here. So this city becomes a safe refuge for all sorts of aristocracy, nobility and clergy.

Elsewhere in the Russian-language world each area is up for grabs once every five years in multi-party elections, with election dates spread randomly, and though the various far-left movements, be they leninist, marxist, stalinist, trotzkyist, anarchist, bollshevik or other spin-off movements do particularly well in the elections in the 1910s, 1920s, 1930s and 1940s, winning a majority in 64 of the 89 areas of Russia at their peak, by the 1970s there is not much left of this, as more and more voters have learned some tough lessons and have turned to parties who promise to seek out the path taken in Western Europe and in North America instead.

Seeing that there is a new danger of persecution of communists arising, trans-eur and trans-sib decide to grant the communists a long-term stronghold in Nizhnij Novgorod, a second one in Krasnodar, a third one in Irkutsk, a 4th one in Magnitogorsk and one in Volgograd, the five areas where their votes remain strongest. And so these cities become the place where for a 45-year period only the far-left parties and their many new spin-offs will be allowed on the part of the ballot that elects 75% of the delegates to their legislature, and then this quota will gradually drop off.

In the end, much like the czarists and the French, Spanish, Prussian, Aragonese, Austrian, Sicilian, Belgian, Greek, Danish and English kingdoms before them, so the revolutionary far left parties of the Russian language world (and of France too) all wake up to a new reality, where the centre-right parties tend to win the largest vote-share, globally averaging 48% of the vote and finishing in first place 70% of the time, all over the world, due to the competent, business-like, law-and-order and tradition-respecting reputations they manage to convey, along with by far the biggest funding for their campaigning, along with other press, internet and media editor's influences, though some of this applies only in countries where there is no distribution of tax-funded campaigning resources or evening out budget cap.

The Japanese influence in Korea, Mandshuria, Saipan, Manila, Burma and Vietnam are also short-lived, apart from some superb mutually beneficial trade deals, trans-pac, trans-ind, trans-oc and trans-malay ensure that all hostile moves are avoided by a penalty fines avoiding wise group of leaders in Japan playing a brilliant game of incentives and disincentives set up by trans-pac that is designed to channel all energy into nonviolent and pro-open-to-all partnership pursuits.

This is put to the test in a big, concerted, secret night-time invasion of Korea and Mandshuria, and within days of this, the leaders responsible for this have been removed from the military and imprisoned, and Japan has been replaced by 8 newly and permanently independent regions-become-countries, Kanto, Kansai, Tohoku, Hokkaido, Chubu, Shikoku, Chugoku and Kyushu.

China, India, Indonesia, Australia, Iran, Iraq, Pakistan, Vietnam, the Philippines, Papua New Guinea, Korea, Afghanistan, Syria and Burma are later sent on similar paths, resulting in a large number of much smaller self-governing states and nothing left by 2020 that resembles the reality B countries of these names.

World War 2 in Asia is wholly prevented by this firm but very justified, bold and firm intervention by trans-pac, in the form of a number of Japan-based peoples militias with international leadership, intel and funding, at a pivotal time in world history. The emperor is forced to choose one region in which to have 100% of the power (set to decrease by 19% per generation), and he goes with Kansai, thus setting the scene for the launching of seven new multiparty democracies. Well, Tohoku is 60%-governed by the nobility and the samurai for a 12-year period and Kanto has a 55% 22-year quota to keep the nobility in power here, both of which fade away in the years after this, but other than this, we have full flourishing multi-party democracy in Japan way early, and with no senseless loss of life and certainly no Pearl Harbour, Iwo jima or Hiroshima disasters.

Also, some completely different political parties and dynamics emerge in different Niponese countries, and before long, there are some very different legal and budgetary set-ups too, with each one ensuing that five or six domestic industrial conglomerates keep the economy and the exports going, while in constant competition with each other.

The world government is launched in 1927, linking together all the world's trans-regional bodies in one partnership of supportive and caring friends. This serves to restore order and loan-stability amid some stock market craziness. With its headquarters in Geneva, and with plans to build further headquarters in Vienna, Nairobi, Teheran, Dhaka and Manhattan, it succeeds in linking the many initiatives of trans-west, trans-brit, trans-eur, trans-turk, trans-mex, trans-pac, trans-east, trans-alaskumbia (previously known as trans-alaskolumbia), trans-malay and the 17 other international cooperation groups all under one heading, a new League of Nations. It pledges never to force any of them to do exactly the same as any of the others have done, but at the same time each region pledges to study the others in search of good ideas and best practice solutions.

Now is the time to slowly begin to bring all the world's militaries, apart from those of seventeen small nations (most of them in North America, Africa, Britain, the Caribbean or in East or West Asia) who have not yet decided to join the military partnership agreement of their trans-regional agreement, together, and to apply a process that will eventually merge all armies and militaries into one, with the broad consensus consent of the world population required for this process to start, and with similar consensus required for each use of force against one criminal leader at a time, thereafter.

Also, national governments are rendered obsolete, as each district, county (shire), borough, kreis, department, state or province now has full power over all of its legal, judicial, electoral and financial affairs, apart from the 0.1% of its GDP that each is required to pay to the world government in exchange for a concerted and powerfully successful effort to bring about world peace, to combat all forms of pollution and international crime, including the mafias, the drug cartels and the factors that cause global warming, while also bringing about better coordination in medical, postal, infrastructure, crime-fighting, drug-control, migration and trade-related matters.

Italy, France, Russia, Britain, Germany, Poland, Romania, Turkey, Japan, the US, Canada, Mexico, China, India, Indonesia, Pakistan, Australia, Greece, Italy, Spain, Sudan, Burma, Brazil, Argentina, Colombia, Venezuela, Cuba, Turkey, Israel, Nigeria, Ethiopia, Egypt, Israel, Zimbabwe, South Africa, DRC, Iraq, Syria, Iran, Libya, Vietnam, the Philippines and Spain are all also prevented from ever becoming one large unified country of the size you would know them in your reality (B), with one ruler and one hostile army, or are sent down the path of devolution into smaller self-governing local people's countries who will never be invaded, bullied, threatened, coerced, taxed, governed, or overruled by the people of a large nation state ever again. Instead, a large variety of smaller and proud to be free, different and distinct areas, with many different political philosophies, all simultaneously flourish where these danger-to-others-and-to-internal-groups-too super-countries would otherwise have arisen. It's not a quick and easy task, but it is a very significant and important one. Only when the nation state has been fully replaced with local power and with a peaceful world order can the hostility and mistrust crap that wrecks everything in reality B be put to bed at last.

In some of these countries, it is the modern-day states, regions, states or provinces, in others it is the counties, districts, oblasts, kreise, maakunta, or local government areas that make up this land's local boundaries that then dictates where the boundaries between the big law-setting areas are, with hardly anybody ending up in a country with over three million people in it, though some later grow to have bigger populations, and with most people living in a country with under 200,000 inhabitants instead, where the chance of one day becoming prime minister is so much bigger, where the press is so much more neutral, where no two parties ever become so big that the others are not in contention any more, and where all these smaller but fully independent lands survive freely, proudly and independently within the many charter guarantees that the trans-eur, trans-ind, trans-malay, trans-pac or other tran-region agreements provide.

The balance of power-principle and the rule by the people principle both prevail, and a much bigger plentitude of countries remains fully independent and fully under the protection of trans-eur (and other, similar bodies covering all other parts of the world) instead, allowing all areas to learn from each other's many different interestingly differently democratic approaches, and to try out their own copy-cat efforts, inspired by what they see in other countries, to improve their systems, policies and lives, inspired by what they see happening in the other areas around them.

Russia never gets to be big enough, resourced enough or united enough to meddle in Georgia's, the Ukraine's or in Prag's, Berlin's or Budapest's affairs. Neither does any other country, with peace, cooperation, friendship and a better world replacing the misery of the 20th century. There is still some antisemitism, and some racist, nationalist, antislavist, antielitist, antigermanist, antigypsy, anti-asian, anti-west, anti-Islam anti-shiite and sentiments in some people's narrow minds, somewhere in this big world of ours, but none of these people ever get to impose mass-misery on their targets, as each little country is ruled by coalitions of the well-informed and is also subject to intervention by the interregional bodies whenever anti-minority sentiments and victimisation get out of hand.

By 1924 trans-east has given the power of self-determination to over 600 areas in its East-of-the-Mississippi realm, and so there no longer is a United States, or a Confederate States of America or a Canada either. Each area corresponding to a US county (or NY borough, Louisiana parish or Canadian or Alaska local government census area) now has the full power to choose its own leadership, and the voting systems vary from area to area, but only very few of them are stuck in a malfunctional US-style two-party system, where hostile heinous lies about the main opponent are enough to win an election. Instead, each area's issues are given proper detailed suggested fixes in the debates and in the now-binding election manifestos, and whoever ends up being elected is then bound to follow through and make those promises come true, unless the council votes a change down or adds in its own changes.

The Olympic Games and their many continental qualifiers now play host to delegations from over 2,647 countries, including Merseyside, Basque Country, Cornwall, Bretagne, Corsica, Versaille et Loire, Omsk, the Navajo nation, Mohawkland, Quebec, Aboriginal NW & Inner Australia, Brisbane, Gold Coast, Chiapas, Kurdishland, Chechnya, the Pueblo nation, and many, many others. The medals table is topped by teams from Brooklyn, Dade, LA, Cook (Chicago), South Holland, Kurdishland, Kansai, Queensland, North Island New Zealand, Oslo, Jiangsu, Rheinland, Volgograd, Hertfordshire, St Louis, Wales, London, Sao Paolo, Mexico City, Buda Pest and Central Hungary, Skåne, Ile de France, Quebec, Dnjeprotrovsk, Seoul, Kanto, Buenos Aires, Croatia, Romania, Catalonia, Bavaria, Silesia, Prussia, Glasgow, Jiangsu, Guangdong, Szechuan, Henan and Moscow. Each of these have made the overall summer games medal table top ten in one of the five most recent games, and no one team has topped the table more than twice.

The soccer world cup, like most other teams sport world championships, is made up of the six continental cup winners and two most successful other area teams from the previous world cup held four years ago only, with one of these 8 areas hosting each group of four teams, and a third area, namely one of the two group winners then hosting the final. In many sports there is a two-tier world cup, held over two years. The first assembles the best prospect challenger teams from all continents of the world, and then the winner (or top five) advance to the elite world cup the following year, where the very best teams await the tough challenge that these teams bring.

The clubs game is remarkably similar to what you may know in your reality, though a number of measures have been employed to ensure that the top five clubs never have significantly more money to spend on pinching and signing players than their nearest rivals have. Also, as there is no England and no Spain, we only have 'local international leagues' so there is no long-distance travelling in the many domestic leagues, whereas the UEFA cups do have opponents so far away that a flight is necessary to go there and play them.

The continental countries cups are massive competitions, with each one containing hundreds of (or sometimes over a thousand) participating teams, which reflects how many free society areas there are in our reality. The format of play is generally cut into tiers assembling the (usually) best (20-30% of) teams in one tier and the next lot in another separate tier, etc, over five to ten levels overall, with each team eligible for promotion into the next level up if it wins its tier, whereas the least successful team over the past 10 years is always relegated down a level.

Most middle and lower tier contests operate with four host venues all hosting big knockout tournaments and then the four winners assemble in one of the four areas' main stadium for the championship finale, while the top tier (at least in Europe) tends to host two stages of round robin groups. The first stage has teams allocated to a group in a all-balls-in-one-bowl drawing, so each group in stage one has parity and the second stage assembles teams according to their ranking as at the end of stage one.

Alternatively, some continents operate a system where all opponents are determined in advance, each team has its five nearest neighbours in the rankings as its five opponents, with the bigger host stadium hosting each clash, and points are awarded for winning the game (500), clinching a tie-score draw (200), for the final margin of win in the final score (max 200) and for the opponent's difficulty as determined by the opponent's ranking (max 100 is given to the team playing against the top ranked team), so each team comes out of each game with anything between 00 and 800 points earned overall. There are also variations in the scoring, with most countries now operating a system that gives certain actions, like a penalty missed, a corner kick or free kick conceived or a goal post hit one point, a goal 25, and a variety of best forward-passing points are awarded in each 15-minute segment, with the best passing in the final segment worth the most points.

Returning to the 1940s, Franco only ever gets to rule over his native Galicia, and after upsetting and then turning his riot police into a lethal anti-lefty force he is arrested, put on trial and imprisoned by trans-eur for 15 years, after having only governed for two and a half weeks and already having been responsible for the deaths of 6 protesters. He is then deemed ineligible for political office, and when his efforts to become a judge also fail, he ends up working in a chorizo factory for 11 years and then in a serano ham aging warehouse until retirement, never attaining any fame or notoriety.

Benito Mussolini only ever gets to rule over Romagna, and here too he falls foul of international anti-hatred and anti-violence rules within his first three years, and he resigns the job once a sizeable fine is imposed on him for his excessively confrontational and violent speeches and behaviour. And so he ends up in a rugby club and working on an olive-orchard, and way out of fame and politics. He joins a newspaper there, but he soon quits this too, having been fined again, making him retreat back to his village of Forli, where he is often seen in arguments in the pub, and then running home when the police turn up.

Due to the forced decentralisation of Germany into 29 small kingdoms and 21 bigger electorally democratic kreise and länder, Adolf Hitler only ever gets into power in the state of Bavaria. Other "nazi" leaders emerge in Brandenburg, Styria, Tyrol, Prussia and Württemberg, but none of these ever has an army, navy or air force of its own, as trans-eur has already replaced all country forces with one international pro-peace force.

Trans-eur has also, very wisely, taken all political militias out of action decades ago, and when Hitler uses his office to try to victimise all the Jews of Bavaria, trans-eur and the world government both soon step in to ensure that none of these leaders is able to do any really cruel or violent things to any political grouping or ethnic minority that resides within its realms, imposing fines and final loss of office warnings.

Also, the genuinely rational and freethinking independence and duty to protect all of all the regulators, the police and the media are preserved, thanks to the efforts of trans-eur, thus ensuring that none of the nazis ever get to hurt anyone, other than through their much ignored speeches, and these are also regulated, so that Hitler and Göbbels both end up sentenced to imprisonment for inciting violence, and all their would-be companions are kept away from the confrontational course they might have taken. No Jews are ever expelled, killed or attacked in any way, and all their businesses remain popular, unharmed and successful year after year.

The burning down of the reichstag in Berlin in 1939 by a Dutch student tourist leads to a period of heightened tensions in this fully independent city, but by having a five-seat talking-chamber for the five biggest parties erected in nearby Potsdam within three weeks, trans-eur ensures that the democratic process is never in any kind of doubt, and that none of the participating parties are ever suspended, criminalized or ejected.

The world is appalled with the nazi's rhetoric on its proposed mistreatment of ethnic minorities, and trans-eur decides to fine and to imprison various nazi leaders, thus forcing the movement to become a considerate and consensus-finding movement, with many leaving politics forever, and quite a few moving to other continents, such as Wisconsin, Chile, Yukon, Hungary, Alaska, Minas Gerais, Belarus, and the Orange Free State, where racist apartheit followers can still fit in, be themselves and feel at home. This may read like a victory for the evil, but think about it also from the side of pro-plurality: do we prefer to live in a world where we treat people violently and harassingly for their views, even if they haven't done anyone any real harm? Is it not better to let people move to a place where they can find like-minded people and to avoid all the hostility, victimization and resentment that comes from living in a winner-takes-all world?

The nazis, the bolsheviks, the maoists, the marxists, and the jihadists all soon realise that, in the world they are living in, one town or province at a time, for a five-year legislative term is the most they could ever have law-making power over, and the fines and imprisonment for ethnic cleansing inciting leaders soon leads to a workably moderate pragmatic and coalition-seeking kind of multi-party-system world instead. Only three people ever die in Berlin's brief skirmishes over the burning down of the reichstag, six more die in skirmishes about the arrest of Adolf Hitler, and only 61 people ever die in the great Russian famine, as international loans flood in, allowing the people to import enough food to live on and more forms of assistance are found and offered at the nick of time. Sure, a total utopia would not have anyone die, but come on, this credible and realistic reality is still pretty good, and the people who govern it can all be very proud of themselves.

Part 2 - The day we all died

In reality B, Cuba was allied with the Soviet Union and as such it was conducting military co-operation programmes of various forms. Similarly, Turkey, Egypt, Greece, Israel and Saudi Arabia were allied to the West, and all five were hosting enormous amounts of ballistic missiles, many of them nuclear, in readiness for war against the Soviet Union, if the cold war ever goes hot. Normally you would expect each powerhouse to deal with its allies in a way that suits it, as was the case, and no distant other powerhouse would normally prevent an ally from working in partnership with the main powerhouse that it happens to be allied to. But then along came president John F Kennedy.

US president John F Kennedy not only decided that he was more than quadrupling the number of nuclear rockets he had in Turkey, Egypt, Greece, Israel and Saudi Arabia, in continuation from where the previous US president had set these base expansion plans up, but he also unilaterally decided to suddenly come out and threaten a global nuclear war that will start immediately, right now, and that will probably wipe out more than half, and possibly all of the human on the entire planet. And this response to news that the Soviets were bringing missiles to a missile base in Cuba, yes bringing missiles to a missile base, just like the US was doing just a few miles outside the Soviet Union. "Turn those ships around immediately" he said "or else we're going to shoot you down!" said president John F Kennedy, and the rest of the world, too dependent on his super-country's loans, its trade, its sports, news, movie and communication programmes, stayed silent, neglecting to call this crazy idiot to be taken far away from all the microphones and from the direct phone line to the kremlin that the white house famously had set up.

So this is where, in reality B, the reality you all currently live in died, or should I say almost died, could and probably should have died. JFK had no jurisdiction over Cuba, nor over the seas, and he overstepped the mark and revealed to the world that he is 100% evil for putting all the lives of all the innocent people all over the planet at risk, for placing all of us onto his gambling table and using us all as chips in a game of high-stakes poker. Now the Soviet leaders were no saints. Joseph Stalin, for example, is single-handedly responsible for the death of more innocent civilians than any other world leader in world history. So you wouldn't really want an evil tyrant like him or his equally evil successors to be the only person who can save all of the human and other major mammal lives on the planet, would you? But that's exactly what we had, for real. I'm not making it up. You see now why we do have an urgent and major need to bring about a reality A type evolution really soon? If we don't we're all doomed, completely doomed!!!!

In the year 1969 we got lucky, really really lucky. Not only did the Soviets turn that ship around and abort their plans to erect nuclear missiles in Cuba, ever, but they also set up a series of peace talks with the US that eventually led to the number of nuclear rockets who were at play in the game to a level that is now no longer big enough to eradicate all humans anymore. So good things can come out of bad situations. But please reflect again on what would have happened if the person in the kremlin making the decision decided to resend the shipment containing the nuclear rocket warhead on a later ship, better camouflaged, better hidden from aerial view, deep in the hull of a civilian container ship, and accompanied by a "no, I'm not turning this ship around" statement determination.

What would JFK have done? What would the Soviets have done if they had a Russian version cloned doppelganger of JFK in power at the time. We can't be sure of the precise actions, but the end result is that our grandparents would all be dead and we would never have been born as a result. This is exactly what you can expect in a world where a few huge powerful nationalistic and inward-looking nations have all the power and where the villages, the counties and the rans-regional and global entities have exactly zero power over the major military muscle and have exactly zero power also over the decision-making involving the use of the immensely powerful military tools. It's hard to imagine a scenario where we could be any more doomed than the current reality we live in, other than the world of the Cuban missile crisis of 1969 and the other great conflicts in earth's history. Bring on a better world! And let's hope it comes soon!

Things like nuclear rockets should be subject to a veto from each one of the world's countries plus from many of its regions too. It's insane to give one head of state or one insane general this much power to kill. What could be worse? Our world knows exactly why and how t will come to an end, and these damned nuclear rockets have everything to do with it.

Part 3 - The True Story Of The Great Apocalyse of 2026 - Can the Extinction of Mankind Still Be avoided?

Told from No Less than Five Points of View at Once

In the interest of point of view sharing, fairness and equality, we have opted to alternate frequently between them, so we can keep track of all the goings on, and convey the rash and likely thoughts there will be on this day.

View 1, Keith: "Was it avoidable? Of course it bleedin well was! The yanks fucked up by going in to invade Iran. The Chinese fucked up by accepting a 800 trillion dollar deal to supply Iran with so many nukes, and got found out by the CIA. All three nations leaders missed their chances to back down and to stop shooting down each other's war ships and planes, and as for the 70,000 nuclear rockets, well these should never have been used. When they were fired, we were all fucked over, good and proper. There should never have been any such option. Now we have two days left to live, and then it's game over. For all of us."

View 2, Sara: "I still don't fully believe it. Or I wish I didn't. The shops are closed. The buses aren't running. There are people preparing for war, and people going over the top, already now, in a bid to join or invade and conquer the secret army bunker project on Hayham Hill. It's mad. I'm just glad I at least know that this bunker exists, as this place might give me, if I make it there, some chance of surviving."

View 3, Greg: "None of this makes any sense to me. The world has gone completely mad. I was perfectly happy, and my life was just coming together, and now this happens! My girlfriend has gone god knows where. I guess my only chance of surviving this next week is if I somehow manage to get recognition for being the guy who joined the army, worked his way up in 2 days of madness. And protected the prime minister, a visiting president, the queen's favourite princess, or the head of a global company, and did it so well that I got picked to join him or her in the bunker."

View 4, Ollie: "Life is full of tough decisions, but the toughest one anyone has ever had to make is here with me now: Do I try to fight with the government, Like Greg, or with the local farmer's militia? If I get this one wrong, I'm toast. If I get it right, I may have a slim chance."

View 5, Kate: "Ollie is right. So is Keith. And Sara too. Not sure about Greg, and no idea why he ditched me for this missing girl? We do all talk, you know. We don't know what each other is putting in the diary, except for me. I have privileged access, as I have the job of collating the entries. We do get together to speak, and to sound out each other's thoughts, as we do all live on the same street in Weybridge Abbey. If we can help each other survive the hell that is this terrible apocalypse, we might actually make it."

The voice that knows: The above was in the evening of the day of the missile strikes, nuclear missile strikes! It was the 17th of May 2024, and it was total mass-nuclear-obliteration. Had they used ballistic missiles, the fall-out would have been manageable, but no. The US used up all the nuclear warheads they had been building up to annihilate all the strategic targets in Iran and in China, and both countries gave as good as they got hit, with more strikes taking out more targets all over the US. Everything was taken out. And the nuclear fall-out was now hitting the air currents and spreading all over the planet. The below statements were collected in the morning of the following day:

Keith: "I can see that the sky has changed, the blue sky is gone forever, and I feel my body filling up with crazy levels of radioactivity already. I don't know how much more of this I really even want to witness. If things get ultra-super-painful long-term, I don't wish to be a part of it"

Sara: "Everyone with half a brain understands that the radioactivity will be lethal to all, except maybe if you are in a tightly sealed bunker." But it all happened so suddenly that none of the big new state-of-the-art bunkers are ready yet, and how long will their stocks need to last? "I hear the only bunkers that could contain any humans who might live to have offspring in the distant future will need to be sealed up already today or tomorrow morning, and to remain fully sealed for up for 35 years, due to the radiation levels that are coming our way. I sure hope they have enough supplies!

Greg: "The tellie is no longer showing anything but repeats, and no adverts, no hosts, no news updates, and no commentary. Most radio stations have shut down. Most shops too. The roads are clogged. The lights have stopped working. The police no longer exists, at least not here in Weybridge Abbey. And the papers have come out with one final farewell edition, which I am going to read carefully now, in case there is any kind of clue in there about how to survive, or, if not, how best to go, …"

Ollie: "Seeing as how the government is definitely intending to put long-established VIPs, leaders and their top-ranking life-long career soldiers only into that survival bunker up on Hayham Hill, my only hope now is to get them lot and these farmer militia boys to shoot each other into oblivion, and only if the farmer boys, my lads, win, and decide to include me and keep me in the bunker with them, can I make it. I am off to join the militia, and to do my all to become indispensable for them. Bye"

Kate: I have always loved Ollie, and my dream is to end up in the bunker with him, giving birth to the two babies who will one day repopulate the world, Adam and Eve, with him and me cuddled together for 35 sweet slow loving years …. If the supplies run short, all the others in the bunker will have to die in order so Ollie and I, or maybe, in those final years, just pregnant me alone(?) may live!

The voice that knows: Needless to say, the scene is similar all over the world. People are preparing to go to war in a desperate last-ditch effort to get themselves into a survival bunker, one of the thousands of such bunkers that are now being hastily dug, engineered, constructed and reinforced. Each country has hastily launched some sort of competition or a points system that supposedly gives the top five or ten winners a place in the bunker. The points system has been devised in such a way that people are encouraged and rewarded with crucial points for helping each other out, for getting the backing of other people, and for supporting the government's efforts to transition smoothly into bunker life.

If the points race winners have much hope, these can only go into bunkers that are built and loaded with supplies in time and are then hidden away or defended, and sealed up successfully, and then the troops who got them in may have the final say and trump card when there isn't room for everybody in these bunkers after all.

What none of them knows, is that no bunker on earth is going to be equipped, so quickly, with enough food and water, a safe, hygienic and functioning system of dealing with sewage waste and with enough anti-radiation medicine to survive. Without each of these, all humans will die of the radiation that is soon to be inside them. Something sufficient might have been built if humanity had had more notice, more time, more focus, and more collaboration. But the way it came, no human is going to survive. But not all of the planet's creatures and plants will be lost and extinct, fortunately. There were 17 space rocket missions in 2023 and in 2024 bringing plant seeds to the Jupiter-moon Europa, where melting ice means that abundant life will soon flourish there. A small number of small fury mammals were also sent, in those last three missions (15 to 17), and they will make it, long-term, but we humans won't.

I hate to be the one to tell you this, throwing a spoiler so early on, as none of our five will have much longer to live. Be pre-warned and prepare yourself. Do not build up too much affinity with them, and try not to think about your loves one, your friends, family or pets either, as this may never happen in real life. Not if this collated diary turns out to be fiction.

Well, dear reader, have you guessed yet, which one of these neighbours from Weybridge Abbey will be the last one left? I won't reveal this now, but I can tell you that only one of them has much more than 48 hours left to live at this point, on the 18th of May 2024. This is known for sure. The final human colony to perish, two years in, in March 2025 to be precise will be a Japanese troop cave-dwelling of dwarfs on a small island near Okinawa, who run out of supplies and open the hatch too early for survival to be possible. They knew this was their biggest risk, and that they could not last another week in their bunker with no food left at this point. The last UK colony, dwindling and going a few months before this, on 19th January 2025, is the one containing the specially chosen points-winning TV beauties.

Everyone from the state, military and official offices died knowing that all hope was now invested in these seven girls and one boy. What they did not know was that the bunker, though adequately stocked, was slowly letting the deadly radiation in through the same pipes that were giving them fresh water and taking all their waste away. I hope you can forgive us for throwing the last big reveal in so early. We miniature guinea-capybaras of Europa are not very good at keeping secrets.

We will see what happened to our five noble youngsters shortly. But first …. Let's tend to the great matters concerning the world as a whole …

Luckily the world did not end in the 1960s. And a lot of progress has been made in each decade in reality A, due to the stronger international co-operation groupings and the better power sharing, devolving and delegating protocols. Everywhere you look, a difference was being made to the biggest challenges of the time. The Chinese famine of the 1970s and the Ethiopian famine of the 1980s ends in similar cooperation-based solutions. The 2010s Korean famine too, is cut short by a well-managed relief grants and loans effort that trans-pac and the UN world food programme co-manage.

A global network of aid, loans, and donations sees each of these parts of the world through the worst of it, with special investment also flowing in to rebuild the devastated farms. Less than 30 people ever starve in any of these disasters as a result.

Poland is never invaded, nor is Czechoslovakia, Belgium or Lithuania either. This is because there is no third reich and no red army. Both tyrannies are everted through a wise combination of having an international adjudicator and hostilities regulator and its successful efforts to make sure that no one man or one army ever comes to rule over more than 2 million people anywhere in Europe.

Stalin rises in power in Moscow, and his reign there is brutal and vicious. This is why trans-eur makes sure that each oblast, kray and republic maintains full autonomy to do things in a more human and cooperative way, and that no faction in any area ever has any form of militia, troops, goons or army. He does upset and threaten a lot of people in Moscow, triggering a mass migration out of the city, but much of this is later reversed, when he gets fined eight times by trans-eur for viciousness and for excessively confrontational hostility and when he carries on transgressing and getting worse than ever before, becoming an even bigger threat to people, he is arrested and locked up in an insane asylum, where he catches TB just two weeks later and dies of it. ironically Hitler dies on the same date, and also in an insane asylum, of hepatitis coupled with leprosy.

The Berlin Wall is never built, as trans-eur steps in when Brandenburg leader Erich Honneker's crazily random orders to build the wall are issued, and this, along with a united response from the Berlin, Saxony, Silesian, Czech and also the rest of the Brandenburg authorities telling the Moscovian special advisors to 'piss off' prevents it from ever being built, and from any of these lands ever being occupied.

WW2 (Japan) is averted, as trans-east succeeds in stirring up a rebellion in the Japanese language trans-pac navy element just as Kansai is about to break with the treaties and start invading other

countries. This leads to a trans-pac blockade of Japan, which is left
with no ships at all when the navy vessels make each civilian ship
coming out of port join its ever-growing alliance. Seeing the lunacy
of the manoeuvre, the rest of the Kansai government turns on the
initiator, deposing him and fining him. Then trans-pac steps in to re-
establish control over all units.

The 1948 takeover of China by the communists is a partial action,
with only two provinces overthrown before trans-pac takes over the
process and makes sure that each province gets plenty of options for
who rules it, plenty of time to decide, easy reverse-back clauses,
coalition-forcing legislative systems and a special extra dose of laws
that make all politicians stick to their promises after being voted in.

Cholera, hepatitis, dengue fever and malaria suffer great declines as
the concerted human efforts of trans-ind, trans-arab, trans-eastaf and
trans-pac inflict defeat after defeat on these terrible viruses. They
even manage to declare each of these ailments, Ebola and zika
extinct in 2018, after a long battle with these diseases.

The Communist invasion of Vietnam takes a more peaceful and
gradual form, after trans-pac makes sure the military option is
removed early on. As a result, only 14 of the 81 communes of
Vietnam go for a socialist experiment during the 1960s and 1970s,
and nobody in South Vietnam is having to flee while under fire.

The cold war is not the same, with only fairly small numbers of
Eastern cities and provinces ever voting to try out any Leninist
reforms, and with none of them, apart from Inner and Outer Moscow
opting to enact Stalinist reforms, until the 2004 trend to revive the
socialist utopia that guarantees everybody a job, an income and a
home is reborn in a new form as a home for x-convicts, or as a land
of opportunities for migrants, disabled people with special needs and
the displaced. There is no need for a NATO ever to be formed in
response, as trans-eur's fines and the news broadcasts from other
Russian-speaking areas are enough to make the people of Moscow
see sense, and they oust Stalin and the communists in the very next
elections.

The Cuban-missile crisis is averted by those Russian-made missiles
landing safely in the leftist-controlled area of Havana, Cuba, where
they soon thereafter come under the international multiparty control
of the trans-carib neutral obervers, and by there not being any one
real target anywhere in North America for them to be aimed at, with
Washington DC never coming to house any form of buildings
supreme power, apart from a small trans-east office, which moves
there due to its delightful quiet parks and their black movement and
first nations revering statues, and there is never a white house or a us
supreme court built, as each county-size area is left to govern itself
without any federal meddling.

There is a man on the moon in 1969, but instead of a US flag, the astronaut plants a Mexican flag (representing his own background), a gay-lesbian-and-transgender alliance rainbow flag (representing the multinational and anti-nationalist pilot and all with bi, trans or guy inclinations all around the world) and a nine-in-one flag to celebrate the nine areas, located in six continents, and with most of them located in what you might know, in your world, as the US, Russia, China and Mexico, who co-funded the space programme, in selfless friendship and partnership. 93 other areas contributed funding or scientist resources, but the nine gave more in overall terms or in per capita terms that anyone else.

By 2021, there is now talk of building a self-sufficient community of earth plants, fungi and insects on a planet, moon or space station in the near future, and this project will definitely succeed, albeit with many base layer stages requires first. Once this is up and running, they reckon, it may one day be possible to settle some mammals, fish, birds and lizards there too. It could one day serve as a survival back-stop in case life one earth ever ends, and perhaps humans are best omitted, for a while, as they cause so much trouble and eat all the other animals, or spoil their habitats. But this will require a lot of further research, and it is unlikely to be up and running before 2038.

The Iranian Revolution only ever happens in three of the Persian provinces, and trans-ind makes sure that no guns, mobs or weapons are involved, apart from when the protesters are being protected. After 15 years, the voters in two of these three provinces opt to shake off the shackles of having a clergy-led state, and they move over to giving the multi-party legislature all the powers that one would normally see it get. The elected candidates still incorporate the main Shiite beliefs into their manifestos, but not at the cost of excluding any progressive plans.

Britain's many little successor states, shires and boroughs all follow Norfolk's, Lambeth's and Wales' lead and decide to join trans-eur, and its commonwealth country friends also decide to stop being aloof from their regional neighbours and issues, and so trans-southaf, trans-oc, trans-ind, trans-carib and trans-east all receive lots of new members too, with the x-colonies, such as Hong Kong, Guyana, Georgia, Belize, Cayman Islands and the Falkland Islands reaffiliating across from trans-brit, which they stay honorary videoconferencing partners in to making stronger partnerships and tax-revenue-sharing schemes with their nearest neighbours be the most important thing.

In 1988 London becomes a cluster of 32 independent boroughs, each with its own government, a different immigration policy and with different health, tax, welfare, pension and governance systems, greater Manchester becomes ten independent borough states, and all other regions undergo a similar process. Westminster still hosts trans-brit, but 91% of tax-funded schemes are now 100% devolved, and so having one MP for each one of them proves to be too expensive to be necessary, and the trans-brit leadership delegates are instead chosen by five of the member nations in a lottery.

All other trans-regional bodies follow suit, realising that there are no more major transformations to argue about, and so each one can now, in especially peaceful times, shrink down in size and let other levels of decision-making flourish. This also makes for a depolarisation of the debate about the future direction of travel for the international bodies. Those continents who, like trans-eur, still wish to have additional agreements in place on top of what the current ones and the new global order provide, now do so with an a la carte menu of opt-in and opt-out initiatives, and a parliament that gives its 20 biggest parties' five-person epicentres a percentage of the vote each that corresponds with its share of the overall vote.

There is a vicious verbal hostility from the Sunni Muslims of Western Asia and also in some rural regions in South Asia and in West and East Africa toward the Shiites, Druze, Alawi, Yazidi, and sometimes also toward the Bahai, Zoroastrian, various Christian, pagan, non-religious, Jewish, Hindu, Parsi, Jain, Sikh and other belief groups and so the trans-regional bodies are given special remits by the global UN body to ensure that every person who is being marginalised because of their ethnicity is allowed to move into a nearby free and welcoming cosmopolitan city, town or province that is under the ruling control of the ethnicity (or a coalition including it) of the persecuted, and that the hostile area always ends up financially covering and facilitating all the moving and transaction costs associated with having to sell your home here and to move there plus interest.

This becomes quite a long-term drain on these (mostly ultra-radical Sunni) societies, and they undergo new efforts to tone the hostility down as a best way of winning the right to one day have lower taxes, better reputations and more development aid. Some towns, where Isis, taliban, boko haram or similar dogma and devotionist influences are strongest prefer to opt to stay hostile to other ways of life, staunchly ultra-religious and to reluctantly pay all the fines, taxes and the moving costs that come with it.

When any of these groups do extra-violent acts to adulterous women or to minorities or foreigners, though, trans-ind and trans-arab do feel the need to intervene to carry out a rescue and to make some arrests. It means that all international bodies are viewed, in these areas, with great suspicion and with dislike in some areas, and visitors permits, except for ultra-religious inward migrants, are very hard to come by in these areas. They sometimes even to reject inoculation programmes, and so many illnesses that are under control elsewhere are busy taking down thousands of religious nutters and their innocent children in some of these ulta-Islamic utopias, but the world is slowly starting to get out, as the young generation of ulema and imams themselves are seeing the need to back these programmes at last.

Afghanistan, Syria, Niger, Sudan, Yemen and Somalia are places where warlords, barons and ulema thrive, and where support for multi-party democratic systems are lower. This is why the trans-regional bodies make sure that each province of these corners of the world remains fully independent, with no one province's thugs and troops ever able to invade, pressurise, send military support to a violent militia in or to bring warfare to any other. This way, even though it is not always possible to stay in the area where you grew up, there are many opportunities to work and settle in other nearby areas where the going isn't so tough if you are the sort of person who is likely to fall foul of the ultra-strict rules that the most conservative and religious societies like to impose upon themselves.

Sharia law, in some interpretations of the quran, requires anyone who is raised to believe but then denounces Islam, and any woman who disobeys her husband or father or who has a fling with a lover to be brutally butchered. This barbaric practice presents a large problem, and a number of anonymous phone lines are websites are set up to offer assistance to young women with big problems of craving a man other than the one the father has chosen for her.

The local governments shut off all info about these rescue programmes, and so a long sequence of leaflet air-drops are necessary, with many tens of thousands of young women opting to accept the offer to disappear from these societies and to live a free life in a cosmopolitan and variety-embracing society elsewhere. This in turn leads to a terrible shortage of women in the ultra-Islamic areas, with thousands of men ending up dying either in duels over a remaining woman or in suicides after they have ended up without a wife.

Many good, caring together from different independent societies get together to discuss the possible solutions to this problem, and many ideas are trialled, including some that pair up male singletons with older female widows until such time as when the old widow dies and then a new loving wife may be sought. Even after the quran is slightly changed to make it say that a sinner must be offered the chance to leave town, repent, or will otherwise face a barbaric punishment, it still takes many years for the risk of violence toward women in these villages to sink.

Those women who find the bravery inside them to go to a multicultural society, find the shock of suddenly being without the overbearing and controlling family to be a mixed blessing at first, but fortunately there are a lot of options and a lot of loving affectionate welcoming people out there to help them blend in and to find a good life here. Some even go on to become leaders, authors or heads of social care, counselling or psychiatry once they get the hang of the way free life works, and most do end up making videoconferencing friends with people in their family and in their village of origin in the end, once both sides work out how to avoid offending the other.

Oil money is shared out widely, with trans-arab in control of the Gulf's biggest oil-extraction projects: all communities in Asia and Africa end up receiving equal shares of the profits, regardless of where the oil wells are situated. A double share is offered only by the poorer half of the 25 largest by population, and by the two poorest smaller communities, and only on a 5-year review cycle, just as the overlap between the richest 30% and the smallest 45% of communities are placed on half shares of the oil profit.

Repeated appeals, raids, legal challenges and mobs and militias seeking the take-over of a mine, an oil field, or an airport, city or industrial facility and are dealt with using inter-regional riot police resources, as many as required. It would be lovely to say that everyone agreed to share fairly right from the start, but that's where we distinguish between unrealistic utopias and the fuller recording of history we are talking about here.

Vandals, thieves and corrupt agents are painstakingly identified through a large combination of entrapment, covert surveillance and other evidence-collecting schemes. It would have been nice to bring about a good world entirely through voluntary, spontaneous and instinctively ethical actions, but in the end there are always a few greedy or crooked opportunists who do need to be taken through a court process or two before they learn their lessons and abandon the crooked ways. In a few extreme cases people have had to be settled into prison insane asylums for life, just to prevent them from victimising any more people, and these places have to be well-resourced to stop them from victimising each other in there too.

Even in there, no bad deed goes unpunished, and no cry for help goes un-responded-to. If a person is insane enough to harm or steel, he or she clearly needs a lot of medication and a lot of complex treatment programmes compete with one another in global league tables to see which can get the best calm and civilised outcome stats. The world also receives a lot of complex treatment programme ideas competing, in massive large trials with one another in global league tables to see which can get the best calm and civilised outcome also in terms of the rehabilitation of people after their first or second offence, with new ideas constantly added to the process and with not-so-successful ideas falling out of use.

Other lucrative industries and other forms of mining are placed on similar schemes that share the proceeds out widely across entire continents. Multinational countries are, by 2014, no longer able to choose one country wealthy tax exile country to have all their company profits taxed in. The big IT, finance, consulting, manufacturing, retail and innovative sectors are all placed into a new global regulator's remit, who ensures that the world will never be without competition and choice, and that no company ever pays its owners or its board unreasonable sums, while also diverting the revenues from sales, profit and income taxes on to the benefit of all the elected local community governments all over the world.

On the local level, a round-robin voting system is used to select the head of the executive body of government, and his chosen finance minister and the biggest other three parties in the legislature each get to submit rival budget plans to the voters, who pick the one that makes the most sense to them as their destination percentage split at the end of the upcoming five-year period.

Many self-governing local areas are now holding an IQ test to work out which migrants from other continents to admit, while others go purely by the level of need, the existing links to this area, the shortage category skills they bring with them, or the amount of wealth the person has. With so many different systems in simultaneous use, there is a big new demand for advice-giving agencies just to help a migrant decide which community to apply to move to. Nearly all of them admit people on a ten-year probation that fails them if they commit any form of crime, or if they end up being on unemployment benefits for more than a set percentage of the time.

Trans-brit, trans-eur, trans-oc, trans-east, trans-west, trans-sib, trans-southam, trans-carib, trans-alaskumbia and trans-mex are trialling a number of freedom to enter systems that allow people to move freely between the continents. These do not apply to people from other parts of Asia and Africa, as immigration remains a hot political issue in many areas. While there is a broad agreement allowing the people of many hundreds of areas to roam freely between all these areas, there are also areas with partial admittance and with extra clauses providing for further permits, checks, references or fees.

Nonetheless many areas continue to wish to pick and choose which applicants to admit, with most having such a system for applicants from Asia and Africa (and the top 100 or top 500 applicants per area per year are admitted), such systems are also in use for moving into the non-signatory areas from neighbouring areas and from areas elsewhere. While this is still commented on as being cruel to black Africans, it is slowly improving, from year to year, with people in Africa who have acquired a lot of knowledge about any one city in Europe generally winning the right to go there through the special selection committees route, and similar systems also help people from Asia and from Central America to move to Australia, Europe, or to North, Central or South America, or to an island somewhere that is just right for them, once they have learned a lot about their chosen favourite destination in particular and once they have memorised its taxi drivers map or become able to lecture about its history, even without falling in the special shortage skills categories.

Similarly, if an applicant has learned semi-fluent Finnish, Latvian, Welsh, Irish, Breton, Slovenian, Belarussian, Estonian, Galician, Catalan, Inuit, Lapp, Amish, Hopi, Algonquin, Blackfoot, Seminole, Cherokee, Basque, Sami, Icelandic, Norwegian, Ukrainian, Bulgarian, Albanian, Polish, Greek or Slovak before moving there, maybe through a mixture of distance learning courses, online learning and short visits with intensive courses, or has made a written commitment to learn it within a year of moving there, a five year residency and work permit all-in application that later converts into a permanent residency right is sure to succeed.

While the birth rate remains particularly high in those extra religious societies, a variety of education and birth control option giving programmes are starting to make headway, seeking to stabilise the numbers before irreparable damage is done to the environment by human overcrowding. A combination of tougher measures is also under consideration to bring the villages with the highest birth rates in the world closer to normality, though these debates remain highly controversial, difficult and heated.

For now, only six women in the whole world over the past 50 years (plus 2,600 men, most of whom were convicted rapists or cereal hit-and-run nest-flighters) have undergone forced sterilisation while they were asleep, and these were all cases where the children were destined to be poorly looked after and extremely heavily disabled and in much pain. Instead, the usual solution is to offer a special high-end elite education fees paying, family-get-together-supporting and holidays-improving allowance to people with three children that they will only get at full reward levels if they don't have any more, and this reduces by 10% with each additional child. The only unfortunate by-product of this is that the world finds a few abandoned babies who nobody owns up to, and of course the best provisions it can offer do cost a lot of money, but the alternatives are, on balance, not choose-able.

The UN, once a one-off get-together to see what all needs coordinating, and who needs the most help in getting things rolled out, soon evolves from being a mini League of Nations that meets once a year to talk about whatever is troubling them at the time to a new world government with bigger fuller solutions to bigger worldwide problems in the core of its remit. Rather than having factions, nationalities, elections, polarisations and wrangling, it is soon decided to give each trans-regional body an equal decision-making status and an equal share of the jobs at this new institution.

None should be neglected and none should ever dominate over the others. Each UN job must fully serve the interests of the people of the entire world, and the best way to select the best people to work here is to have a panel of ten top Un staffing and success-finding managers be selected in a process that begins with each trans-region submitting two good applicants into the process, and it ends when all the scores are in, and all those who chose to use their entire packet of scores to eliminate one applicant in particular have succeeded in their quest, while the ten most universally credible applicants have now won a five year term on the world government's executive board.

Pol Pot and the Khmer Rouge may only ever come to rule in one single cluster of villages, and here too not one person is ever to be harmed. When the violence breaks out, inter-malay and inter-pac send in the troops to rescue the victimised and to arrest and send to insane asylums all the culprits. Thanks to their rapid and brave intervention, what could have been a massive massacre was stopped short on the third day, and most of the intended victims managed to get to a safe province nearby, until the time came when it was safe to return home.

Idi Amin, Mobutu, Kabila, Mugabi, Putin, Qaddafi and dozens of other greedy tyrant rulers of African, Asian, American, European or Oceanian societies succeed only in attaining a maximum of four three-year terms of office in much smaller and far less militarised countries, each with legislative superiority to restrict them further, and they end up pocketing only their government salary, as a system of checks and balances, including independent monitoring, tip-offs, trackable traceable cash and secret surveillance ensures that none of them ever manage to steal or redivert the main flows of their people's tax money.

This is more easily said than done, and it does come with its controversies, costs and with the potential that some of the people who are there to police this also end up entangled in the temptation of corruption, criminal, crooked, bribe-able, double-agents or ineffective. But through frequent rotation of staff, hidden cameras and bugging devices, along with high-tech upskilling, training, creativity, good funds traceability and frequent trap situations that test the integrity of those in positions of power, a much less corrupt and much more ethical system of government does indeed come into being, with the people who need the most help benefitting the most from these clean-up initiatives.

Iraq must never all fall into the hands of any one group, be they pro Saddam Hussein bathists, members of his earlier alliance of parties who he later the out of the governing alliance, Kurdish tigers, ISIS, centrist or leftist moderates, Shiite militia, religious or secular new or old Sunni factions or Shiite hardliners. A wise trans-arab super-body enjoys the powers to step in to make sure that each political and ethnic group has plenty of areas where it can govern, that the people in each of these differently governed areas enjoys plenty of genuine choice in their elections, and that none of these groups is ever cruelly overrun or mistreated by any of the others.

In the year 2013, a miracle happens in the great plains: Realising that they have been left out of the big discussions the world is having, the big exchanges of data and the big partnerships that genuinely do solve society's great problems, and occurring immediately after a trans-west summit of republicans, 37 of the 39 the last remaining county-size strongholds of US-republicanism who have, until now, refused to join the UN and in some cases trans-west too, situated in the remote and agricultural valleys west of the Mississippi river, now decide to join the UN.

To celebrate this bringing in of over half of the world's remaining non-participants, all in one month, a lavish and colourful new UN HQ, packed full of meaningful artwork and furniture conveying optimistic progress-seeking messages is opened in New York, making the existing HQ in Geneva take on a secondary role. The United Nations, having already been launched in 1914 as a League of Nations, now grows to have new ambitions: better coordination of information regarding the evaluation of various products, services and pilot-trial tested schemes, programmes and ideas, a new plan to create a "language for the world" and a new "currency for the world" are launched, and a set of global regulators whose role it is to bring about a fairer and better-functioning tax and spend system worldwide, including also the elimination of tax exiles, loop holes, monopolies, cartels, and the sale of unsafe and unreliable products.

The new worldwide currency comes into being on the 1st of January 2024, using a mixture of ten recent and less recent dates' exchange rates as the permanently set conversion rate and by the 31st of January 2024, every single jurisdiction all over the world has "opted in" and is now using this new currency only. The new language comes into being gradually and very slowly, but over the course of a 95-year period, from 2023 to 2118, undergoing a process of only three words at a time being replaced worldwide, once every three months, with one and the same word to be used from now on everywhere, complete universality of communication without the need for translations is truly achieved worldwide.

A panel made of government, university and dictionary master people who speak, between them, each one of the world's 100 most-spoken languages well, while also speaking English, French, Spanish, Mandarin, Russian, Hindi or Arabic. This specially assembled global people's body, known as trans-glob-lang ensures that each language has an approximately equal number of its words chosen (with double quotas given to the top 20 most widely spoken languages) as the new global word for this, while also making sure that words that sound nice, are easy to pronounce and easy to spell, and are comparatively shorter and less confusable with other global words are chosen every time.

There are, of course, more than 95 x 4 x 3 words in any language, and so the final 25 three-month periods each contain one word more than the previous, each time, and the final stage contains all the rest. The decision-making panel members spend all their time evaluating the options for the next three words, with all translations considered and evaluated using ten criteria to score them all on, in search of the best one to pick for global use. At least three of the final five options in this process is always from one of the top ten most widely spoken languages in the world, and one of the final five is always found from among the least widely spoken languages in the world, the ones who were not among the 100 languages to be on the decision-making body. This allows all sorts of indigenous people to be honoured and praised for having the world's best word for this, so good that the entire planet will one day be using it.

A simplified form of grammar is applied universally, with specially written software converting all books and news into the new global language, and the very last stage, bringing in "the rest of the dictionary" into the global language ends up being a tournament-shaped vote of the top 16 languages, competing to get voted into the quarter-finals, then semi-finals and then the final, where it ends up being English and Hindi who are put to a global vote to select the final words to make the new global language complete at last.

This eventually kills off all sorts of concepts of being different, separate, mistreated, distinct nations, and from now on there is no longer a remoteness in places that speak other languages. It means there is never again a shortage of TV programmes, cinema films, books, news and magazines to read, or people in special-interest chat rooms. The world becomes a much better and more united place.

It also ends the need for translators to exist, except, in the first few years, as a way of capturing what the elderly, who still speaks the old languages only is telling us. It makes traveling so much easier, and having global discussions about politics, the news, science, social trends, travel, cooking, work, study, research, hobbies and other topics. Schools no longer need to teach any more foreign languages, which frees them up to teach people more about the decision-making processes, advice and tools that can help them in real life.

Only three new words per three month period, over the first 70 years and then a few more words per month thereafter are "brought in" (merged into one world-wide) and dozens of widely spoken languages all around the world will each contribute equally to this new language: When the English word "peace" , the Spanish word for "friendship" and the Hindi word for "cooking" are rolled out in the first weeks of the new world language's gradual existence, all translations of this new word, in all press, book, email and internet writing are automatically "translated over" to this new word, so that by the middle of week three, even a Somali, Korean or Burmese news headline using any of these words now automatically substitutes the new *globalese* word for peace, friendship and cooking into all its news articles, along with all books, including the quran, Shakespeare and the bible. Europe, China and North America have already been starting to gradually roll out, through forerunner initiatives that did not know this was coming globally, a common language, using similar evaluation principles, technology and pace of change controls, and the words they have chosen are automatically entered as front-runners and finalists, but never as the only option, in the global process to pick the one word for each meaning.

23 years in, there are still a lot of localities who have voted not to go along with the change, but eventually, they see sense, allowing all children to learn and use this new language. Those same localities become the places not so many people wish to visit, which affects their tourist and conventions trade heavily, but eventually each of these areas has a change of government, either to a left-centre grouping who understands the benefits of joining this movement, or to a new generation of more globally aware young leaders, who now do all their reading, TV viewing and thinking in the new global language.

By the end of year 35 it is no longer awkward expressing yourself when travelling around the world without multiple language fluency, as, regardless of which border you have crossed, the new global words, given plenty of time to slip into your vocabulary, are now exactly the same (plus or minus some persisting but rather pleasant local pronunciation accents) all over the world.

Whereas, in reality B, many words have two or more very different meanings, which makes confusion more likely at every turn, this new global language is specially assembled to be truly brilliant, allowing all listeners all over the world to know exactly what the person speaking or writing this means, even if irony or ridicule is implied but not obvious, for which a simple "ovek" sentence ending is brought in globally.

Further changes are made on a slower pace, after the year 95 full step 380 launch, with only one word every 15 years being replaced with a new one hereafter, often picked from a more old obscure language, or specially invented, just to ensure that further improvements in the conciseness, clarity, shortness, pronounceableness, unconfusableness, the systematic and logical relationship with other words and in the poetic sound of the world language can occur, and then, after five such 15-year periods, it is decided to add one more year before each further review, so a 16-year period of no changes follows, in 2193, and then a 17-year period, etc.

The world government, made up of a fair balance of representatives from all of the world's religious, political, old lingual and regional groups, has many challenges, issues and struggles to consider making a wise intervention in, or not, and in doing so, it must always make sure that it does so only to give people and localities more options, more help, and better-informed options, rather than to remove options, overrule and prescribe.

Best of all: There are no veto powers, and so the law, the global human rights charter, the recommendations and the availability of help for the most vulnerable applies equally all over the world. Every jurisdiction area initially pays just 0.02% of its GDP to the UN as tax, rising slightly to a new mutually agreed 4-tier system in later years, and 57% of the areas qualify for a 30% reduction in this tax, as these areas offer all migrants and all residents guaranteed jobs, income and housing as part of the highly successful universal system of local-area-owned business with an unlimited intake of labour to share the work between. Of these, 22 areas even qualify for a 0.0% rate of tax, as these areas contribute satisfactorily and fully both to the x-offenders super-welcome-scheme and to the world army recruitment system, while also coming under the poor region heading in the UN's global anti-poverty initiative that extends tax decreases to help more money stay in these areas.

Guns and Hunting: Although some forms of pest control, meat farming, endangered plant helping entrapment, bear, crocodile and lion tranquilizing and limited ethical and sustainable fishing are still in use at first, all guns and all big game-, bird-, fox- and rabbit hunting are completely phased out worldwide, over a three-year transition programme, with a few exemptions and non-participating areas to mop up later. It started with a ban on the manufacture and sale of all firearms. Then it got expanded to a number of cash-paying trade-in options, and then to full confiscation. Even sharp knives are no longer publicly accessible, and people now go to special places to have bread, textile or wood cut up for day-to-day use, which is a pain for some, but it makes life for our youngest and oldest a lot safer, a lot.

Completely de-gunning society was never going to be quick or easy to achieve, and it was always going to encounter a lot of entrenched resistance, especially in the Americas and in Africa, but it had to be done, as human society was completely out of control, and organized criminal gangs were in no way tolerable, subjecting a lot of people to a lot of horrific coercion, and it had to be accompanied with a lot of digging around, as the crafty people then buried and hidden their weapons from trans-west, from the police and from the other degunning and deweaponizing authorities for a long time.

This gave rise to new problems, including a rise in night-time and holiday-time burglary, which required launching a better bedroom alarm button response system in response. Also, rat, rabbit and fox, mouse, raccoon, possum, squirrel, beetle, ant and deer populations were now becoming so big in some areas that people were starting to panic. But there are a number of solutions to each problem, and in most cases a catch, sterilize and release program is enough to bring these populations under control.

On the opposite side, this still did not solve the problem of critters getting run over in traffic ever so often. Well, fortunately, with trans-eur, trans-east, trans-brit, the UN, and other backing, initiatives to construct protective fences, tunnels, netting, perches, hedges and trenches were brought in worldwide, thus saving billions of innocent lives and sparing billions of bird, mammal, turtle, insect, frog, crab and other youngsters from the grief of losing their mummy or daddy or baby.

 Many pockets of mass human migration, including Tower Hamlets, St Dennis, Lyon, Queens, Bronx, Manhattan, Dade, Philadelphia, Toronto, Dublin, Bruxelles-Midi, Hamburg, Köln, Berlin, Moscow, Istanbul, Athens, Johannesburg, Guyana, Fiji, Hawaii, Ibiza, Singapore, Mumbai, San Francisco, LA, Detroit, Vancouver, Mexico City, Rio, Stockholm, Vienna, Leicester, Hounslow, Tower Hamlets, Thetford, Yarmouth, Cambridge, Slough, Portsmouth, Birmingham, Burnley and Bradford, Lisbon, Danzig, Sarajevo, Hong Kong, Shanghai, Sydney, Dubai, Lagos, Casablanca, Kuwait, Qatar and Brussels are all placed under a special electoral system that guarantees that its 10 biggest minority groups (defined in terms of being different ethnicities or family beliefs from the surrounding hundred mile areas) get to govern these areas, with the ethnic majority only electing one third of the delegates to their 15-member city-parliaments. Some of these, such as Bradford and Tower Hamlets even go so far as to set up an all-Muslim second legislative chamber with a veto and a rewind option on all changes.

The continuation of mass-expulsions from areas in Africa and in Asia that vote to have a society based on Sharia law leads to each of the above hyper-cosmopolitan areas being overrun with thousands, and sometimes millions of displaced migrants who soon become additional euro-Muslims. The growth of this population in Europe does not go unnoticed, and a number of county shires, departments, provinces, kreise, oblasts, voivodeships, estadoses, local authority areas, districts and boroughs decide to set up a new quota limiting the number of new Muslims allowed to move into the area per year to 5, 10, 20, 50, 100, 200, or 500. While each of these specific quota limits is only brought in in a few places, it does give places that are particularly anxious about the prospect a chance to control the pace of the influx. It also creates a need for special new panels, scoring systems, refences and evaluation entities to be made up in these areas to ensure that the application process remains as fair as can be.

Overall, this scheme is regarded with widespread support, though many experts still argue that whatever the "best way" is, should be applied everywhere, not just in some provinces. There are two instances in the 2030s where areas who are currently experiencing their Muslim population rising from recently still under 45% to now over 50% are met with such a stressed out and hateful response that the interregional sees no alternative but to intervene. In addition to this it also intervenes in 17 places in Asia where tensions between secular and reformation-orthodox Muslims has led to such escalations in tensions that a two-state solution ends up being necessary. The two-state solution is an effective way of giving each individual and each family a safe place to move to, where their way of life is under no threat at all.

Other provinces end up receiving a three-chamber legislative system instead, with one chamber for all, one for the Muslims and one for all the others, where both ethnic group, sectarian, ideology or belief communities are able to block, water-down, modify and to reverse changes that they were against all along, and where each is given a budget to spend and a set of government posts to fill. A third set of solutions we see being occasionally applied is to scrap all barriers to inward migration of non-Muslims, though some of those do find it hard to work out which of the applicants was lying on their application.

ISIS ends up with a homeland granted in the Northeast corner of what we know as Syria and with a second in Chechnya, a third in Southern Afghanistan and a 4th in Niger, allowing its adherents to live a pure, clean fully Muslim devoted devout sin-free life-style. The decision to grant these is much criticized, but it is done in good faith, as hating any group of people and depriving it of its own specially crafted utopia is not really the true human way. Other right-wing societies, including scientologist, Montana freeman, ultra-libertarian, ultra-orthodox Jewish, Aryan evangelical, Amish, branch dravidian, mayan, voodoo, rastafarian, anarchist, pre-Christian druid, falun gong, kuo min dang, mormon, taoist, zoroastrian, and many other fringe groups are also allowed and granted a true homeland where they can build their unique version of utopia.

This does make it harder to bring everyone together when a global problem-solving effort is under way, make no mistake, but in a world where most solutions have to be pragmatically made in a multi-wave timetable way that only includes the willing in each wave, that's how it needs to be, and besides: what's the hurry?

Leicester becomes the first city to put a gathering of Hindu scholars in as its second legislative chamber that also has the power to overrule the verdicts of its judges for up to one year. This leads to a number of other areas putting all-migrant, Jewish, African, Muslim, oriental, indigenous, pro-gay, feminist, vegetarian, x-offender and pagan bodies into their local province government's policy-formulation committees, which leads to a very large number and variety of new schemes and rules being trialled, all over the world.

In Libya, where trans-arab has been keeping an eye on the rise of supporters of change, Qaddafi is made by trans-arab to accept that he can only hang on to one small corner of Libya, and only for his life time plus two years only for a chosen successor. When he sees his movement being toppled in elections everywhere, he reluctantly agrees to retreat into this region, along with all of his loyal forces and bodyguards, and with his nearest and dearest. This one SouthWest Libya area, where only 6% of Libyans live, is where his reign will continue, but within the constraints of a multipart electoral system that gradually gets 25% then 48% then 52% and eventually, 45 years later, 100% of all power in this area over the course of a slow but safe and mutually agreeable multi-stage transition period. There he lives on, freely able to write his books and to speak to the media of the world.

The ayatollah of Persia undergoes a similar "managed retreat". So does Mugabi on SE Zimbabwe and the Castro family in Cuba, who both find themselves voted out and suddenly no longer welcome in the government they worked so long to build, but luckily the inter-regs saw fit to give them the security of a retreat-to, so they could be safe, themselves and not dead or in foreign exile.

The tragedy of the 9/11 disaster in Manhattan in 2001, which was not prevented, sadly, tragically, reveals the need for a tougher system vis-à-vis extremists. It also changes a lot of self-governing provinces, self-governing boroughs, self-governing districts and self-governing counties all around the world into "no more than five Muslims per year are to move here" resistant and standoffish lands. The world has been giving all the most extreme and hostile groupings a place where they can flourish and from where they can dump all their lies onto the internet from. This is further exacerbated by the Charlie Hedbo murders and by a number of rock concert, city bridge, city square and road system bombings, all over Europe, Israel and New Zealand, which the interreg system, the police intelligence system and the media never saw coming and which the entire world reacts to in total shock.

It leads to a lot of soul-searching, a lot of debate and a lot of anger in the big discussions that shape the world's response to these. It strengthens the reactionary and hate-fuelled far right in most elections, while also weaking the centre-left. The wise majority of the planet does eventually realise that it is never right to punish the many for the actions of a few, which means that stripping all locations of some of their electoral options, or of their chosen elected leaders is not an option.

Instead, we see a raft of new laws, criminalising all sorts of complicity, assistance, influence-giving, radicalising and keeping secret from the police a number of relationships to these attacks. Unfortunately, this requires not just local but also international taxes to rise, to fund these actions, which is such a shame, as we are getting a little more like East Germany and Moscow (in reality A 1950-89) by the day. Let's prey it never goes all the way, as it would mean the loss of almost all our rights, freedoms and the loss of trust itself.

After a lot of surveillance work, there are a number of arrests of minor, marginal and major contributors to these terrible attacks. And much progress is made also in making the ingredients for bomb-making much less widely available, much more controlled and measured, and in putting road blocks in some spots where cars and pedestrians should never overlap. Tough decisions have to be made, and in the long-run, no onslaught to eradicate these groupings completely can really be made. Well, not until such time as when one of those groupings, ISIS, goes completely rogue, vicious, deadly and non-compliant, in 2017. This is when the world leaders unite, with a 473-0 UN vote to support an exceptional move to ban ISIS from all governments, all forms of gun-ownership and from all elections globally for a 10-year period to allow all weapons, all militiamen, all bomb-making tools and items, and all its propaganda to be found and exposed, and to free all those who were being held hostage (or who had their doubts) from having to bear life in those tough locations.

By the year 2009, the last remaining vestiges of residual one-town-only powers for kings, nobility, barons, dukes, popes and for the successors of dictators such as Franco, Lukashenko, Putin, Kim-Yong-Un, She Jinping, Menangagwa, Kabila, Zuma, Castro, Chavez, Morales, Qaddafi and Mussolini finally ends, with locally elected multi-party systems, using many different electoral methods, rising and flourishing everywhere, now that the last of the autocrats has been retired. In the 2170s the world government pledges to let each locality, borough, district and province have a voting system election, to choose the same as now or a different way of holding elections. This gives areas that have fallen under one or two party dominance the chance to open the door to better ways, while also letting the most misfunctioning gridlocked large coalition systems try something else for a limited length of time and then get the chance to switch back if it wishes to.

Many great men such as Kofi Annan, U Thant, Ban Ki Moon and Boutrous Boutrous-Ghali (no relation to me, though I was named after him when I changed my birth name) have served in reality B as UN secretary generals, and these were great men with impeccable morals and with a daring devotion to tackle the difficult and controversial issues of their time in search of a mutually beneficial best for all solution. You and I can only hope that maybe one day some of us can match their wonderful input into the pursuit of world peace and a better dignity for all living beings in the world. We can only hope and aspire to the fate that maybe one day our efforts will be recognized as making a big difference and for our contributions to building a good world government. It probably won't be possible for us, but we can try and by releasing this book I feel I have done something to hopefully help the world out too.

Venezuela's 26 states (much like also those of Brazil, the US, Mexico, Germany and Australia), in reality A, all go very different routes, depending on how the voters respond in the ballot box, thus leading to some areas where nationalisations are comprehensive, some where they never started to happen, some where they are slow cautious and not as far-reaching, and others where they were backed but later reversed. In doing so, they allow a larger number of people who are closer in so many ways to the issues that local people face to make those big decisions that help empower the local people and the dialect-speaking and immigrant ethnic groups to build a far better system that responds better to the lessons it has learned and that offers people more ways to flourish and be free, economically independent and politically influential at the same time.

Syria, Lebanon, Iran, Iraq, Turkey, Russia, Vietnam, China, Mexico, Nicaragua, Venezuela, Korea, the US, France, Britain, Germany, Spain and all sorts of other places never end up existing as one mega-state with winner-takes-all power struggles. This has been said once before, but it is worth repeating. As a result of having so many smaller regions, the potential for confrontation is so much smaller too, and so is the scale. It also allows different groups to fully flourish, rule and put their ideas into action simultaneously, and without spoiling it for the others. It also allows people who have run for office or supported someone who ran for office and did not win to move into a nearby country where the kind of things they believe in are the norm anyway. This makes for a much better world, one where there is not winners and losers, as in reality A after every election, but rather there is winners and the different winners next door, setting up something they can support in their area, while watching how the other way they did not want to be a part of fares from afar.

Pollution: all forms of pollution are a terrible thing, and they cause both immediate and long-term harm, especially when their cumulative scale is allowed to get out of hand. This is why certain filters have to be mandatory world-wide, and this cannot wait for those who opt-in only to take part. Similarly, emissions from all sorts of facilities, industrial plants, chimneys and fires all need to be monitored, not for its own sake but to ensure that as soon as we humans of earth fins a better way, a way that works in a cleaner manner, this way is rolled out worldwide, making the world cleaner.

We cannot have opt-in only systems regulating the fumes that come out of cars and the industrial wate that goes into rivers. It has to be a proper worldwide high standard that prevents all the bad things from happening in the first place, while also making a good standard of living still feasible for all of us, and this, in the end, can only be done with a world government that is big enough, strong enough, well enough informed and tooled up and enabled to get the problem solved in all parts of the planet, and to do so <u>before</u> lots of needless deaths and illnesses can occur, preventatively. This is why we do need a global world order of tax-funded pro-earth actions, and there cannot be any disagreement on this, not unless you are totally evil, suicidal or misinformed.

Drug crime and mafias: well, this is a global problem too, transcending borders and continents. We could opt to save money and to let them continue flourishing and ruining people's lives as they currently do in reality A. But why the hell would we choose this course of action? They are a huge problem and we do not need to wait for two thirds of us to have experienced it ourselves before we take concerted international action to solve it.

Company profits: A number of independent provinces and other entities have decided to enact the smart-override system to company profits. This varies by sector, size of company, age of company and economic recessionary climate, but it tends to place a three-way split of all company profits: 82% go into taxes, 04% to the shareholders and 14% into the rainy day, foundation use and better future fund, at least for larger, long-established companies in not overly volatile and recession-affected sectors. Other countries have other systems in use, but I do wish to point out that the smart-override system does allow all of us to suffer less of a tax burden on our day-to-day earnings, shopping, renovation, expansion and licence renewal actions, as most of the tax revenues your society needs can be harvested in this way, rather than letting it all go to people who do not work for the company and who have done nothing to help it or the society at large by buying some company shares.

Ejected serial killers, armed robbers, burglars, paedophiles and rapists often tend to get barred from living in the city they call home, which is all good and well and understandable, but what happens in the next place, the place they end up going to live in next? Well, that's a good question. We don't want a world where the same sort of crime is committed again and again, and this is exactly what would happen if we did not have much sharing of information between the independent authority areas.

Well, trans-eur, trans-pac and trans-east have each pioneered a scheme that places additional tracking, surveillance and bugging into x-offenders devices, even if they now live in a different remit area. This is a great way at stopping them from doing it again, but what happens when they either find a way to fool the tracking device, take it off, hide their true actions from it or move out of the continent to a region that does not operate the same system? Well, there are a hundred answers to these questions. I can't pretend these are simple and easily resolved, but efforts to improve the way these people can be monitored for their actions without impeding their career options, and new forms of transcontinental cooperation and information and advice sharing do all contribute greatly to solving these problems.

Public sector debt: Even in the utopia that is reality A, we still cannot pretend that there is no issue with local, regional and global governments ending up spending way more than what the collected taxes add up to. And so, as the years go by, an ever larger percentage of next year's tax revenues will be needed to pay for the overspend we had years ago, plus the interest that is payable on this debt. So how do we solve this problem? Should each entity be restricted to having no increases in spend until it has the money it will need in the bank? Or is there some clever way that we have not thought of that may make this problem a thing that has finally been solved? Well, I would love to have your input into this if you have the answer (I am reachable on fanofgreatsportingaction@gmail.com).

Trying out the five or six most brilliant ideas, all simultaneously, just to see which one works best may be the best way to solve this problem. Some of the big ideas involve either annulling some of the debt, not paying it back, declaring partial bankruptcy, setting up a second central bank that issues money that pays the debts off, or creating a second currency that is just for owning land, private additional pensions, distant future holidays, special shipments and company shares, in order to have different rates of inflation and different hand-outs to all in one currency that does not affect the other.

A lot of thought is needed to work out which the best front-runner scheme could be, and trial and error is a good way for less genius people like me to work out which way works best. But overall, I would be very surprised if letting the debt keep on growing forevermore turns out to be the best way. Plus interregional or global cooperation may be beneficial here, especially if we are now in a world with one currency and one central bank interest rate only. Maybe it could be better solved by having some of the debt turned into five-year bonds that are funded 90% from newly created money and 10% from tax hikes, or some tweak or augmentation of one of the above ideas, maybe?

In addition to the many different electoral systems that flourish in the world we live in, of which proportional representation is the best way to get a lot of groups to have some of the say each, but round-robin (eg a vs b + a vs c + b vs c) systems are probably the best way of electing one overall leader, budget, plan, solution, governing team, etc. The median numbers vote system has been massively underutilised in helping to set the scale of a new budget, the penalty or age cut-off or other quota on anything involving any sort of number in the decision-making process; jury systems and mini-referendums, including elections through opinion polling would be a terrific way of letting the people choose between the two possible routes to go next; a ransel party, where it main decision-making leaders are all chosen by a lottery is a novel but special way of making sure that the decisions and advocated actions of a party truly reflect what the wider society would have wanted; interselection tournaments among all applicants, of strangers, and among all who turn up are a great way of finding those who people tend to trust and to pick as their prospective leaders in a way that may find a better leadership team than any other way; and the use of intelligence, relevant knowledge and best solution finding exams, quizzes and contests could be a better way of finding those candidates for office who have the brain power to find new and better solutions and who have a better understanding of the problem as it currently stands.

Having made life so much better for all humans, let us return now to the plight of our cattle, pigs and poultry birds'. They too should have certain inalienable rights: Once substantial rights to a decent life are made global, requiring all kept birds and all farm animals to have seventeen rights, from birth to harvest, which make up a good and decent life with space to roam, dignity, clean ground, treats, ample perching places, and a painless death in their sleep, if they have to die prematurely at all. Don't get me wrong, there are still some appalling conditions in use on some farms, in 2023, all over the world, and there is a long way to go, but overall trans-eur, trans-east, trans-pac and all the other bigger bodies, plus the local authorities' actions have already made clear, big, substantial improvements in the lives and deaths of farm animals, and there is never, in recent memory, a decade where further real clear progress was not made, and so the future does look bright for all creatures now, at last, especially when the world government acts to bring best-practice to the places that have not spontaneously opted in, because they wanted to keep their costs lower.

Forests: The UN made every inch of forest land protected from ever being built on, way back in 1918, when it was first founded, and from ever being polluted, plus all hunting is also ended, following a three year transition programme, worldwide; fishing is phased out in most spots, especially in reefs and in rivers and anti-vermin and anti-insect products are made to be subject to a much more considerate, nonlethal, nonpainful and humane list of criteria, which is now being brought out worldwide.

There is still a world population problem, as the number of people on this planet is now dangerously close to 15 billion, which cannot be sustained with all the food, waste-collection and water-supply issues a population of this size requires. This is why some very difficult decisions have had to be made, and the three-child policy, now that it has been rolled out worldwide, along with the birth control options menu, is making a huge difference in this. But what happens when this is not enough, and the population shoots up to 38 billion?

Many a meeting of world leaders and of subject matter experts has grappled long and hard with this difficult subject. In the end, the only way to achieve a slow-down in world population growth is to have one, two, or three child households become the norm and for anything else (having more than three over a lifetime) to become rare. In achieving this, we needed to roll out a number of optional education, birth control and lifestyle option changes, bringing to an end the shaming of those with no children in regions where this was a big problem, by bringing in a system of escalating fines for the insult-slingers.

By making it so that the number of children a person has had now determines the official pension (and other allowance) category status equally as much as the number of contribution years (and the criminal record) does. This then determines the parents' pension amount. All young are given ample access to good education options, so we are not returning to the days of the one child policy, but we do need to keep the numbers under control, and men and women who have had children with more than two partners already are now starting to be given medical intervention to prevent them from having many more after this, until they have spent 15 full years in a perfectly functioning long-term loving partnership of parents first.

In areas with a large death at young age from diseases rate it would be too cruel to impose a two-child policy; but a four child policy, along with a massive upgrade in their healthcare systems may be right for these, while places where death under the age of 70 is extremely rare can be given a two child policy more easily; and the tolerance for people who have ended up having more children needs to remain soft, supportive and human, even when the overall figures are having to be kept a close eye on.

The problems of loneliness, singletons and a lack of desirable males or females in certain areas has also arisen in the UN get-togethers, and here the array of solution ideas is so dazzling that rather than reject all but one at stage one, the best thing to do was to start off by having each local authority area encouraged to try something different out, and to make each one hire 'someone from outside' to help evaluate its success or otherwise. Then the more in-depth evaluations can follow, and the better ones can be identified empirically (like with lab tests).

Solutions in use include some cities and countryside towns trial-legalising the seven husbands on seven days of the week system, which only around 2% of women would ever want to enter into, and even these would only want this for a short period of time before they choose one of them to be their hubby. A bunch of introducing single people to potential suiters who meet the main requirement criteria schemes, some of which involve video dates only at first, a scheme of allocating dates by age, location and lottery; and the trial partners six-month reducing list size "tournament system", where the last person still to be on the list at the end of these months becomes the fiancée, are all new and exciting contenders currently competing with many others on this list.

A whole load of systems of putting potential pairings together from within commonality categories is allowed to flourish, mostly through the private sector, all three of which serve to make sure that all people do find good long-term companions, affection and love. And each of these arms its participants with ample birth control, topic suggestion options, date venue options, and with a 'go away, meddling parents' option that, if used, can make them finable. It also arms them all with a "leave me alone, I said you're off my list" option, to make sure it all stays consensual, with no xs allowed to turn into stalkers or anything like that.

Guaranteed jobs, work, housing and income for all schemes have become rather popular, as the world government has been incentivising the use of them with tax and spend incentives, in order to generate more places people who find themselves displaced can flee to. More and more areas that don't yet have so many migrants living there have made the decision to become special socialist 'welcome here' places, in which all the jobs and all the income are dished out fairly and equally, according to how many people are available, who has signed up for which training, and how much work will need doing in this sector this week.

One in three areas worldwide, areas where all land and all businesses are either state-owned and employee-run, on a gradual transition in this direction programme, or are out on 10-year loans to privateers. One in 15 local authority area worldwide is now designated a 'welcome to all' place, which means that people with heavy criminal records are welcome and supported to get into respectable honest work here.

Global tax rates vary from 0.2% of GDP in 'guaranteed work for all' places, 0.1% tax levels are in place in the 'welcome to all' places, which are fantastic towns for allowing x-convicts who have lost their welcome where they have come from to work their way back into respectable society – the ultra-close monitoring system here, with cctv cameras inside and outside each and every building help to ensure that none of them are tempted to re-offend; the shortage of younger women in these x-offender towns is resolved with a seven-days-per-week wide-sharing scheme of the single older (mostly widowed and divorced) women, from whom a good reference can go a long way, and who are to be empowered and treated ultra-well at all times.

With the younger women and future wives choosing their husbands very carefully and gradually, and with the older widowed or divorced ones swapping out one of their seven one-day-per week husbands every two years for a new one, things are quite interesting in the lands of Kern, Massapequa, Irkutsk, Uppsala, Cadiz and Naples. But most jurisdiction areas are instead opting for a solution that simply makes everyone choose five (to ten) good sets of friends (who tend to come with a partner) to keep in constant touch with, and it allows them to pick their favourite four of these once a year and to swap out the fifth lot of people for a new pairing that is recommended by a special computer formula system based on what it can be programmed to know about your type of person, the kind you get on best with. A version of this for matching up single people is also in use, and further improvements keep being added to it every year, making it a fairly good and reliable way to meet new people who fit well with you.

The global tax is currently set at 0.3% of GDP in lands where land and businesses are owned by local individuals, rather than by the state, and 0.4% in lands where land and businesses are owned by individuals and companies who do not necessarily live locally.

To be eligible for any of the categories below 0.4% a society must also have a clean outcome when it is examined for birth rates, pollution rates, crime rates, corruption rates, income and wealth inequality rates, good-regulation rates, good mediation schemes, women's empowerment, birth control, victim-help promoting part-time-working, and freedom of expression civil liberties, with the required levels of each rising further for areas applying for the coveted 0.2% and 0.1% tax rates. The ability to pay is also taken into consideration, and temporary adjustments of up to 0.07% upwards or downwards are applied in response to localised times of particular wealth or hardship, with the funds these taxes raise used to benefit the people and nature everywhere in the world.

As there are now, in 2024, over 17,130 completely free and independent countries in the world, it is deemed unnecessary to have one representative from each one sitting at the world government at all times or at any of the trans-regional bodies, and so five overarching neutrals are employed to oversee each trans-reg body's work instead, with the selection process allowing a variety of quotas and regional interests to be applied in the gradual elimination of applicants, until the five are found who best represent the entire world's true interests. Elections are also held, not so much to determine who fills which post, but more to help decide which initiatives need to receive more of the available funding instead.

A new trend of temporary and partial mergers of like-minded local authority areas, boroughs, counties, provinces and districts, such as in rural Kansas and Nebraska, in the New York City area, in the Thames Valley, in Central Finland, in most of Korea and Vietnam, and in Nordrhein Westfalen have made a lot of accelerated progress through a pooling of resources, an increase in specialisation and an increase choice of providers a big win for all. It is a brilliant new form of partnering up and making the best use of common resources, commonly used contracted out services, commonly used computer systems and more a wisely used and targets workforce that achieves more through better specialisation of job roles.

We expect this trend to further accelerate, as there is now nothing stopping two thousand communities, spread over four of five continents from forming one, two or three big centralised, temporary, voluntary service buying alliances on a trial-basis, with a joint leadership to tackle certain problems they all have and will all want handling in a similar and ever-improving way, making the people of the cooperating areas better way off together. After all, it's not like there will still be a language barrier, a plug-types or legislation-based systematic barrier, any residual mistrust or animosity, or a clash of national or trans-island systems.

The only thing preventing it from happening right now is fear of the unknown and a stupid reluctance to try something promising and new out. I notice that places who no longer have political party factions are far more open to try such progressive things out, while those who still have parties are also good at this when the same party finds 'very similar to me' twins elsewhere. As the same sort of grouping tends to be in power in a whole bunch of countries, these then find a way of bagging lots of gains by joining forces. When, a few years later, there is a change in who is in power over the area, a realigning tends to follow, with new international partnerships being brought in or switched over to, under which there is also much to be gained by pooling resources and by procuring the best solutions together, as part of a wider and better resourced management, buying and contracting team.

Covid-19 is a tough blow to the world in 2020, and it takes the world a long while before it develops the most potent of vaccines. But fortunately, those people who require a tighter lockdown in 2020 and those who require a looser one, can both, in our world, in reality A, if they so choose, move away to a differently governed land, not far away, for a while, which nobody can object to and which kind of works better for everyone, much like the way the huge variety of gambling, drugs, censorship, rehabilitation, welfare, and birth control laws seem to actually work much better for the world overall than having just one solution applied to all.

The main downside of the opposite simultaneous solutions approach is that the countries who have brought covid under control through cutting off personal contacts and human to human exposure are left with a huge challenge when trying to keep all goods and people who enter from places that have gone the other way from getting in too easily, before they are properly examined, and declared checked and clean.

Mobsters, now, in 2025 are being caught very soon after any sort of bank robbery, human smuggling, abduction, extortion ring or other robbery. They sure try to evade the trackdowns system by selling off their stolen goods quickly, or with a long flight to a new identity in another continent, but thanks to some very high-tech face recognition, finger print and DNA recognition software, a newly globalised system of tracked money, interlinked cctv cameras and a wide use of covert recordings, we are catching them quicker than ever, with better evidence than ever, which is winning wide support, even from those who at first objected to being surveillanced at all.

A bunch of new trade agreements have been struck worldwide, with a World Trade Organisation system ensuring that every kind of trade deal on the table anywhere in the world is made available as an opt-in for a bilateral add-on deal everywhere else too, so this has helped to link up the achievements made by each regional trans-org locally at first, now going global. It means that goods and services are now widely available internationally, with a good list of options on everyone's menu now, along with a good variety of impartial examiners who can warn a person, organisation, council, department or company when they are about to order something that does not work in the reliable way the seller presents it.

The whole of Europe has long had a general right for all non-migrants and non-x-convict EU citizens to roam freely all across all of the continent. This is now being expanded to a nearly global new expanded mega-alliance deal, called the Atlantopacific, under which people who come from areas where the main language used, before the global convergence into globalese, used to be any European, Japanese, Korean, Malaysian, Australian, North American, Slavic, Latin American, Celtic, indigenous, Spanish or British language can now move freely between all of these wonderful vast areas, though there are a few special limit restriction exceptions retained, such as a limit on the number of people moving to North America from Central America and the number of people moving from Urdu and Arabic speaking areas to cities that have suffered from terrorist attacks.

This goes alongside an existing agreement on the free travel of goods, services, finance and labour, from which all these regions have been benefitting for some time, achieving lower food, appliances and building material prices, more choice and far higher standards of living as a result.

Realising they have been left out, the Asian, African, Turkish and Arab regions have struck a massive free trade deal with each other, allowing all kinds of commerce, lending, investing and know-how borrowing to occur right across all these areas. They are also about to bring out a free movement of people agreement, with each area only to limit the number of new arrivals from two of its neighbouring states, and not to anyone else. A mega-link-up between this and the atlantopacific free trade agreement has just recently been reached, creating a global free trade zone that will help the system of aspiring ambitious and growing companies from warmer and colder countries find many new clients elsewhere in the world, bringing about a much better-served world population overall who has a much-improved choice now when it comes to buying anything it is thinking of buying.

There are still many issues around the African-born visionary ideas of a worldwide free-movement of people deal, as we have fiercely guarded quotas limiting the number of people (other than top doctors, artists, sportsmen, engineers, scientists, school principals, IT experts, architects, TV-show makers, nurses, carers and other listed shortage area members) who may migrate to Europe, Siberia, Oceania, North America, East Asia, wider Turkey, North Africa, South Africa, South America, the Caribbean and West Asia at present, and these rules vary widely from one destination province, state or borough to another.

But all this is under review, and a fairer way is destined to be found soon, under which people will at least be able to visit the area they have always wanted to visit most for a few weeks, and if they still love it as much as they thought they would, they will at least be able to sign up for a temporary guest worker's work permit for this destination, if they have a clean criminal record and the local knowledge, for ten years. Then, if this is not renewed, they can either go somewhere else they have always been interested in next or return to where they lived before until retirement and then return to their top pick place to live permanently.

The rise of Nigel Farage, Boris Johnson, Donald Trump, and some other narrow-minded bozo in Hungary, Turkey, Belarus and elsewhere is not such a big news story in reality A. For a start, they could only ever govern over an area with a population of less than 1 million, the international bodies would never let people like this work in them, and they all have powers that are also limited by a number of rule-enforcement and electoral-promise enforcement bodies. as well as by the wider legislature itself too.

Tighter new immigration restrictions are on the rise, as a result of the few recent and tragic terrorist attacks in Kabul, Bagdad and Paris, but a growing shortage of people to do the dirty and hard jobs is making the most restrictive cities and areas reconsider how many places of origin to keep on the most restricted list. And so most places have recently put a long list of places or origin on the totally unrestricted list for a few years on a trial basis, while also ensuring that the most dangerous people and ideologies can come nowhere near their lovely cities, and that a few top applicants from all other areas are also allowed to come and work in their first preference destination for a ten year trial period.

Most of the locations who, in the 1990s or 2000s decided to quit their interregional agreement or just its free trade element, or to quit the UN, have since changed their mind, and the effects of missing out on the security, the shared resources, the extra low tariff trade, the joint working on fighting crime and the many other benefits have made nearly all such areas decide to rejoin the eurotranspacific agreement, to rejoin their trans-reg body, and to rejoin the UN. Some are even rejoining the old Southeast North America Confederacy. In fact, as the UN anti-pollution, anti-gangster, anti recession and disease eradication programmes are only going to work as well as they ought to work if every person and area takes part. It is not unlikely that the UN will soon decide to make unjoining some of its action areas an option that no longer exists.

After all, letting a few rich selfish narrow-minded people, somewhere, who refuse to pay a single penny toward making the whole world so much better for everyone, opt to pay no taxes at all toward keeping the entire planet alive, inhabitable, safe, clean, salvageable, and in order for their families' and for everyone's benefit is not something you could say they don't benefit heavily from.

And making the paying of the low but crucial taxes that make saving the planet happen optional is almost like giving up on making anything good ever happen. Letting the richest opt-out of paying toward making it happen would be the same as abolishing all forms of cooperation, including roads, waste collection and the police overnight. So maybe it's finally time to use the world's biggest army, now firmly in the hands of the UN, to make it clear that you can choose between a lot of courses of action, and between a lot of different policy, appointments, law variations, schemes, partnerships and a to a lot of different solutions to various social issues, but you cannot opt to no longer be part of this planet, where the air we breathe and the water in our rain clouds and in our oceans is common to us all.

Just a brief note to say that a lot of team sports and individual sports have scheduled a lot of brilliantly planned and well-presented truly exciting events soon, from rugby to baseball, from chess to handball, from volleyball to basketball, and from golf to tennis (and many others!). Each of them is open to all, and each of them has a number of trophies available to those with fewer resources to throw behind their team too.

The next FIFA world cup will go to either Croatia or to South Holland, in two days' time, which will try its best to be as great a treat for all the viewers of the world as the Sao Paolo versus Wales showdown we had last time around was, or the Lombardy versus Zambia finale in last year's global opportunity cup, or as last week's UEFA Champions Cup final between Atletico Madrid and Manchester City. Regardless of what happens on the night, we just know that it is the millions of spectators all around the world who will win, as the whole thing will be broadcasted on so many channels worldwide that it will be easy to channel hop away from all the adverts.

Part 5 - Now back to the excitement of hopeless survival desperation that reality A would, could and should have completely prevented:

In the evening of the first full day after the bomb blasts:

Keith: "The sky has now vanished, I hate to say it but most likely it is gone forever, under a huge wall of grey clouds. No crops can grow any more. I have been thinking about how I will choose to die. I have also been indulging in my meat, cannabis and alcohol stocks with Greg, who told me about a fun way of making an exit that the government (or the press) supposedly recommends and supports. This will also be my one last chance to finally meet that pretty celebrity TV show hostess who I have always fantasized about, and who I adore so incredibly much."

Sara: The government has admitted that it is about to seal off its bunkers. According to the last ever newspapers to be printed, it will wait nine days before it seals the last one of them off for a 35 year period. It has launched a new system of letting people all score each other to see who goes into it: Each person gets to give out 10, 5, 3, 2 and 1 points per day to the five people who they feel have behaved the best, and a further 10, 5, 3, 2 and 1 points to whoever they feel looks strongest, healthiest and prettiest and who would be best to be kept for repopulating the world in 35 years' time, but the app prevents people from giving any one individual both kinds of points on the same day. I have just been on the website and have installed the app, and I see that there are people with over 90 points already, so it will not be easy for any of us to 'win on points' but it is being presented as the only way to be in with a chance.

Greg: "I have seen some lovely ideas in the paper on how best to go, for a single guy of my age: One suggested method is to go to this creepy prison up Elm Hill, which has been converted into a safe house for celebrities. I don't know what they've done with the inmates who used to live there? Maybe made some sort of cargo carrying unit to support the army as it defends our princess, our prime minister and the points leaders? There, at the Palace of Pleasures, which is occupying the very spot where the Elm Hill Penitentiary was, we get to choose the two most beautiful celebrity women, and well, this is hard to say out loud, so I will whisper it: You get to choose a pretty leggy bird to have her legs around your throat and a cute curvy gal with a nice ass to sit on your face and while the two ladies you choose finish you off, you do your bit to save these heavenly women, as they get 295 points each from your ultimate sacrifice, as long as they are of the most fertile, healthy, young and strong category (or 45 points if gifting yourself to your own girlfriend, daughter or wife or to anyone who comes under some other category)"

Ollie: Gosh, things move quickly these days. The militia boys have already given me my weapon and most of my training (no uniform, as we go incognito!), and we will burst our way into that survival bunker on Hayham Hill at 0500 tomorrow morning, occupy it, kill all outsiders, take their bodies away, then get our supplies in, plant land mines all around us, in keeping with our secret map for when re-emergence day comes all those years later, and will then seal it up. Job done. I will be there, though I hope to somehow manage to end up somewhere other than the firing line at the very front when it all kicks off. It's the only way I'm going to make it in one piece.

Kate:" I too have been given my weapon and my training, but I think I will lurk near the back and say 'it's ok guys, don't worry about me, I am protecting our flank from attacks from behind'. My gamble is that Ollie and I will be away from the deadliest bits of gunfire, but close enough to get in when the bunker is taken. There are also some boxes of supplies hidden away in some houses, but I don't yet know how I am going to get all this stuff into the bunker? ….   Ooh, I know, I'll get us a van! And then we could do multiple trips and really shift those supplies quickly!"

Part 6 - In the morning of the 2nd day, the 20th January 2025:

Keith: "The bad news is that I now know that today is the day I am going to die. The good news? Well, I am going to meet, and not just meet but even have an intimate life-saving (for her) encounter with the woman of my dreams, yes that ultra-gorgeous TV show presenter slash weather girl slash shampoo model slash twitter star, panel show contestant and my does she look great in the newspapers and in the magazines. She's the one that I have the really biggest hardest fullest crush on! She's the one I want to save!"

Sara: "Sh. Don't tell the others. I have decided to build my own bunker, and I will fill it with all the things I like to read, eat and do. It's going to be hard work, but I've bought a 20-ton digger and I've already started making the cave, deep in a nearby large abandoned field. This will be my salvation. I just hope my prince charming turns up. Oh I just know he will, I won't settle for any old passing male. I will pick one with potential" (giggles).

Greg: "Me and Keith have both signed up to the thing up at the prison. This way, even though we will not make it ourselves, we can die in an arousing position of pleasure, under some famous leggy curvy TV goddesses, and we can go to eternal sleep in the belief that these fabulous girls will make it, using the points they earn from having us go there and choose them. First we given them some immediate pleasure, and then we save them long-term. That's how a true valiant knight goes out".

Ollie: "The battle began at 0520, just a little behind schedule. We were well equipped and we had a good plan. It was all go. Our surge of improvised explosives took out the entire government and military contingent, we think. Though we did lose many brave fighters in the skirmish, we seem to have won the bunker, fortunately. And we hope we haven't damaged it. This means we will be saved. But first we need to figure out how to open the damn thing up, and how to get all the supplies that our boys and girls have brought inside?"

Kate: "I have found us a working van, and have loaded it full of supplies, twice so far. Now I am guarding it and that second load of goods carefully, while the militia boys are out in the town, preparing the boxes of goods to fill it up a third time – there are lots of scary looking people around, and the boys have been gone for a long while. I'm now just waiting for word when the bunker is opened up, so we can get our supplies and ourselves safely inside. Maybe if I move the van to be completely hidden and camouflaged, these creepy weirdos will stop eyeing up my precious stockpiles."

Part 7 - Around midday:

Keith: "Well, I am now third in the queue, and then it will be my turn. I can now confirm that these lethal ladies are definitely the very celebs I fancy most. I have seen them coming out to grab their next donor. I am giving them all the points I can, in the hope that some of these amazingly talented beauties will survive. There are my two daily allocations of 10, 5, 3, 2, 1 to give out, there's the 295 each for doing the ultimate deed on me, and then, the menu chart on the wall over there says: There are also some 5 point, 10 point and 20 point gifts I can give by also sacrificing my ears, toes, and even my trouser onions just before the final choke begins. Tough one. ….. Well, seeing as it is my one supreme dream girl in the world, who I am giving these to, who I may be hereby saving, long-term, I think I will say yes to the loss of my ears and of both my trouser onions. I am not going to be needing them in those eight minutes I'll have left to live. But my toes? I didn't choose this option, as I could not bear the pain and the needless suffering. I hope they'll understand."

Sara: "After these two unknown girls and a bloke turned up unexpectedly, the bunker-building project on the farm sped up nicely. My next worry is: where are we going to find a door that can seal us in? And do we have enough supplies for the four of us?"

Greg: "I only ended up signing up for the loss of my ears and the squashing of one of my onions today, as a points donor, which will happen in a few minutes from now. I am right after Keith in the queue. He's doing a 295 today, and will not going to be coming home. My choice went to a different bird than Keith's, as he's into skimpy blondes and I'm into curvy brunettes and redheads. I will go home afterward and will finish off the last of my booze, all the good meat cuts in my fridge and of course all my drugs stashes, before coming back here tomorrow for my final surrender deed. That's if I don't find a bunker I can survive in by then. I still hold out some faint hope that maybe fortune will save me, and that would be my preferred route to travel."

Ollie: "Can't speak now, hard at work." Grunt. "We're digging our way around the bunker door, as we can only open the flippin' door from the inside … Damn, this is hard! We must hurry. We can rest once we're sealed inside."

Kate crying, sobbing intensely: "I tried so hard to fight them off, but the van and the supplies are gone, my hand is a bloody mess, and I fear Ollie and the guys won't want me in this condition. Crap! I should've driven off before they got close enough to open the van door. They had a road-blocking pole and heavy stand structure, blocking the road off, but I should've crashed into it as hard as I could, and maybe I'd have got through. I nearly did, but then I fell for their we're on your side spiel. Now I've messed up big time and

they boys will all hate me, and will send me out to go get it back.
Shit."

Then Ollie and the boys give the signal that the door is finally open!
But they have the shock of their lives, when they find that there are
people inside the bunker already, and among them are none other
than the British royal family! "What?"

Part 8 - In the evening, a particularly fateful evening it is indeed:
immediate death for some, just so another human might live

The finger of the one he longed for most waved Keith in. His turn
had come at last. The waiting was over. It was time to make the
ultimate sacrifice, so his biggest crush might live. There were no
spaces left for males in the main bunker of the state, as the thing will
be sealed off from the air for so many years that it makes sense to
bring women in instead, who will one day be able to repopulate the
world, if all goes well. But which women will make the cut?

Meanwhile, Sara is now bringing all the supplies she can find into
her brand-new mini bunker – apart from the medication to keep the
radiation in check, which she has not found much of, it's looking
good … maybe she will find another way of getting more of it …
Let's hope she has found a way of dealing with sewage waste …

Greg is now back home, having donated a high-heel flattened ball to
one tall, attractive cutie, and his ears to another, which made him
look badly mutilated, mostly because he was. He is now finishing
off the last of the booze in his home. There is no point in wasting
any time on sleep tonight. Greg will have plenty of time for this after
tomorrow, when he is done in, so there's actually time to watch his
favourite movie one final time, properly, while smoking the last of
the weed, gulping undiluted gin by the gallon and enjoying some
intense one-ball self-arousal time, for old-times' sake.

Ollie and the farmer's militia have managed to get the door open and
have gotten themselves into a deadly skirmish shoot-out with the
king of England's entourage inside the bunker. The beautiful,
pregnant and not long out of breast-feeding royal princess grand-
daughter and her royal delegation had been in the bunker, all sealed
away, with 35 years' worth of treats, or so they thought. Well,
neither side had much ammo on them now, that anyone could locate

in such haste, and so it turned into a jiu jitsu mass brawl inside the bunker, while another militia that neither side knew about, made up of teachers, coppers, shopworkers and lorry drivers, was lurking outside, about to make its daring move on this same bunker.

The voice that knows: With complete human extinction now probably imminent, all our five subjects were triangulating: Ollie and Kate were busy triangulating a soft spot on their opponents that they could target and so take them out. Sara was zooming in on all the pharmacies in the area. And Greg was trying to convince himself he was going to go out with the biggest pleasure anyone has ever had, when he goes back to the Palace of Sins one more time. Now back to the excitement:

Our Weybridge Abbey Kate is in a hair-pulling and eye-gouging brawl with the Dutchess, the one who is meant to give birth to the future king, and also with her butler: all three are taking quite a beating, and Kate has used a bottle strike to take out one butler already, and has, in full flow, deployed a deadly karate move on another, which took him out instantly.

Sara had done one round of triangulating to choose a good place in a quiet field for her bunker and then another round of dazzling triangulation to find all the supplies, which now that all the shops were only open for ten minutes a day, as required by a new law, with nothing much left to sell, was an act of near-miracle and of much breaking and entering. The medicinal anti-radiation supplies were, in the end, not found in shops, but in the vehicles of the soldiers who had died in the recent skirmishes. Taking them without making any noises was not easy.

Greg was zooming in on his favourite woman's best body parts, which is where he longed to spend the last of his moments: He wanted to go out with his lips in a kissing position, attached to the body of his favourite TV personality, and he was pleased that his last glances before he went down and under her were filled with the sight of a warm, soft, girly, attractive, familiar, long-desired, much-admired woman who could enjoy receiving the affection and the final joke-telling of a man who devoted himself to her.

Sara is now defending her bunker from an unwanted intruder. She has hit him with a shovel, eight times, but he has kept on coming at her, so desperate to climb into the bunker with her was he that he just kept on coming, and there just isn't room for five in her tiny little bunker! She sees the chance to stick the shovel in his throat, and put him out of his misery, but does she do it? Is she the killing type?

As the girls of the Palace of Sins all got together for their lunch break. They had a chance to admire each other's outfits, while also giggling about the experiences they've just had as the femmes fatales who were active as angels of death at the Elm Hill Palace of Pleasures today. All of them were looking superb, just like they have just stepped out of a shampoo advert. They were clothed variously, wearing sensual white high-end patterned lingerie, some in swimwear, others just in regular underwear, each with their hair done up to look sensationally semi-curly, semi-straight, part tied up but with parts dangling down, which the majority of the girls were wearing today, in the hopes of luring any undecided males under their deadly spell. These extra-stunning girls wore short red skirts that barely covered all their "charms".

Intricate patterns of pink thread adorned their skirts, which if one sees them from up close, but not too close, spell out "to die for". This worked well as patterns that were woven into these skirts. The girls' socks were clean, soft and pink. This was pleasant for the doomed boys to experience. Everything had been thought of and prepared specially to make them look as appealing as possible.

Their hair was long, well-grouped and wavy; and these girls' tops were white, with plenty of skin-reveal holes and V-shaped slits in-built into the design, helping to turn some already super-sexy young women into irresistibly gorgeous killers, who no man could ever say no to. In today's world, their clothes resemble an abbreviated tennis dress, enhanced with beautiful pink girly designs. In their stunning looks, they really were, as their skirts implied, to die for!

The officials were only here to keep score, and so their dress code was totally different, with simple black t-shirts and jeans. It was unclear, what their reason for sticking to the instructions was, as they were not accruing survival points. Maybe some sort of lie about going into a lottery, if all goes smoothly. Or something.

Sophie was determined to get herself an equally striking skirt for tomorrow's sessions, so more of the men would choose her, and if it means she will do better in terms of her kill count, it will win her more points too, giving her a better chance of making it into the best bunker.

The floor in front of the tightly packed try-out area viewers rows in the conference room had become a deadly deed chamber. All the girls who had come to try out and to show they were good enough to become a full-fledged angel of death were busy demonstrating their killing techniques, as a panel of judges made notes on a clipboard.

It was like this throughout the whole of Elm Hill palace. According to Rachael, this was the way things were going to be until the end of the following month. The people in power had decisively defeated several planners who had been arguing for other schemes for dealing with the issue. Now that the points system has been agreed on and launched, it was the be-all and end-off for everyone to live and die by.

Those with other opinions were now either in custody, behind bars, or in the buses going to the survival bunkers, if they played their cards right, moving in unison with the designated military units; and there were millions upon millions of prisoners, neutrals, add-ons and spares who were now surplus to requirements and no longer needed. For those who were not offered a place in the bunkers after all, even after helping set everything up, they were not to be kept alive, lest they damage a bunker when the lockdown begins. The government has started to reward their angels of death cooperative for their good work by being given these people as bonus death sentence prisoners free-of-charge, each of whom was worth 4,000 vitally useful survival points, to be collected when doing the deed on them.

Many of the suitably instinctively overly submissive men had been brought in to work in the angels of death cooperative palace as special house prisoners, security guards, officials, cooks, body-shifters and other supporting roles until such time as their time to "go under" comes. It was useful to have them around, as they could bring out clean sheets every so often, prepare the food and take away all those made freshly lifeless to the disposal site. But if any of these house support team members did not behave and work exactly as was expected of them, or if they failed to obey a single command, the girl cop rulers of the site, heads of the angels of death cooperative, the authorities, and ultimately, the girls would get them and would take them out.

Nicola, her three daughters and the maids had a GREAT home life together, at first, living in the angels of death cooperative, taking the lives of two to seven men per evening each in their boudoir girls' room, and then reading girly magazines in between kills. It wasn't an uncommon sight to see a mother, finishing off a victim, while she breastfed her newborn. The apocalypse had brought its own normality with it.

Giving life and taking life, all within the same cycle. The oldest daughter, Elle, was likely to be bringing another male to death at the same time, right across from her, in the room right opposite Nicola's, right at the same point on the hallway, but then on the other side. Both of them would enjoy none of the potential pleasures that come with their work. They would check their new points balance quite often, fixated only on upping it as high as it could go, so they might have a better chance of being included in a good survival bunker.

The second-oldest daughter would alternate between the two angels of death, providing the legs around the throat assistance that goes with the finish, which seems to come more quickly when there are two pairs of angel of death legs all squeezing the one throat. They came across like a happy family and they worked well as a team. No male ever lasted more than 20 minutes in their room with them.

Keith went out with a smile on his face – his last thoughts were: she's quite a big lady down under, soft but solid, and a little bit hairy too … so lucky to be allowed to do this … into position goes everything … she's powerful down there … blimey, those legs, that's a tight grip! I never knew my goddess of desires' legs were this strong … and nice to know that … oh crap, can't breathe, not at all. Is this some sort of sumo giantess with her foot on my head, stopping me from lifting me 'ead? No, just an average build girl, and I don't seem to have the strength to … urgh … dying … dying … what can I do? May as well try to let her do her thing … it's really her that we gave ourselves up for. I only wish that she makes it…. urgh … my angel, the goddess of the TV world, and my, can she squeeze hard with them legs of hers … going faint … fading … sleep time …out. Not long after Keith's passing, the corpse-shifting team came in to check he was done, and to take the body away. He was still warm, when his hands hung over the sides of the wheelbarrow as what was left of his body was being taken away.

Greg made his final visit to the former prison and chose a woman who he wanted to make a 295 point donation to. He even got to look at her pretty face as she fired the gun, six times, that ended his run (and extended hers, but only by an extra week!). This was one of many cases this week where it just wasn't working, and nor did the rope she had tried to strangle her previous visitor with, so she ended up having to finish one of them off with a gun, and when it ran out of bullets, she then went on to use a knife and two spears to finish her last kill of the day off. This was hard work for Suzette. Greg was still so drunk that he never fully knew what hit him. But his manners were so well raised and switched on that he helped his woman out all the way, even when it was time to give her the throat and the chest and then the throat again. An easy and willing target, helping her do the deed. What a way to go!

Everything had gone along so wonderfully. All the women had even adjusted to the frantic pace of points-claiming that was now demanded of them, if they wished to stay anywhere near the leader board. Sophie found she could easily put away 3 to 4 males every 60 minutes without feeling exhausted. Due to this constant killing, Sophie and the other angels were now in an almost continuous state of fury, and this helped them sleep ever so well when the shift was finally over.

Life was now so beautiful to Sophie. She decided she was going to win her place at the top of the leaderboard and to make it. With this thought, she no longer felt the least bit remorseful taking so many victims' lives when she began another day's shifts in the angles' palace of sins. She, and the rest of the glamorous women who had won the right to operate here, were sparing them a slow horrible death from radiation poisoning in the cells or out in the streets. They were playing an important role, and giving the boys a pleasant enjoyable and meaningful exit, in her presence, rather than out there where a bleak slow agonizing decay would have befallen them.

Sophie couldn't finish any victims at all off if they cried and begged for mercy. Each victim, without exception, had to gladly submit to the gentle, affectionate, caressing death this glambabe offered. Most of them did. If ever one of them did cry, struggle and beg for mercy, which was rare, Sophie's partner in their angel of death work, Céline, would have to jump in and finish the male off, usually using her tight lethal legs around his throat, until he was no more, no longer posing a moral dilemma for Sophie. Céline also had a knife, in case it ever became necessary. And it did!

One such occasion arose in the morning session, right after returning to their designated room after delivering the demonstration to the visiting crowd of new applicants chasing just two final places as angles of death in this palace, in the conference room. A man in his 20s who has been reluctant all along, started to fight when he was in position. Céline tightened the grip that her legs had around his throat, determined not to let him get out, and she waved her left hand frantically, signalling to Sophie that she needed her knife.

Sophie hesitated, but seeing the grip of the legs be subject to persistent thumps and a lot of leg-flick jerks designed to break her hold and to throw Céline off, she ended up giving Céline her knife.

And Céline plunged it into the male's heart so quickly that she must have been holding the knife for less than one second before plunging it deep into his chest. This worked, and it did the trick. The male's violent fights were over, and now Céline's legs were able to choke him out.

Seeing that he was defeated and on the way out, the male glanced longingly up at Sophie, who saw this and knew what it meant. The man was now ready to die for his dream girl. Sophie sighed. She would have wanted to spare the male, or at least to prolong the encounter for a bit longer, to receive more pleasure from it, or to go out with him. But stalling, slowing down and letting the other girls run up an unassailable lead was NOT an option. It was time to move on to the next victim, who was sitting outside and reading a girly magazine, ready to enter the moment he is called, just like you would see in a doctor's surgery.

Then, while he enters, the assistants drag the newly departed out and sling him onto a trolley for further removal and disposal. A carpet has been hastily moved to cover the majority of the blood stain on the floor. It was a busy day. This one turned out to be way more compliant and gentle, and Sophie was able to control him as she went in for the kill, which more than made up for what the previous guy's offerings were lacking. This sense of euphoria spread, and the dying man managed to go out with a central body part arising, in the middle of the angels of death applying their kill on him.

The girls had time to engage in chitchat: "Oh, that one was so much better! Why can't they all be like him. Oh by the way, I've just got to get my hands one of these splendid little outfits you're wearing, Céline." Sophie stated. "I love the way it accentuates your curves, your tummy, your hips, abs, cleavage, and your legs, all at the same time! It's perfect!"

"No problem, we know just the shop," replied Céline. "It's no longer open, but we can maybe gain entry through a broken window in the rear. We'll go there tonight!" They exchanged compliments around how well their lipstick matches their skirt, shoes and earrings, and also around how dazzling their eyes had been made to look, and then they gossiped about the men who were sitting outside and waiting in the queue, speculating on how far they might go on a date with them under pre-apocalypse circumstances.

The twins had the room next door. They worked hard for their points, and were amassing up to seven kills a day between them. They were among the most successful of all the girls who were employed here as angels, as their poster on the entrance hall wall makes them look so dazzling, in their carefully staged two-girl wavy long hair and sexy outfit making them look so nice and appealing pose. This invites many of the men who are not sure when they first arrive, which of the girls they will give themselves to, nudging them to make the decision to pick them.

Many of the chosen girls also benefit from having a very good picture up in the entrance hall. By getting picked more often, a girl can really soar up the rankings, clocking one lot of 295 survival points after another, all day long. It's hard work being so damn pretty and cute!

As the next two men, a bunch of convicted crooks who had been sent here to be finished off made their way to the angels that awaited them, Sophie thought of those poor dirty convicts being led into their cells, not for being paedophiles, thieves or violent, but probably for being with an opposition party, or for made up charges. Perhaps she might be made to take some of them out today.

Or maybe these two who are coming in now are nothing better than a bunch of stalkers, rapists, killers and robbers. This latest thought cheered her up immensely. Sophie's recollection of her life before coming to the angels palace of Elm Hill was no longer very clear. She did remember much about going to school, getting a house, getting a job, taking driving lessons and moving in with a boyfriend who later left her. But it seemed so long ago, now that she was lying in bed, trying to get to sleep, reflecting back on the day's events.

All her bed-time memories were now more recent: of striving to improve her precise kill time, of kills that went wrong, of Céline wrestling down and killing those who squirm too much, quickly and violently, and of those blissful moments of relief, when it was a done deed. Thinking back also to that handsome and cute compliant visitor, one of many that day, who gave himself over completely to her deadly squeezes on his unprotected and willing neck.

A new male visitor to her parlour, the kind who wanted to sit and chat, rather than go straight into the required position, would be quickly brought down by Céline's marvellous legs sweeping his legs out from under him, as she crept up from behind him while he was facing Sophie, and her grabbing hands controlled the angle she wanted his head to be in as he fell. He would then be leg-scissored by Céline, while Sophie had to help her by stepping on the part of his throat that was still within reach once Céline's deadly leg choke was fully applied, while also treading on his hands or feet, so he could not stray from the position they needed him to stay in.

This was the usual way to welcome a new visitor into her room, into her angelic chamber of death. No man would last more than 18 minutes max in there on a busy day, when these two girls, Sophie and Céline, working as a team, had ever so many bookings to get through. Sophie surmised that her style of killing would offer a more refined, relaxed, sophisticated and fulfilling finish than what some of the other girl angels in the palace was using. Most of the others were a bit rougher with their men, as they lack that air of trustable, divine, gentle control that makes most men surrender themselves fully to Sophie the moment they meet and fall for this angel of elegant angelic doom.

This difference is very much apparent in the try-outs, which were still going on at the end of the corridor in the conference room, even now as the top of the leader board was weeks worth of bonus kills ahead. There, victim after victim was being brought to his death by so many aspiring applicant girls, performing to the cheers of the officials, while being tested and assessed. But only very few of them had that aura about them that made the men they were putting out surrender themselves fully, gently and willingly to the girl who was depriving them of air. This difference was being noted, and it was going to make the difference between getting the position on offer or not for quite a few of the women in the audition.

One of our five main characters at the start of the story, Sara, was among the many women trying out here today. She was not just here to explore the only way of surviving the next 30 years. She was also interested in finding her inner femme fatale, having thought, dreamt and fantasized about being a deadly girl angel of death many times. But she comes here without much coaching, training, experience or advice. And there is a lot of competition. For this reason, she is unlikely to win the contest here today. But she and all the other girls are sure to get one kill under their belts during the try-out, which may be very enjoyable for some of the girls, as it involves using her body to quell a dying man's struggles.

As the man has been allocated to her, rather than choosing her, the girl taking him to death's door in these try-outs will only get 140 points today, while the woman he picks as the cutest and best-looking, the one he would have wanted to 'go under' most, wins no less than 2,000 points from this, whenever one of the try-out girls is picked, which not only improves her survivability score. It also helps her greatly, in the battle of the many try-out contenders.

The palace is spacious and lush, with an inner courtyard, a neat and lovely garden of plants and flowers and a fountain. In the garden, the birds were tweeting and some children were playing, obliviously unaware of the fact that hundreds of men were being brought to their deaths inside the building right now. It wasn't relevant to them, as they were the young of the angels, the angels who had good score tallies and were expecting to have a good chance of making it into a top-notch survival bunker real soon.

While the girls in the garden, wearing tiara crowns of daisies, were chasing and playfully catching some smaller and younger boys repeatedly, giggling as they went, the grown-ups inside were busy inflicting a final demise on men who were destined never to rise again. The kids were happily at play, unaware that while mummy was busy bringing some man to death, daddy was already dead, a victim of a kill inflicted by an ambitious and points-hungry girl in the first group of try-out girls in the conference room today. The fabric of society was changing fast, and the population figure was dropping fast.

Inside the conference room, the many try-out participant applicant women and girls are arranged in a pattern of positions along its main central floor, reminiscent of a tile pattern from Spain, while the spectators, mostly made up of supportive girly friends, officials and applicant girls were studying the techniques and were hoping to be in the next try-out the following day, are lined up along its perimeter.

Quite a few of the male supportive friends and family who had come to be spectators, cheering their girl on as she fought her way through the try-outs, have themselves been claimed by one of the other participant girls from the try-outs, with a soft yellow silk scarf placed around a man's neck to denote her choice. None of these chosen men will be alive by the end of these try-outs today, as each participating woman is entitled to complete her kill and to go for a good score from the judges. Sadly, this means the end of many good boyfriends, husbands, dads, uncles and brothers in there today. And tomorrow, there won't be enough males here so each new applicant girl can have a go, not unless the try-outs are changed, as one might have thought, to non-fatal by making each pairing decouple after 90 seconds or so.

A raven-haired beauty such as Sara could earn incredible pay as an angel of death, with looks "to die for" as one of the sponsor's slogans up on the back wall reads. Sara understood the humour of the message, and she grinned, as she saw the last of the dead male victims from the second try-out group being lifted onto trolleys and taken away.

Sara glanced around and noticed women of a select young range of ages, the third group, now all wrapped around their latest victims. Some of the girls were quite young. They may be lacking in her killer instinct skills, but presumably they get extra points for the fact that they could still be of child-bearing age in the distant post-lock-down future, when it is finally time to emerge from the bunkers. Well, if the menopause is usually at 50-54 and we subtract 35 for the number of years the lucky few will be in those bunkers, this requires some seriously young girls to be picked and brought in. Hopefully the selectors will have thought of this.

Sara wondered how could the lighter and smaller applicants ever even make a kill of a male who is sometimes nearly twice their size, or significantly stronger than she is. Then she noticed one young thin girl, possibly 18 and not very tall, busy choking a male out, with her arm wrapped tightly around his throat. She was frantically squeezing hard on him, keeping him from getting any air as her arm stayed tight to his wind pipe, as part of the try-out. That answered Sara's question.

Having been here to see the previous round of try-outs performed here moments ago, in which there were numerous kills of various techniques, Sara was now familiar with the positions the women were using. The common choke-outs all deployed either upper thigh head scissors, or arm chokes like hers. Sara saw both of these positions being used and among these were a few slight variations in technique, some acting as new positions she'd never thought of. As expected, most of the male victims were not laying still and so dealing with the way they were resisting was turning out to be a crucial part of the try-outs test. For the ultimate winner, their opponent wouldn't have even needed to be bound. But they had all been bound, as a procedural precaution.

Sara's group is up next, how exciting. Younger girls and boys, stadium attendants, were busy removing bodies and directing fresh victims to the various rooms. They normally get a nice and slow pace of work in the boudoir rooms, as there are so many angles to share the work between, but during a try-out there is always an awful lot of bodies to remove and a lot of people to shift, which makes the try-out days by far their hardest shift to work.

They are also the most perilous, as those thin yellow soft silk scarves can be placed around any male's neck to denote a smothering woman's choice, and it is not unusual to see a bunch of helpers 'go under' after being thus picked in these massive try-outs. Very often, it's the newest male recruits among the team of helpers, who had not known how the try-out girls' selection system operates, who end up with a soft silk yellow scarf placed around a man's neck to denote her choice, which means the male has less than a quarter of an hour left to live, and he will have to spend it all in positions of struggle and of worship of the woman who has chosen him!

Pay for the helpers is poor, but the lunches could sometimes be quite generous and after a full week on the job, a special package of perks, vouchers and survival points was to be earned. For the lucky few who do end up becoming glamourbabe angels of death, there is a mountain of survival points, potentially thousands of them to be earned, a guarantee that every court case will go her way, and an automatic exemption from all low-scoring citizens' duties to give themselves over for the kill. Sara was pleasantly surprised about this revelation. Glamourbabe status is not easy to attain. You have to earn it through mastery of the walk, the dress, the pout, `the look', the takedown, the finish, and so on.

When Sara's try-out group was invited to start selecting their target males, which was after a line-up of men, all tied together in one long train, had been brought out, they leapt into action. Most of the girls quickly returned with a cute male claimed through the yellow silk scarf method. But there were more girls in this group than boys in that train of tied men, and so, after missing the dash to claim the last one of them, as they had already run out of specially brought in men to use, Sara was left without a man. Sara sighed despondently.

Then she remembered that all males in the room and beyond were choose-able targets. Luckily, there was a handsome helper close by, who had just finished piling up three of the dead onto his trolley. In a haste, Sara slung her soft yellow scarf around his neck, narrowly beating two other girls, who were now left having to claim one of the four men in the spectators rows instead, who had been left to last because they were sitting there and holding hands with a woman they love, or because they looked scary and big. Sorry, guys, but you know the house rules? Well, here's a copy of them on a card for your girlfriends, while our female helpers are helping the choosers bring the last of the chosen males to their positions.

Everyone ready? Go! While most of the chosen males were already kneeling and kissing the baby bump regions of the girl who had chosen them anyway, and these males were easy to push over onto their backs, there was also the ones who were still on their feet. This included the three puzzled males who were picked last. In keeping with the house rules, these three stayed near the women who had chosen them and they were all spectacularly swept off their feet by some very determined and attractive females, who now had all the men on their backs and ready for choking out.

Sara's chosen helper boy made an audible gasp when he was skilfully thrown onto his back by Sara. He looked up to her, admiring every inch of the sensually curved body of Sara bathed in the bright spotlights from the conference room ceiling. Her eyes felt like they contained a mood hue of moonlight that was making him want to stay down and await her mighty legs shortly descending down on his throat. Without saying a word, he lay down at her feet.

Sara then pressed her legs together as hard as she could, praying she had wrapped them around the right bit of his throat to do the job and to do it impressively, her skirt going all around his head like a curtain. The feeling was so overwhelmingly delicious to have a victim's neck pressed hard and his heaving chest pressed tight to her body as she had let her long, lovely legs descend down around the north end saddle point of his body, without thinking about it. This showed a natural instinct, which the judges will like.

She then began a slow deep squeezing on the male's neck. It was not long before her sweat glands erupted, as she was exerting so much effort, with a big driplet of her sweat seen running down the helper's face. Sara was a little embarassed by this, but again the judges looked pleased and were giving her some good points, or so it looked.

We were now in the final try-out group of the contest for a place in the angels of death palace, and everywhere around the floor, girls were again finishing off their victims, while also trying to look like pros who can do it all with little effort, whatever that looks like. Many girls in this group ended up with no victim left to pick, and the look of disappointment on their faces was clear to see, as their try-out was over. They were not even allowed to go and get each other, for some reason.

The applicant girls managed as best they could to seal off all male abilities to breathe, using the power of their legs alone. As there were so many girls here, chasing so few winning posts today, it was not surprising that the judges never gave all those who they had already marked down with deductions in the first move a second glance. It was not so important for them to get the race for 29th place to 108th place right. What mattered today was that they were well enough informed about the top few best killers that they can then choose between them.

Some might say, come on! if some of the girls are already out of the running before they have made the kill, maybe they should be tapped on the shoulder and sent home, thus sparing the male. Well, this is a discussion that may have been different under other circumstances, but given how none of these people will live to go in a bunker anyway, you might as well give them all the thrill of the kill and let the girls think they are still in with a chance, for now, while letting the boys go out with a feeling of defeat for a bigger cause amid their demise.

Sara was lucky enough to be one of the twelve girls who made it through to heat five, the finals. She did very well to get this far, but only two will get the official state-backed angel of death girl job here in Elm Hill today, so the fight is not over. Sara was looking around for her supportive x-boyfriend, her uncle, her brother and her dad. But unfortunately they had all become a part of the game, and were now either lifeless bodies being loaded onto the trollies to be taken away, or they had been claimed already by another one of the finalists for the next round. Only Sara's sister was still there to cheer for her.

As usual, a row of allotted convicts with their number and their crime on them, was brought out, and Sara was able to pick a comparatively nice-looking guy for her next kill, leaving the fiendishly ugly brutes for the other two girls, the ones who had

progressed from the 4th heat. All the other girls now had to sit the
rest of this one out, but were free to stay and watch from the stands.

In a rare, funny, incident, one of these girls, Kelly, accidentally
choked a man who had "exempt" written on his chest. He had paid a
fortune to be exempt and was the general manager of the site. But
nobody noticed this when he was protesting at her yellow scarf
being tied around his neck and it was far too late when the helpers
realised.

On occasion, one of the women would receive a kick from
somebody's victim in his death throws, but in the heat of the
moment, his vain resistance was not noticed much by her at the time,
though the loss of control would lose some poor girl a ton of judges'
marks. Besides, he was under another girl's spell and he now
belonged to her alone.

Having been brought to a place of doom for all chosen men, by the
chosen angels themselves, and having been written upon with a big
red marker pen, clearly, on the mens' chests, each male getting the
names of the three ladies he had chosen for her looks in the catwalk
show earlier on today. As it was clear that, in this instance, an honest
mistake had occurred, and the crowd was chanting "honest mistake",
it was agreed to dock Shelly only 0.3 point for her mistake, and to
award her the rest of the points won from this kill.

Now only eleven of the 61 men remained in the queue. It was
starting to look like some of them might still be alive when the gong
goes. The rules state that any who are in mid-struggle at the time of
the gong, may continue with their kill until the male's ultimate
sweet surrender, the time of the final capitulation being crucial
where two girls have the same number of kills, and if there are any
left in the queue at this time, they are to be awarded one to the
winner, then, if there are any more, one to the second-placed girl,
one to the third, … as a `victory lap' celebration that may also serve
as a judge-off.

Handsome Stan the rodeo star and car salesman (swindler)
was pleasantly surprised by the sudden and unexpected kiss from a
magnificently beautiful glambabe. She had come to collect him,
yellow scarf in hand. Looking forward to an encounter with such a
vivacious and laughy chick, he let her get him, thus beating four
other girls who were heading his way off. In the end, he was easily
felled and soon he too was in his final throws of useless struggles.

Eventually Sara got into the swing of things, but she never made
it out of the bottom three in the final of this event. She struggled to
get the kill time she would have needed, as he victim, an x- burglar,
had made it hard for her by not staying down the first time she nailed
him. Just like Sophie's leggy partner Céline, who at the same time,
in her boudoir, was busy compressing another doomed male's throat
between her '10 out of 10' lovely legs. Other crooks would just walk
along in silence, sharing a burning passion for the beautiful glambabes that were about to attack them. Bert proved to be no match for
Nicola's prowess, which truly was everything he had ever dreamed
of in an all-powerful set of legs. The deadly legs of her partner Elle
were also a dream come true in action.

The crowd, mostly made up of officials, tier two pretty women
hoping for a turn tomorrow, and local women who were on their
breaks from hauling away bodies all day long, was chanting "kiss
that girl, kiss that girl!" – They were well into the excitement and the
heat of the moment now.

Obeying did not spare anyone's life, but supposedly it will win him a
better start in the after-life, and it bestows a lesser amount of shame
upon his name. This is what it said on the leaflets and on the posters
at the entrance. Most of the offerings seemed to have no problem
with the logic of this.

Quite pleased with herself as she finished him off, Sophie and Céline
were soon done with finishing off a pilot, and then they moved on to
their final victim of the day, a taxi driver and engineer, specialising
in car radios.

In the final minute of the game, all the women were
frantically working their lethal legs and their deadly arms, trying to
finish their more man off and to move on to win a room of their
own. In the final 15 seconds, three more girls managed to finish one
off, have the kill confirmed and to go up looking for another crook
to take out.

Two of these criminals were quickly snatched by an eager for
points female who wrestled him down, in partnership with her co-
angel, onto his back and went to work on finishing him off right
away. It was little Rachel and the blonde bombshell Brittany, who
were now joint leaders with Sarah-Jayne and her partner.

Then, just ahead of the buzzer, sweet Suzy, who had just run out of
men with her name on them and who had already clinched 4th place

came and took one of the open selection men back to her spot, where she and terrible Tara threw him over and descended on him. Within seconds, they had him in the desired spot, his face under the sweet bottom of sweet Suzy and the terrible legs of Tara pressing down on his throat. His air supply was cut off. This gruesome twosome was about to kill him off, and to earn some valuable points.

When the time finally ran out, just two of the males remained unclaimed when the gong sounded, and hence they were going to be victory laps or play-off deciders for two of the top three finishers, which turned out to be Brittany and little Rachel, ahead of Samantha and Amber in this event, mostly because of Sarah-Jayne's costly slip-off, which gave her final target costly extra minutes through one last bonus breather.

 When the final standings were read out, and the top two planted a victorious foot on their prizes' faces, while the others planted a foot on their last victims' already surrendered faces, the crowd cheered ALL the girls well, and chanted "super babes, super babes" every chance they got and some chanted "that's a good innings".

Lovely curly lethal ladies wearing black evening dresses were dragging the choked out males out of the arena and over the edge of a nearby cliff into an empty outdoor swimming pool. More and more defeated males were being chucked off the edge and were piling up inside the empty pool. Sophie was amazed at the huge heap of seemingly dead men (but surely most were merely unconscious? or maybe pretending?) already, and the night was young yet.

The crowd euphorically chanted "You go, girls!" and when it was over, the glambabes' own remix of the Space Girls' Classic Hit "I really, really, REALLY wanna sit-a-sit-ah!" was played through the sound system, while all the bodies were taken away, presumably to be turned into a variety of nifty uses, from gastronomic delicacies, to beauty products like skin cremes and shampoos, to stuffed toys and trophies for walls, to food for crocodiles who were being bred and raised for the women to eat when they were ready for the butchers. Or maybe for no use at all.

But the loudest cheer of all so far, topping many a really big, loud cheer already so far, came when the ring announceress pointed out who the winners were and how soon they could take ownership of a room, adding how many more men still awaiting their fate in those boudoir rooms here tonight.

The chosen glambabes' names are written on the whiteboard in big red letters, just after the deliberating at the end of the competition.

The names are Kate and Millie, who will form a new partnership, taking over the new killing chamber boudoir that was once known as the broom closet instead. Sara and the many other girls who came close but missed out were then sent home, their heads hanging in shame. Their contact details were taken, in case a smothering opportunity were to arise in any of the smaller new fringe locations in the area.

Then the two victory-lap trophy-boys were slowly and pleasurefully being taken out, kindly and mercifully given a couple of sit-up breaths before the final sit and leg squeeze combo, in which all nine pairs of glambabes were allowed to sit on the chests and legs of these prizes, while Brittany and Lil' Rachel ensured that their throats were suitably constricted.

The competition was over. Everybody came out of the conference room, apart from those who had been choked to death in the finals. They were not about to get up and go anywhere.

In The Pageant, each male chooses his top five picks from among the girls during a lingerie catwalk show, and is guaranteed to get one of his picks, so the more often a girl is chosen, the better are her chances of scoring the most from her kills, after all more men to take out means more points, not just potentially, but for certain.

Young Carlos waited patiently to be led in by one of the cute teenage girl attendants. It had been a long and difficult journey for the youth. He was a Hispanic, born and raised by an indifferent peasant family along the lake's coast. His father was a brute that drank up the family's small income, for which he had to be sentenced in court. His mother took to drink herself and left him and his 11 brothers and sisters to fend for themselves. Her only diversion from drinking was knife-throwing. In one of her rages she knife-throw killed one of his younger brothers. It didn't seem to bother her in the slightest that she was had just killed one of her own children. That's just mum being mum.

One day a buyer came to town and young Carlos, along with two other brothers, was sold for a few loaves of bread. He remembers how happy and gleeful his mother was as she tucked the loaves under her arm and ran back to her dilapidated cottage. She was accompanied by a swarm of begging street merchants. Just as she entered the cottage, she grabbed one of the boys and pulled him forcefully inside, in her usual way. So far nothing of young Carlos's life had been fun.

His only joy was to look out onto the vast expanse of the blue lake and imagine himself as a brave sea captain rescuing beautiful women from evil pirates. This was his favourite escapism, one he longed for most.

Now he faced a slow, painful death in the legs of some woman, and he longed for a glimpse of her boobs, as he had never seen any in all his life. All of the prisoners were sullen and resigned to their fate. It was as if they were already dead and just their body hadn't gotten the message yet. After being fed a horrible tasting gruel, they were loaded on a large cargo lorry. Being prisoners, they were stuffed into the black cramped depths of stinking cargo unit. At least the gentle vibrations of the journey had had a soothing effect on him for he, as with most of the prisoners, and they soon arrived at the try-outs arena within the Elm Hill palace of sins.

Carlos's mind went blank. When put in a position such as this, beaten down, unloved and forgotten by the world, you turn inward. His young mind was virtually blank. All thoughts of escape were laughable. The prisoners were so weak from malnourishment they were barely alive and utterly defenceless. How could they overcome well-armed and perfectly healthy guards, with weapons designed to maim and to kill. He was jarred awake when the slavers opened the hatches. Bright sunlight, like a searing intense beam penetrated into their lair.

All chained together at the ankle, they slowly filled into the waiting cells. A big fat red-haired wabbly fatty brute of a woman looked them over one at a time. Every so often, she would select a slave and one of her assistants would unchain the slave and make him stand in a separate group. Finally it came time for Carlos's turn. All she said was "This one goes in the next event" to her assistant and moved down the line. Carlos found himself separated from the main body of prisoners. His fate had just been sealed.

There were perhaps 11 of them chained together, separate from the rest. All of them were quite young and many of them were innocent, obviously unfit for the life out there. Carlos didn't get his hopes up, for the lot of prisoners was a very cruel one, and any unspeakable fate could await. Much to his surprise, they were loaded into a cosy living room area, furnished with comfortable settees. Much to Carlos's surprise it was clean. They were even fed a decent meal.

Hundreds of other young prisoners were already in the waiting cells. For the first time in his life, he felt a spark of enthusiasm. Then he heard the word angels whispered from slave to slave. "angels" - he was to be choked out. His spirits soared. No slow death in the mines or a dog-like existence in some dirty hot dry slave pen. The prisoners began to talk amongst themselves. They were all excited, elated in fact. True they would die, ah, but such a glamourous girly death was aspirational for a hopeless young male like him. A slow sensual choke-out by a beautiful woman was not such an awful fate. They were mostly looking forward to it, even more so since it would be performed by some golden-haired American beauty named Amber.

After docking, they were unchained and led in large groups to a bath. This was the first time young Carlos could ever remember such a warm relaxing bath. A stern matronly like women checked each boy to see if he was clean enough and many were sent back. After the bath attendants handed out new cloths. It was nothing more than a white cloth that went around their waist. Then they were fed and what a feast.

Carlos had never seen such a display of food. A long table covered with only a meagre supply of not at all delicious food stretched out before him. The young lads ate like wild animals and Carlos was no exception. They all knew this food and the decent treatment would end in their kill, but they welcomed it. It would be the crowning moment of a fantastic dream. A majestic encounter with a girl would tie it all together into one beautiful package.

Carlos and several hundred companions were led through the clean and neat alleys of the arena. Prisoners being led to a cooperative of angels was a normal everyday sight and the proper citizens showed no interest in them at all. None of the lads were chained and there were occasions when a slave could have made a break for it. This was the furthest from their thoughts. They welcomed the sensual deadly embrace of the glam-angels.

The column stopped momentarily when a housewife with a fancy hair-weave up-do indicated to the guards she and her two teenage daughters wanted to look over the lads and to select some victims. The women, though in her early 30's and their mid teens, were very beautiful. Her beauty was also enhanced by the fact she was wearing Victorias Secret underwear only.

Both her daughters, also wearing this, had immaculate bodies any
lad would gladly go under for. She and her daughters briefly looked
over the prisoners and made their selections. Then six five pound
notes changed hands. Carlos passed the door of the women's home
when one of the boys, the women's captive, turned and smiled. He
was obviously pleased to have been selected and was evidently
looking forward to the encounter.

The large group of prisoners was further broken down into groups
of two to three hundred and led off either to the various angels'
boudoirs throughout the palace, or the waiting cells of the try-outs
arena. Now and then, the column would be halted by an
animated housewife waiving her hands about while making her
point, or by a young maiden, so she could select a victim for her next
points haul. In most instances, the selected youth would turn
and waive to his companions.

Carlos, through all the confusion, had lost sight of his pals. He
had hoped to perhaps catch sight of them before his end came. Once
again, the column shuffled to a halt as two young women looked
over the victims. A tall sexy blonde pulled his pal Markus from the
line. His young face was radiant. Carlos felt a strong tinge of
jealousy, especially when she and her companion turned to lead the
youths away.

Both young women had the most magnificent and perfectly formed
posteriors you could imagine. As Carlos passed, he
called to his pal. Markus turned and smiled. The women seemed
nice and attractive. Carlos patted Markus affectionately on the head.
Markus waived and shouted "good luck!" The column moved on and
soon the young women and their victims passed from sight.

At last they arrived at their destination. Carlos didn't get to see much
of the building. An attendant came around and offered them water or
boiled rehydrated fruit. Young Carlos had never at any point in his
brief life known such kindness. He knew that he would pay for this
with his life, but that was of no consequence. He thought it was
much better to be sacrificed by some majestic beauty than to suffer
for years as a nameless slave.

One attendant, a young girl, was making her way amongst the
prisoners, putting a light coat of fragrance on their frontages. Over
the next few hours, an older woman or a young attendant would
come in and select a few victims to be distributed to the angels. At
last it was Carlos's turn. His short journey through life would come
to an end.

He was led down a long Sorority House hallway. Along the hall were a number of rooms, or rather more like open stalls. He looked inside and saw some intense leg-scissoring going on. Many of the women were being quite loud and angry about it, and he imagined that the males might be moaning in pleasure as the feeling of being taken all the way swept over their bodies. He saw them struggle and thought that this must be the polite and protocol thing to do. Attendants were exhausted, dragging body after body away – there was sweat in the air, as women's hard squeezing efforts were bringing it out of the girls. "Here" the women said pointing to a stall.

Carlos's breath was taken away when he saw her. She was a tall Mediterranean beauty with long black hair. In-shape and retaining all of her feminine charms. "Over here, lay down here" she said impatiently. The youth regained his senses and obediently lay where indicated. He placed his head on a large soft pink pillow. She then lowered herself down, glared briefly over his face, sussing out how much of a fight this one was likely to put up. "Not much, if I keep telling him what to do" was her verdict on this matter.

This raven-haired goddess had a glistening thick cloak of long wavy curls plunging down her shoulder, an hour-glass figure of curves and long legs, and her lips and nose were adorably small. She was very commanding and that twinkle in her eyes said 'you will want to stay on my good side, boy!' The dilation in her eyes was accentuated, probably from the "excitement" of all of the kills she'd performed so far and just now on this shift. He had watched in almost slow motion, as she lowered herself down and closed her legs in around him. He felt her gently wiggle her hips, working his neck deep inside her kill zone. This was such a treat for him – she was amazing! He just wanted to be near her.

"Ah, oh, this feels SOOO damn good. You shouldn't be so damn fussy. Ya gotta take your pleasure wherever you find it. Jennifer Klissoris was deep into her kill, and Carlos was nothing more to her than one of many conquests that week, as this was not the try-outs arena after all, it was the deadly buy cosy boudoir of one of the established regulars. As she clamped her legs tight, she then smoothed her stylish orange-coloured dress around herself, which kind of meant that it was all that Carols could see. As he was soon going to be gone, it did not matter a jot what he could see, including the colour of Jenny's underwear, which was very rewarding for the dying boy to gaze upon, or what he is told, which is very little.

Sophie and the eccentric older lady talked for some time. It seemed that a band of raiders had recently swept through the farmland up ahead. They didn't do much damage, but concentrated on taking

anything edible they could find. This in turn meant that supplies in the palace were even shorter the next day.
Sophie then excused herself and wished the old lady a good spell of luck and moved on. The thought of a whole vast area stripped clear of food was frightening. It was about mid noon when she came across two women arguing over a small boy.

Both of them were uncalmable, and the boy was long gone, having had a one-way trip to the palace of leggy angels with his aunty, when she came up for an audition. It was quite a heated exchange that might eventually lead to a fight. The women of this area, deprived of males, would soon get desperate - who knows what would happen then.

Sophie then observed a tall 17-year-old typical piano student type girl rounding her bend onto the hallway. She almost stumbled onto a young boy, before snatching him up and dragging him into her boudoir. The door closed behind them, and there was some commotion in there, followed 17 minutes later by another corpse being taken out of this room, that of the boy, and another kill-load of points being added to yet another girl's survival points tally.
This one was even quite a lot younger than her. It seemed like in no time at all the last male in the region will follow his gloomy fate. With the kill,
she began to feel her female needs satisfied. Every good day would currently be one where many a male succumbs to her. One has to wonder, whether this insatiable killing spree would end, once safely in the confines of a survival bunker. One tends to doubt it, as the yearning for more has now been programmed in.

Aside from being young, he had also been very frail.

Sophie's last visitor for the day was delivered to her room. She had to be careful and not get carried away. With choice victims in short supply, she wanted this one to last a bit, to get the most out of him. After two hours she decided to unlock her legs for a 23rd time and to climb off the lad and look over just what she'd captured. This one was going to be taken to bed with her, and by the morning, or possibly by the 4th morning from now, having complied in many ways and fulfilled many a sticky favour, his time will be up. Such is the life of all who accompany an angel of death.

He gasped for breath and coughed. His soft blonde curly hair was all matted down. "Sorry about this." Sophie said apologetically. He didn't say much, then
looked up at her. He saw the yearning in her eyes, and knew it was his duty to accompany this princess of his fantasies to wherever she

wanted him next. Off they went to bed, and he turned out to be of many uses in the night.

The next morning, after hiding what was left of her toy beneath her bed for the day, Sophie and Céline then directed a farmgirl to go for a swim, while her brother was taken in and locked in by the yellow scarves of both Sophie and Céline. The girls' next young victim was instructed to lay down in the face-down position, leaning his young neck over Céline's extended left leg, while a queue of specially delivered men forms behind the door to this boudoir. The old lady handed Sophie a thin white satin cloth skirt. "Better cover him up good" she said pointing to Sophie's victim. "Them's scarce around her and lot'sa women gonna get REAL excited over a cute one like that." She said. "also, we don't want to be giving too much away to them guys waiting in the line!"

The old lady then raised one foot up slightly off the floor, glancing down at Sophie and Céline's latest victim, who was now fatally trapped between Céline's killer legs, while sat back, with the dagger in hand, in case. "You want water or something honey?" she asked looking down at him. The victim, as much as Sophie could see of him, had light brown hair and was about the same age as Sophie's hidden bedroom captive. The two might even be classmates or something.

A small weak voice replied "no, thank you." "Suit yourself," replied the old woman sitting back on her chair and letting the thin white satin cloth skirt be flung onto his face. With Céline's victim safely concealed under a blanket, her legs tightened securely around his throat. The old madam sat back and enjoyed the view, as the death grip took its next victim, creating a most pleased grin on the face of the old lady. For some reason, witnessing this was giving her the good sensations. We prefer not to speculate too much about why, but it was clear to see that she was not a neutral official – the thrill of the kills, and especially of witnessing the younger males die, was somehow doing it for her.

After a few minutes later, Sophie saw a woman in her 30's wearing red, a necklace and large circular earrings thank the woman in front of her and help her off an exhausted but still living victim. The lad was in a bad way, and the leg scissors hadn't worked, so this vixen decided to kill him with her sword. She pulled her shiny sword out of its sheath and had the poor lad completely surrounded. He dropped to his knees to beg for mercy, clearly having changed his mind about whether or not he was willing to die here today. The old lady scorekeeper winked at her, saying "definitely another willing one in my book!" Then the sword went right through his skin and deep inside him, piercing his heart. The kill didn't take long and soon she was back on the prowl for another victim.

Not far ahead, five ordinary looking men blocked a path, with dozens of death angle women sitting down for a snack in front of them. The men were standing there, sensing the deadliness of these women. The men turned to run, even though they didn't look threatening or particularly dangerous, just curvy and soft like girls do. The men made their way to a door that they had entered this wing through, but it was now closed, locked and sealed. There was no window and no other escape route, other than going past ALL the snacking girls somehow. This was going to be tricky, especially as there were now 22 girls and they were now up on their feet, having left their snacks behind in order to pursue these new targets.

The men didn't have a chance. With so many women simultaneously chasing them down, the only possible outcome was that each one of them would soon be trapped between various pairs of legs and were being turned into points, as the kills were inflicted in a relentless push to spare not one of them, and with none of them even destined to live to see the 20-minute mark from the moment they had first been spotted.

Sure, this was the angels' palace, and these guys had probably come here, knowing this was going to happen, but maybe they had been hoping to make it to the special boudoir of their favourite TV celebrity girl – we'll never know, as their demise was swift and comprehensive. The girls had struck again! This time, all over a hallway, with all kinds of visitors gazing on. While each newly felled male had two or three pairs of legs wrapped around him at once, yet more girls attacked their heads and chests, treading or stomping on their chest, seeking to gain some of the kill points or maybe just seeking a satisfactory win. It was all over in seconds. Sophie never gave them a second thought and resumed her journey to the ladies loos, having only just stopped for a coffee, and ended up becoming part of this deadly onslaught when the opportunity arose.

Man after man lay stretched out in boring repetition. Then she perked up when she noticed many new delicious males about. At first, just a few, then more and more. She decided it was time to return to the room, to join Céline and see how she was getting on. The room was filled with four dead male's bodies, as the removal service had failed to keep up with Céline's incredibly deadly dispatching of men – the place felt like a war-devastated area. While walking along, she noticed the bodies of three freshly killed young males, all laying on her bed. This gave Sophie a panic, as she was hoping to se her bed-time toy again, so she could have more fun with him – but it was not to be, as Céline had not known that this one was for keeping, and she had put him into the great big dominatrix dungeon in the sky, as his last breath was spent admiring Céline's shapely legs.

When Sophie looked out the window, she saw in the distance that a woman in her mid 40's was struggling with a heavy pack. She was dressed in a black dress skirt. A tall blonde woman in her 20s was travelling with her, hair piled high on her head – a hockey team star she knew!

The two girls had evidently just lost their boyfriends and their brothers, as each male in the area has been brought up to the palace by the army and have turned into completed kills. For this reason and others, these two women were resuming their journey, off to seek new opportunities and to see if there were any men, food or bunkers to be found in other regions.

Perhaps they could make a living as an angel of death, they had wondered. The girls had been especially excited over such a prospect. They had given it their all, showing with what ease they too could kill males when they took part in the try-outs. Piles of men lay before them, when they awaited the results. They had spotted one or two still living ones among the piles of fallen and used up men, but a frenzy of frantic girls ensued, resulting in fresh new kills, as a result of which any hope of escaping with a rescued and living male evaporated, and so now a whole new adventure was about to unfold, with the women heading off to seek their fortunes elsewhere.

A similar system has also been up and running for women like them who are done trying to make it to go and gift themselves to the country's best-looking, best-known and most fancied men, but there is only one such site in the country, which is far from here. The angels of deathstiny men of Weston are also competing for selection and survival, and this is located a very long way away from Weybridge Abbey. Some people, be they gay, lesbian, straight trans, bi or just huge fans of one of our sublime and amazing deadly angel celebrities, do opt to "go down" for a candidate of their choosing for the survival points that this gives them. Such kills of the same sex as they are do also exist, but none of the people heading to the Elm Hill palace of pleasures tomorrow, when we take a closer look around, comes under this list of people.

Thousands of ordinary people have, instead of ending up in the palace of sins, gifted themselves to their spouses (usually to the wife), girlfriend, sister, niece, offspring or to their close friends, to a long-admired school mate beauty or to a sorority group, in the hope that these 450 points will help catapult this other very cherished person into an angels of death shortlist and then on to ultimate long-term survival.

Part 9 – The end of Keith

Keith went out with a smile on his face – his last thoughts were: she's quite a big lady down under, and a little bit heavy too … so lucky to be allowed to do this … kiss, kiss, … over goes her leg … it's tight in there … blimey, that's a tight grip! I never knew her legs were this strong … and nicely formed … oh crap, can't breathe. Is that some sort of sumo giantess with her foot on my head, stopping me from lifting me 'ead … dying … dying … what can I do? May as well kiss her once more … it's really all for her. My angel, the goddess of the TV world, and my, can she squeeze hard with them legs of hers … going faint … fading … sleep time? …out.

Keith's body was already cold and discarded. They had thrown it onto a massive pile in the dry swimming pool, around the back of the last corridor's cell blocks. He was down and out. He died in the belief that he was saving his dream girl and giving her a treat. Greg's much messier and still warm body was now being carried away to the same pile. Well, actually he was on a trolley, pulled along by his femme fatale. It made no difference if he was fully dead or not. Any re-arise-ers would be stabbed in the routine morning sweep.

The Nest Master, Valeria, ordered the next shipment of men to get ready to disembark. She was tall, powerfully built. She took no guff or slackness from anyone and it seemed her only pleasures in life were to enjoy a smooth handover of another entire shipment.

One by one the doomed males approached Valeria to receive their shackles, ready for the next round of try-outs. Corporal Cammie-Sue barked out "hurry up, hurry up" to keep the males moving along. Cammie-Sue was a perky brown haired young girl that had tremendous energy. One thing about her - she was human. She had been through domestic abuse long ago and was raised as a housewife. To everyone here, she was truly a Neo-Amazon and as fit as the rest of the girls, but deep down, she longed for the normal life of affection and partnership between a man and a woman. Though human, she helped see to thousands of victims, as professionally as the rest.

She harboured no special affinity for most of them, as they fellow humans and loathed settlers in most part. But from time to time, a male really took her fancy and sometimes she would try to keep him in her room, or even to help him to escape. Escape was not easily achieved, as a band of Warrior Women knew where to lurk to catch each escapee. Trying to help her special sweetheart get around them, meant everything to her. These illegal escapes infuriated her bosses, and they never figured out how Valeria had been behind them. The band of Warrior Women destroyed the environment, tearing through the bushes in search of the one who got away. Many of the local inhabitants were suspected of harbouring him, or of not cooperating enough with them, and so fatalities did occur.

But Simon the purehearted had somehow, by frequently crouching down and sussing out the next area ahead of him, managed to find the right moment, and he was now on a ship, heading to Portugal. The craft grew a bit unsteady as it began to settle down. The ship's navigator, Nicole, had to put a hand against the hull of the ship to steady herself. Suddenly a green light came on and Nicole began to shout "Go, Go". Without warning a blast of hot humid air hit Nicole square in the face, which almost took her breath away. She ran into the ship and watched through a window as the escape shuttle disappeared into the depths of the distant seas. One second he had been on this ship and now he was gone, seeking a new life for himself elsewhere, possibly in Asturias or Galicia.

But for every one who got away and made it, there were a thousand who didn't. Nicole adjusted the straps of her legs and secured a tight new Velcro seal around her latest victim, her third for the day. The new Velcro-assisted leg-kill method was working well for her, and her next victim, one who had also been given assistance to escape, but who had then been caught halfway down the mound and brought back, was now in his death-throws. Several more who were destined to be up next were currently assembled in the hallway with the others. None of them suspected what carnage this same hallway had recently seen.

Everything was set up so as to free the girls to concentrate only on hunting and on finishing men off. Their points tallies were updated instantly, and the dwindling population in the area made the food that gets delivered to the palace daily by the military last and fill all the angels up and keep them all going.

Foraging trips, where all men that a unit of girl warriors could fin
would be rounded up and brought in had been kept at a minimum,
but now, as the supply of men was getting low, they had been
increased, further depleting the area of its remaining males.

 The jungle creatures and insects were too afraid to go anywhere
near these warrior girls, so quick were their reflexes. If any males
are spotted, this troop will soon take care of them. Valeria said that
probably within a few days nothing much would be left of the males.
Once again, they resumed their torturous journey. After a few twists
and tangles of paths and dried up riverbeds, all seemed to become a
monotonous blur. It was getting near dark when the warrior girls
came across a well-travelled path. Dozens of settlers used to walk up
and down this path, completely unaware of the presence of the man-
snatching Neo-Amazon warrior women. The march ceased when
they came upon a small grassy clearing, a perfect place.

There seemed to be a new eternally bleak break in the traffic and
much to the girls surprise, two talkative young males approached.
Valeria was quick to duck down and to get set for an attack. She,
Vanessa and Etar were at the front, ready to lead this attack.

Vanessa had light red hair, a good trim figure and was an
excellent athlete. She had a deep and burning hate for settlers for
they had murdered her
parents some years back. Nicole could see her virtually licking
her lips in anticipation of a catch.

After two hours of steady marching a unit of Warrior Women pulled
off the trail they had been on. The Nest Master walking in the lead
had heard something. Two young males, their chosen prey, were
approaching. With quick military precision, she motioned Chantelle
and Clarissa to reposition themselves quietly to the front for the
attack.

Clarissa was shorter, more sassy, wiry and very aggressive. She
loved a good fight and often took on opponents much larger than
herself, as she knew exactly how to deal with them. Nicole
wondered why those two girls were chosen to receive the honour of
first capture of this trip, while on the mission. Then she noticed both
girls' skin had taken on the most camouflage pattern, while her own
skin was still several shades of white.

Oblivious to the silent death lurking off the trail, the two
young males laughed loudly. As far as Nicole could determine, the
youths were a few years older than most of the warrior girls and so

much less fit, as a result of which they should make easy prey for the warrior girls.

Vanessa and Clarissa burst out of the dense brush and dove towards one of the males. She had been premature and almost blown the ambush. The youth turned to run, but she grabbed him by his hair and dragged him into the bushes.

Our Nest Master, Valeria, a veteran of many such ambushes and Chantelle had to chase after the other male. They soon caught up with him and pushed him into a large-leaf bush in the jungle. Lying on his front made him easy to pounce upon and to tie up. Once he was totally defeated, they picked him up and easily tucked her victim's ankles under her arm and carried him off into the underbrush like a sack of potatoes.

One second, the boys had been on the trail, then the next they had been pounced upon and had been dragged off into the underbrush. "What the." was all that one frightened male had been able to utter, and then he was taken. All the girls gathered around to inspect their latest catches.

Lance Vixen 4 was examining the many bulges on the body of her captive, who was tied up and facing her. Valeria knelt down near her, giving her helpful hints, or so she thought. The victims were no longer struggling, instead standing still and accepting their fate.

Both lads were shirtless and Nicole watched the heaving chest of the victim positioned firmly in front of Lance Vixen 4s' powerful body. "She could make quick work of him", one of the girls said softly. He would disappear from view, taken to her bedding spot pile of leaves, and there she would trap him, while she had her wicked way with him!

"My turn next!" Valeria said urgently – the three girls she had spoken to all laughed aloud with wicked grins. To emphasize the point, rude signs were shown, including one involving a tongue. By the time these two were handed over to the palace of angels to be enrolled into servitude, it is fair to say that Lance Vixen 4 and the girls had made them give the girls a wide variety of rude favours. A girl has to seize her opportunities wherever she can! And these guys won't be telling on them, or if they do, it won't make any difference, so all's fair in special circumstances.

Once her toy boy was in a disoriented state, you could change positions on him without fear of him trying to escape or putting up a major struggle, especially as his ankle was now firmly tied to a nearby tree. That's all we can disclose about what happened to them before the handover of the captives was completed. A girl's urges MUST be satisfied first.

The males, though, quite disoriented by their sudden capture, showed no fear. One said softly "Neo-Amazon Warrior Women" and acted genuinely impressed by his captors. The other male, the youngest and Valerias' and Chantelle's victim asked politely if they were to be taken to the palace of the angels of death. Valeria smiled down at the young male, nodding and pointed to the ground, saying "but not before you satisfy my urges first". With an audible "gulp" he laid down flat on his back. His companion then obediently lay flat on his back too, awaiting the favours he knew they were getting him to fulfil.

Greg made his final visit to the former prison and chose a woman who he wanted to make a 4,000 point donation to. He even got to look at her pretty face as she fired the gun, six times, that ended his run (and extended hers, but only by an extra week or two). Even with six bullets inside his tummy, it still wasn't working, and nor did the rope she had tried to strangle him with, how awkward! So she had to finish him off with a knife and with four spears. He was still so drunk that he never fully knew what had hit him. But his manners were such that he was still trying to help his chosen woman out all the way, even when it was time to give her the throat and the chest and then the throat again.

Vanessa knelt down and began to rip the shirt off her victim. He was trying to help by unbuttoning it, but received a hard slap for his efforts. The youth gave a quick glance at his companion, but he soon vanished from view, behind Vanessa's impressive posterior. She was about to get him down in a reverse straddle, her favourite position, and her bits were all that these guys were going to have on their menu from now on.

Neo-Amazons, particularly Neo-Amazon women, have long sharp toenails. Vanessa had such an enduring urge to satisfy that she began to rake her victim's chest with her toenail sharpies, without necessarily aiding her kill in doing so. She made move after move, while he withered in pain. Generally Neo-Amazon warrior women were known for their

aggressiveness, but not torture. This might become an exception, and it was only because it had been so long since her last male encounter that her cravings became more violent over time.
... ...

Back in the palace boudoir, Chlessa was presented a fresh victim. The man's eyes lit up with excitement when he saw the curly blonde emerge to wave him into her room. Before long, his throat, too, was positioned right underneath the powerful firm and formidable right leg of this tall stunning beauty Chlessa. Every woman has her own particular finishing position. Chlessa was well known for her expert both legs on top technique, whereas most of the other angels preferred the tried and true one leg on top and one behind approach. Both worked equally effectively, and won the women many points, in the grand race for a place in the survival bunker.

Chlessa finished her kill off and then arose to hug
her daughter affectionately. A brief and precious visit from Cloette was such a boost for Chlessa. She was glad to see her still alive and well. The same could not be said for the morning batch of males, who were now deceased, while the afternoon batch was in the waiting room, awaiting their call-ins.

It was a very beautiful sight to see the caring loving mother side of Chlessa. All too often it was just busy women rushing around to grab another kill. But today, for a few short but precious seconds, it was affectionate hugs and words of devotion, support and caring for each other that rang out in this boudoir. Even those who were dying could sense that something deeply meaningful, affectionate and pleasant was in the air today, as women were supportive of each other and helping each other out.

When Chlessa then turned to her next kill, little Cloette was playing with the coloured beads, waiting for her to finish. It was during an affectionate motherly glance at the child playing with the beads that Chlessa made an embarrassing slip, resulting in her victims' throat being free of its leggy onslaught for a second or two. That was one of those embarrassing moments that women hoped no one ever saw. A woman was supposed to be in total control of her victim and a leg slipping off a throat, away from its designated strangulation location was an awkward unplanned mistake.

The man's throat wasn't free for long and Chlessa's usual boudoir-sharing kill buddy Sabrina, who was already moving her next victim around the room in readiness for an upcoming kill of her own, figured he'd hardly had time for two full breaths of air before Chlessa reacted quickly and reinserted her leg back onto his throat to continue her kill. Chlessa and Sabrina made eye contact and both said "oops!" and giggled aloud, while the male lay beneath Chlessa's long womanly legs dying. The little laughter worked wonders in giving all five people in this room a boost, and soon the happy vibes were back.

Little Cloette wanted to be allowed to get more deeply involved, and so both Chlessa and Sabrina decided to let little Cloette whack the dying men in the face with Chlessa's designer handbag, once they were properly stuck in the kill position. This little something meant the world to both Chlessa and to little Cloette, whose mother-daughter bonding bloomed like never before, as the bag-buckle was pelted into the dying men's face, and giggles were shared by all three women, happy as happy can be. There was also a sharp-tip sword, and the women let little Cloette stab the man with it, once he was secured into position and half-way passed out already.

Chlessa, showing a bit of embarrassment, turned toward Sabrina. Sabrina had been introduced to them previously, but it had been a cordial formal introduction with minor small talk. "You didn't see that, did you?" Chlessa asked, looking over her shoulder smiling. "Not a thing" Sabrina said with a grin.

President Gabrielle then gently reminded Chlessa to always concentrate on her kills, as the points talley is all that counts when this is all over. "If yah don't make the cut, then it was all for naught, me dearee!"

During the course of their conversation, Sabrina casually mentioned her "hunt" through the hospital. Much to Sabrina's amazement and pleasure President Gabrielle asked if she and her daughter could go along on the next trip. Hunting victims through the hospital with the President and her Daughter almost sent Sabrina through the roof with excitement. She smiled to herself when she felt her body twitch with a sudden shudder, as her victim's final struggles had rather satisfyingly awakened the 'o-moment in her'. Her victim wiggled around a bit. Evidently it was getting a bit drippy for him down there, and hitherto unknown flavours were now front-most in the "demise-ling's awareness".

Nancy and Dr Sanchez were both out looking for their next kill, and so Sabrina was thrilled when, for the next hour or more, she got to talk to her two prestigious new roommates, chatting frankly and exploring many a concern, feeling and sensation, while more and more men kept being brought in and dying at their cosy settles arms, legs and weaponry, each time boosting their survival scores further, while also getting something satisfying out of it themselves.

As the overall scores were kept but not published, and so none of the femmes fatales knew whether they were anywhere near the lead nation-wide, there was a deep sense of uncertainty and inner panic in all of them. Had they known that not one of the girls in the venue we have been covering will end up anywhere near the lucky few, when the cut is finally made, and that it will be too late by then anyway, as too much of the lethal radioactive element will have entered their bodies by then.

So it is with a sense of deep regret that we must draw our attention away from the sad ending that is imminent for all the characters we have been covering, and as we return to the real world of the here and now, the world that does not yet know at all what is coming its way, as it lives its unpanicked ordinary lives. We can now finally understand the wider context and start to ask the big questions.

Part 10 - How do we go forward now?

Going forward, the challenges are many and great:

How do we bring in the lowest carbon emissions form of car engine ever to be invented worldwide, without making the company who had it first and who patented it lose out?

Surely we award it's key people a tax-funded reward and compensation payment that is almost equal to what is stands to lose by us letting hundreds of other companies all over the world simultaneously (and very soon) roll out their own quicker, cheaper and more intelligently and high-quality maintaining mass-produced copies of the best product. This is fair, and it is right.

We cannot wait 75 or 150 years for all patents and copyrights to expire, before bringing in the best functioning car engine systems with the lowest pollution emission levels worldwide, so this is roughly what to do, and we have to do it in the way the world's smartest people recommend we do it. A similar process is needed also in boiler/furnace production, in loft insulation production, in HVAC production and in the regulation of all forms of industrial fumes and waste, as well as with garden and household waste and recycling initiatives, water purification systems and in all other forms of infrastructure improvement too. Only by rolling out the very best way ever found everywhere in the world do we get everyone the best outcome they deserve.

How do we bring in the cleanest form of electricity production worldwide?

It's not a quick and easy roll-out, but with the guidance of some really smart, devoted, impartial people acting on our behalf, we can get there soon.

How do we improve the rehabilitation of x-offenders who have been committing crimes both before and after prison? This too requires the entire planet getting its most intelligent people to work together in trialling and evaluating the 300+ ways it could be handled and then making sure that the truly most effective, affordable, results-achieving and ethical solutions are gradually identified and rolled out where they are most needed.

How do we bring support for the new world government and for the new world language, army and regulators up to the target levels of 99.99%, or up a little closer to these levels anyway, quickly, before there are riots and uprisings of those who do not understand that this is all for the best for all of them?

This requires tackling disinformation and fake-news stories. Most of the mass-panic we have found is based on people saying things that are not true, which is hard to regulate well. We advise rolling out some very small fines that do not decimate anyone, do not turn us into tyrants and do not leave those who do harm fully unpunished either. Most people don't realise what is true and what is not true, and that's a problem we will struggle ever to fully solve, but it will help to make the right answer more easily found in internet searches and in libraries. We must always encourage people to remain sceptical and to learn they are not being forced to trust anything. In the end, they will only carry on believing a small number of lies and untruths anyway, which does not do us much harm, and which is the human way, the way of a planet full of varieties and of different philosophies, ideologies and hobbies and interests, each of which are to flourish in a perfect world.

How do we help people who are rolling out good new and old products to get the importation, sale and health system coverage process ok'd by the regular of more countries more quickly and easily in a world with thousands of independent jurisdictions and countries? This needs to be facilitated by all the trans-regional bodies, as well as by the voluntary opt-in partnership buying alliances, but it cannot ever be made compulsory for any entity to forego its powers to block something it deems as harmful from getting into its country. Much to the contrary, if something is harmful, high-risk, addictive, dangerous, a bad influence or non-functional, we should let all the other trans-regional bodies know about this too, so they can also take action to protect all their regions full of good people too.

How do we get the best vaccines and the best medicine out to everyone who needs them? This requires a lot of cooperation, collusion, pooling of powers, resources, intelligence and capabilities. It also requires competition and evaluation, and the winners of the competition need to be rewarded well, while we also ensure that all parts of the world who need a form of medicine, a vaccine or a cure or prevention tactic do get given access to it, including the chance to borrow the money to fund the rolling out of the best solution for all programmes, and everything that goes with it.

How do we best democratise the world government, without letting it become a vicious rule by one faction who hates the other factions and refuses to help their main causes kind of system? This is a very good and difficult question, and one that requires some brilliant minds to make some deep evaluative comparisons between a number of particularly good specific nitty-gritty proposals. I would strongly hope to see something built into each of the winning proposals that ensures that the people of each and every country in the world who disagree with the views of the world leader are allowed to try out their other solution ideas instead, for a while.

I also hope to see a system in use that gives maybe 100 political parties and alliances of parties from all over the world some proportional voting power and say in this virtual world legislature, and that gives the candidates for the top head of budget-setting and government posts a round-robin voting system (not one that costs more to run than current systems), under which the ultimate winner has to beat all of his opponents in A or B and A or C type two option head to heads, attaining more 50+% vote wins in head-to head one group against another votes than any other group gets. In the end, we cannot have any one country rule over another, and no one faction may ever become so strong as to harm the others. Instead, we need to make it a world where any truly good new ideas do indeed succeed in winning over the panels of experts who then in turn recommend to the voters of the world to back these bringers of good new ideas, as well as those others who also find a place for the good solution ideas to be tried out in their plans as well.

How do we eradicate the mafias, arms-traders, the espousers of terrorism and the drug cartels? This requires a lot of bullet-proofing and a lot of intelligence. Once we have gathered all the intel, at whatever price it takes and offering all the rewards and sentence reductions we needed to, we can then take them out by converting each participating member of these criminal organisations into a 'good dad and good worker' type person who gets all his income from legal mainstream professions instead. If we find that the only way to ever achieve this is to remove cash worldwide and make all transactions electronically traceable, then this is what we must do. When the battle has been fully won, I hope and believe that it will become clear that it was all worth doing.

In all of these, there are a number of good solutions already, and by trying them all out in a wise way that then learns which are best and rolls them out all over the world, we can achieve the 100% optimal outcome that everyone in the reader's world (B) will keep on promising but will never deliver. Only a world unity cooperation system in which <u>all</u> options are on the table and are examined before we decide which the best solution is can take us to the best possible of worlds.

Part 11 – In the heat of the struggle - A free for all fight to survive

Poor Kate is now in a death-choke hold sleeper grip move that the pretty royal princess herself is administering – her hands are trapped under the side of a piano and of no use – will anyone come to her rescue? Or is this the end of another one of our main characters?

Sara manages to finish her intruder off, and to seal her bunker. She does so with her female friends, a rope, a shoe, a sock, and lot of womanly hands pressing down on their target's mouth, for a long time. "It took 25 minutes of time and a whole lot of energy to finish him off. But he's no longer a threat now, the bastard!" concluded Sara. She looked around for other invaders, saw none, and threw some camouflage and some old junk up to make the area look like just a small patch of trees with nothing worth having under them.

Others were planning, building, arguing, battling and working to try and get into one of the bigger and better equipped bunkers. What they sensed a risk of but did not know for sure was that before long a fatal dose of radiation will, most likely, have built up inside all of them, not enough to kill them straight away, but enough to mean that 35 years of lurking in a bunker, alive, was not likely to happen, unfortunately.

Ollie tries hard to save Kate from the hold she was in, and he would have made it too, had it not been for the gun-fire of the newly arriving militia, now making their move, now that all their opponents were sitting ducks, and Ollie's back was their very first target in the lair. Just as the defeat of the royal family and their entourage was within grasping proximity, the arrival of these gunmen that nobody knew were coming was the death of Ollie, who took several bullets and fell, bleeding to death on the bunker floor. Most of the others, and all the militia men soon followed, as this other militia was now going to be replacing all these residents. They might make an exception for the pretty pregnant princess though, carrying the heir to the throne, as she will have her uses, they thought.

Soon after Ollie, Kate too was sadly shot, and so were the royals. All apart from the pretty princess, who worth keeping. The mysterious late arrivals were in such a hurry to get yet more supplies in, the dead bodies out, and to seal themselves in that they did not take time to get rid of the last two of the bodies. The following day, realising that it was going to be getting very smelly in there very soon, they decided to cook all the dead'uns for supper.

This was ok for protein and carbs, but it raised the CO levels in there, as they were cooking, and it also raised the amount of bone waste that they could not get rid of so easily now that they were sealed in. Then, another day later, they realised that the water supply system was broken or stuck, and so they had to open the hatch again, to try to fix it, while taking in all the deadly radiation they had been sheltering from. Sadly, this incident shortened their life span from years to weeks. They did all they could to nurse the royal princess back to health, and to turn her into their supreme leader, but then they all fell into rapid decline, and those last days were proper depressing like, as none of them had the strength left to nurse the others.

Sara did manage to wave goodbye to the outside world, take a deep breath, and to step inside her new home. The group of four worked together to double-check they had everything and to seal the door. From now on, they knew nothing about what is going on elsewhere. And they were all fully committed to surviving at all costs.

Two days later, Sara got so angry at the one male in there with her that he nearly died, at her unforgiving martial arts prowess-filled hands. He should have learned his lesson then, and turned into a faithful servant, but he didn't learn, and his terrible behaviour was wasting precious supplies at very unsustainable rates of consumption. He had failed to do what was expected of him, and he was of no use, the crappy excuse of a man that he had been! It was time to start keeping him tied up from now on, and to put him on minimum rations. If he struggled, she would have no choice but to KO him or worse.

Sara soon realised that her supplies were only good for a couple of years, and that her bunker might not be fully radiation-proof. So she decided to just make the most of each day she had left. She dived into her fantasy book world, while lying on her tied up man who had to keep really still. She loved these books, the world they were set in, and she analysed each line for hours, before reflecting on how to use this wisdom in raising these young'ens she had in with her. She was convinced she was pregnant, and so it was now ok to straddle squat smother her tied-up male out of existence, which happened at night. She had plans for getting rid of one or two of her other fellow co-residents as a way of making the supplies last longer. But it never came to this.

Not long thereafter, five weeks into her bunker-dwelling time, Sara started getting more and more consumed by the lack of a single living male in her 35-year den. She dreamt of stepping out and finding some fertile, handsome and not particularly strong guy nearby, who was dying like everyone else of the radiation, and of throwing him onto a car and having her way with him right out in the open, without saying a single word.

Sara was in her den for a good number of days, with the two girls who had turned up the previous day, living out their last days in girl chat, book talk, reminiscing, and dishing out as much mutual praise and encouragement as they could. But her lair was attacked several times more, and each time the girls, knowing that their door was by no means unbreakable, had to open the door, whack some half-dead sick zombified blokes into oblivion with shovels and planks of wood, maybe take one in with them if he was cute, submissive and weak enough to tie up, control and instruct (This happened twice!), and they lived out their den days in as much partnership, chatter, massages, good energy and sexual pleasure as they could possibly have, while the radiation was slowly killing them off in their sleep.

It started with these primal cravings and with the fantasies, including a worryingly sick fantasy to 'have some fun' with the body of an intruder man that the girls had just bludgeoned to death near the entrance to her cave. And it turned real when one of those who had been locked out of all the safe dens somehow arose from where he had fallen after an earlier invasion attempt and started banging frantically on the door and using a crowbar to rip it open.

This guy, and another one who turned up a week later, had their uses. Sara was lusting "after that male touch in her woman regions," and she failed to resist these urges for more than a day after she realised there were still good-looking boys alive out there, desperate for shelter, and willing and able to give her a good time in between book club chats and reminiscing sessions.

Sara always did it "her way" which involved her tying them up, just in case, with the girls nearby to help her kill them in the event of a struggle, which they knew and understood, and it involved Sara sleeping fully on top of them, both men, full weight, all night long, and then making them pleasure her with more body parts, from nose to mouth, from willy to toe to finger, and in more ways than I care to list. She never turned kind, and she never gave them a break, not even when they were covered all over the face in her juices and she was having a period and had a flatulent spell to boot. To object to whatever she wanted to do to you was to die, they thought, and they much preferred to keep on pleasuring her for now.

Half a year later, Sara and the last of the girls both faded away, all in the same night, in their sleep, in January 2027, with a let's do another book club night tomorrow last thought. They never found out about each other's similar timing. The last of her sex slaves died in the October before, of strangulation after a disagreement, and he even helped Sara get her legs around his throat so she could get rid of him when she had found that the supplies were running short, and that he had been secretly sneaking off with the forbidden snickers bars, and in his mind the women in the den were all preggers by now, and there just wasn't enough food left now so all of them could make it.

The voice that knows: The final human colony to perish, two years in, in March 2028 to be precise, will be a Japanese troop of cave-dwelling dwarfs on a small island near Okinawa, who then run out of supplies, have issues with their water supply system and are overrun with wastewater flooding and sewage waste inside their cave hideout, two years in.

They are left with no alternative but to open the hatch and hope to make it on the outside. But it is too early for survival to be possible. They knew this was their biggest risk, and that they could not last another week inside their bunker with no food left at this point.

The last UK colony, dwindling and going a few months before this, on 19ᵗʰ January 2028, is the one containing the specially chosen points-winning TV beauties, in a mountain cave bunker near Snowden called Noah's Ark. Its supplies are ample, but its water system was always destined to be lethal. It was bringing the lethal radiation in with it, making the residents ever more ill, until the last of them, a pretty pregnant beauty queen and model, died, peacefully in her sleep, at 3 am on the morning of the 19ᵗʰ January.

Everyone from the state, the military and from the main official offices of government died knowing that all hope was now invested in these seven chosen girls and one boy in the Weybridge Abbey bunker. What they did not know was that the bunker, though adequately stocked, was slowly letting the deadly radiation in through the same pipes that were giving them fresh water and taking all their waste away.

I hope you can forgive us for throwing the last big reveal in so early. We miniature guinea-pig-capibarra-cross critters of Europa, assembled by this brook to tell you this sad true story, are not very good at keeping secrets.

Various efforts in the US, Russia, China, France, Spain, Germany, Canada, Bosnia, Belarus, Kazakhstan, Peru, Nepal, Iran, Australia and Argentina succeed in surviving the first year, but are insufficiently sealed off from the radiation overall to avoid succumbing in the second perilous year since the apocalypse.

So you must make the most of every day you have on earth, as it may well be quite close to your last day alive, everyone.

Let us not end with a sad note. Humanity has messed the planet up, behaved terribly, and paid the price. Humanity has also saved a good number of gentle, cute, fury earth species in its ambitious space programs, plus one day, centuries from now, the earth, too, shall bloom again.

And some crazy dreams came true in those last mad days; it was not all bad for all of our characters, especially not for Keith, Greg, Ollie and Sara. They all showed tremendous courage and compassion, a capacity to plan ahead and a determination to do all they could to make the most of their final days. I think we can be proud of all of them. I also commend the way that, in the very end, the women finally found empowerment, and put the males into devotional subordinate positions.

Had it not been for the nuclear strikes, the future would have been bright for all, well, for a few more centuries, before the accumulation of pollution, plastic and emissions wrecks what is left of the planet. And given that none of them were destined to survive the 35-year fallout period, or even to know that this was going to be the minimum length of time they would have to stay away from the surface of the world, we can close somewhat pleased that each one found joy in something very special in their final days.

Ollie has managed to defeat two of the guardians of the royals in a messy and exhausting struggle. But three more of his farmer's militia goons are dead. The jiu jitsu is brutal! And full of desperation! No fancy footwork, just arm chokes, desperate full-force furniture whacks and hard thumps to any body part they could get to, taking their toll on both camps. What a mess! What mayhem! What carnage!

Keith's body was already cold and discarded. They had thrown it onto a massive pile in the back corridor's cell blocks. He was down and out. He died in the belief that he was saving his dream girl and giving her a treat. Greg's much messier and still warm body was now being carried away to the same pile. Well, actually he was on a trolley, pulled along by his femme fatale. It made no difference if he was fully dead or not. Any re-arise-ers would be shot in the routine morning sweep.

The angels of death girls were working long hours and giving it their all, as they knew that only those with the very highest scores were going to be invited into the survival chambers come next week. What they did not know was that by next week a fatal dose of radiation will have built up inside them, not enough to kill them straight away, but enough to mean that 35 years of lurking in a bunker, alive, was not going to happen, unfortunately.

Poor Kate is now in a death-choke hold sleeper grip move that the pretty royal princess herself is administering – her hands are trapped under the side of a piano and of no use – will anyone come to her rescue? Or is this the end of another one of our main characters?

Sara manages to finish her intruder off, and to seal her bunker. She does so with her female friends, a rope, a shoe, a sock, and lot of womanly hands pressing down on their target's mouth, for a long time. "It took 25 minutes of time and a whole lot of energy to finish him off. But he's no longer a threat now, the bastard!" concluded Sara. She looked around for other invaders, saw none, and threw some camouflage and some old junk up to make the area look like just a small patch of trees with nothing worth having under them.

Ollie tries hard to save Kate from the hold she was in, and he would have made it too, had it not been for the gun-fire of the newly arriving militia, now making their move, now that all their opponents were sitting ducks, and Ollie's back was their very first target in the lair. Just as the defeat of the royal family and their entourage was within grasping proximity, the arrival of these gunmen that nobody knew were coming was the death of Ollie, who took several bullets and fell, bleeding to death on the bunker floor. Most of the others, and all the militia men soon followed, as this other militia was now going to be replacing all these residents. They might make an exception for the pretty pregnant princess though, carrying the heir to the throne, as she will have her uses, they thought.

Soon after Ollie, Kate too was sadly shot, and so were the royals. All apart from the pretty princess, who worth keeping. The mysterious late arrivals were in such a hurry to get yet more supplies in, the dead bodies out, and to seal themselves in that they did not take time to get rid of the last two of the bodies. The following day, realising that it was going to be getting very smelly in there very soon, they decided to cook all the dead'uns for supper.

This was ok for protein and carbs, but it raised the CO levels in there, as they were cooking, and it also raised the amount of bone waste that they could not get rid of so easily now that they were sealed in. Then, another day later, they realised that the water supply system was broken or stuck, and so they had to open the hatch again, to try to fix it, while taking in all the deadly radiation they had been sheltering from. Sadly, this incident shortened their life span from years to weeks. They did all they could to nurse the royal princess back to health, and to turn her into their supreme leader, but then they all fell into rapid decline, and those last days were proper depressing like, as none of them had the strength left to nurse the others.

Sara did manage to wave goodbye to the outside world, take a deep breath, and to step inside her new home. The group of four worked together to double-check they had everything and to seal the door. From now on, they knew nothing about what is going on elsewhere. And they were all fully committed to surviving at all costs.

Two days later, Sara got so angry at the one male in there with her that he nearly died, at her unforgiving martial arts prowess-filled hands. He should have learned his lesson then, and turned into a faithful servant, but he didn't learn, and his terrible behaviour was wasting precious supplies at very unsustainable rates of consumption. He had failed to do what was expected of him, and he was of no use, the crappy excuse of a man that he had been! It was time to start keeping him tied up from now on, and to put him on minimum rations. If he struggled, she would have no choice but to KO him or worse.

Sara soon realised that her supplies were only good for a couple of years, and that her bunker might not be fully radiation-proof. So she decided to just make the most of each day she had left. She dived into her fantasy book world, while lying on her tied up man who had to keep really still. She loved these books, the world they were set in, and she analysed each line for hours, before reflecting on how to use this wisdom in raising these young'ens she had in with her. She was convinced she was pregnant, and so it was now ok to straddle squat smother her tied-up male out of existence, which happened at night. She had plans for getting rid of one or two of her other fellow co-residents as a way of making the supplies last longer. But it never came to this.

Not long thereafter, five weeks into her bunker-dwelling time, Sara started getting more and more consumed by the lack of a single living male in her 35-year den. She dreamt of stepping out and finding some fertile, handsome and not particularly strong guy nearby, who was dying like everyone else of the radiation, and of throwing him onto a car and having her way with him right out in the open, without saying a single word.

Sara was in her den for a good number of days, with the two girls who had turned up the previous day, living out their last days in girl chat, book talk, reminiscing, and dishing out as much mutual praise and encouragement as they could. But her lair was attacked several times more, and each time the girls, knowing that their door was by no means unbreakable, had to open the door, whack some half-dead sick zombified blokes into oblivion with shovels and planks of wood, maybe take one in with them if he was cute, submissive and weak enough to tie up, control and instruct (This happened twice!), and they lived out their den days in as much partnership, chatter, massages, good energy and sexual pleasure as they could possibly have, while the radiation was slowly killing them off in their sleep.

It started with these primal cravings and with the fantasies, including a worryingly sick fantasy to 'have some fun' with the face and body of an intruder man that the girls had just bludgeoned to death near the entrance to her cave. And it turned real when one of those who had been locked out of all the safe dens somehow arose from where he had fallen after an earlier invasion attempt and started banging frantically on the door and using a crowbar to rip it open.

This guy, and another one who turned up a week later, had their uses. Sara was lusting "after that male touch in her woman regions," and she failed to resist these urges for more than a day after she realised there were still good-looking boys alive out there, desperate for shelter, and willing and able to give her a good time in between book club chats and reminiscing sessions.

Sara always did it "her way" which involved her tying them up, just in case, with the girls nearby to help her kill them in the event of a struggle, which they knew and understood, and it involved Sara sleeping fully on top of them, both men, full weight, all night long, and then making them pleasure her with more body parts, from nose to mouth, from willy to toe to finger, and in more ways than I care to list. She never turned kind, and she never gave them a break, not even when they were covered all over the face in her juices and she was having a period and had a flatulent spell to boot. To object to whatever she wanted to do to you was to die, they thought, and they much preferred to keep on pleasuring her for now.

Half a year later, Sara and the last of the girls both faded away, all in the same night, in their sleep, in January 2024, with a let's do another book club night tomorrow last thought. They never found out about each other's similar timing. The last of her sex slaves died in the October before, of strangulation after a disagreement, and he even helped Sara get her legs around his throat so she could get rid of him when she had found that the supplies were running short, and that he had been secretly sneaking off with the forbidden snickers bars, and in his mind the women in the den were all preggers by now, and there just wasn't enough food left now so all of them could make it.

The voice that knows: Let us not end with a sad note. Humanity has messed the planet up, behaved terribly, and paid the price. Humanity has also saved a good number of gentle, cute, fury earth species in its ambitious space programs, plus one day, centuries from now, the earth, too, shall bloom again.

And some crazy dreams came true in those last mad days; it was not all bad for all of our characters, especially not for Keith, Greg, Ollie and Sara. They all showed tremendous courage and compassion, a capacity to plan ahead and a determination to do all they could to make the most of their final days. I think we can be proud of all of them. I also commend the way that, in the very end, the women finally found empowerment, and put the males into devotional subordinate positions. Had it not been for the nuclear strikes, the future would have been bright for all. And given that none of them were destined to survive the 35-year fallout period, or even to know that this was going to be the minimum length of time they would have to stay away from the surface of the world, we can close somewhat pleased that each one found joy in something very special in their final days. In a way, they had a better life than they would have had, had they spent 35 years bored to death in a tiny cramped den with terrible air quality and then come out to find nothing much out there that they can use to live on, other than ivy and dandelions.

It was better for them that they had human company and high quality supplies to live on right to the end. And it is better for the planet that it shall, from now on, be home only to plants, flowers, trees, cockroaches, woodlice, worms, squid, crabs, snails, ants, wasps, bats, flies, and coconuts, living happily in a world that does not seek to run them over, spray them with pesticides, squish them, shoot them, trap them, bury them under concrete, drown or electrocute them or expose them to death by dogs, cats or ferrets any more. And while earth, in this new form, flourishes again, so too does Europa, where the last mammals left, from a variety of small cute fur species, sent off on a routine mission that wasn't meant to be the final one, nibble without stress or danger on endless pastures, meadows, forests and wilderness. This is a happy ever after that carries true value, just not for those species who, like humans, did not make it. I hope you are able to see this too.

And me, well, I have symbolically inserted my soul into one of the miniature capibara guinea pigs that went on the rocket that has taken us to a whole new world of nibbles and munchies, where there are no predators and no pick-up trucks to run us over. You may cry now if you like. I wonder if they have greengrocers where I'm going? And what sort of den shall we build there, you and I, in our happy new world? The world where all are friends who live in harmony.

Part 12 - The Truly Wisest Route to Democracy

<u>How We Can Strike a Deal to Get from The Present to The Brightest Future Ever Imagined</u>

The above terrible ending in parts of Southern England and in a few other strategically targeted and tragically decimated areas have no more people left to ponder their futures. But other parts of the world continue to live on as normal, and here is where things are going with their bright new ideas:

For ever so many years, the Beijing politburo, various even more power-grabbing opposition killing tyrannical and authoritarian regimes all over the world, the supreme leader in Pyongyang, in the Kremlin, in Havana, in each of the stans of Central Asia, along with a number of monarchies and military dictatorships have controlled every decision-making process in their country, for better or worse. That's an awful lot of power to have concentrated in one pair of hands, considering how biased, subjective, greedy, selfish, tribal and corruptible a human is. Especially a human with immense power over money taken coercively off other humans, as taxes and raids of domestic conquest both by definition always do.

These rulers have hoarded scary amounts of power, enough to make it very dangerous to speak out against them in any way. They have come to dominate every new project, budget, reshuffle, appointment, event, bid, assignment, initiative, response, show, exercise, lesson, any action to arrest a critic in the media or an opposition politician, and have kept their ability to override and alter any change that goes on in these communist party, military-run and dictator-ruled nations.

Such concentration of power in one man's hands is extremely dangerous. This is apparent to all. To oppose, criticise, question or challenge the leader has long been an exercise in self-harm and self-destruction. To emerge as a critic is to go on the list of people who must vanish, in these societies. Only those who never catch the leader's eye for any such reason survive in these countries. Dissenting opinions are banned.

This forlorn and sombre fact was not about to change, not of the incumbent leaders' own volition, or was it?

Well actually, believe it or not, it was! A smart new deal was struck on the 17th of December 2024 between the leaders of the G7, their allies in the G20, their contacts at the UN Development Agency, at ASEAN, at the IMF and in Beijing that was about to bring to life a totally new way of ordering things. Further deals struck in later years miraculously combined to affect each one of the world's worst dictatorial regimes.

The international community's offer came with a firm reward and punishment system. Those countries who do not sign up to any part of this gradual and moderate civil liberties improvement plan will be hit by ever harder sanctions, tariffs and trade barriers, rising at a rate of 1% a year forever more, and will be under arrest when they next travel, while those who sign up will benefit from a beneficial new free trade agreement like none there has ever been before.

In addition, the offer came with a very well worded addendum explaining how the people of the country will gain in several ways from participation in this non-prescriptive new transition plan, while the old rulers will live on fabulous pensions (starting now, if over the age of 60 and if stepping down) and will (otherwise) have great opportunities within the ministries under this new system too, thanks to their reputations and their experience. After a lot of back and forth, China, Russia, North Korea, Saudi Arabia, Cuba, Brunei, Indonesia, Myanmar, Vietnam, Syria, Jordan, Libya, Morocco, Yemen, Iran, Qatar, UAE and seventeen others of the world's most authoritarian and undemocratic countries spectacularly signed up. They were all keeping a close eye on each other, the domestic media and the exit door as they did so. They understood the positive side that the offer and the transition plan's many options bring with them.

In order to qualify for a lucrative and desirable new trade deal with Japan, Europe, the Americas, South and Southeast Asia, the communist party rulers of the world agreed to something it had never allowed in its country before. After taking in expert evaluations, it just simply made sense to give this a go. The worst that could happen was spelled out on pages 81 to 103 of the evaluation report, and it would take less than three years and less than 0.1% of the national budget to reverse should this be needed.

Was this a hostile action, forcing these countries to adopt an imposed system? Read on and decide then, dear readers! If it achieves the right thing in a gradual and victim-free way, it may be the best route to democracy ever conceived.

Consider also that even the freest of Western societies have rule books and constitutions that were imposed on the country by the leaders of the biggest political party in that country at the time of the nation being founded, with opportunities rarely missed to build in rules, stipulations and voting systems that will always favour this one grouping, or in some cases, the two biggest political parties in the country, at the expense of the aspirations of all the others. We're not saying that all democracy in the world so far is partial, is completely failed, but some of the below ideas could certainly take us in a better, more pluralistic direction. Then, once the basic system rules are optimised, we could then look into ways of throwing the corporate lobbies out of democracy, which would finally bring about something resembling true democracy.

This mass-sign-up, with even the Saudis, China, North Korea, the stans and the land of Putin ending up convinced to sign-up, occurring at long last in 2039 was not easily achieved, as the regimes, especially the Chinese, North Korean, Turkmen and Saudi regime, were not happy to share or to surrender power so easily. That's why the five-step transition plan had to be formulated and mutually agreed in various slow-moving and handover-enabling ways, as a compromise deal that gives both sides (those who have been seeking power and those who have been hogging it) a reasonable amount of leverage, opportunity and security. Its five stages allow for the coexistence of forerunner regions and late change regions, where the old regime can carry on ruling in the old way for many more years to come, while a number of further guarantees and pay-outs had to be agreed too, before they were ready to sign up. Of course a heavy dose of carrot and stick had to be in-built too, to bring them to the decision to go ahead with these changes. All the details of those will be revealed in the sequel, if ever it is written.

So how does the new way of working actually work?

Well, it's main concept is fairly simple: Instead of just having one big united communist or regime-run party and a bunch of tiny independent persecuted opposition parties, the plan, format-wise, is completely different: In effect what we get is the sudden launch of five or twelve more or less identical communist parties, and rather than ask every person to choose which one of these to be a member of, the core principle is that one simple number determines which party each and every individual is a member of, and that number is the year you were born in, OR, in the case of Cuba and one of the stans (Uzbekistan): the month you were born in. In most countries, the standard year ad (running from the 1st January to the 31st of December) is used, but in China we use the 12 Chinese calendar years instead (year of the dragon, year of the ox, year of the rooster, year of the snake, year of the tiger, ….) , which is why there are 12 year-of-birth-related parties in our system in China.

The five or 12 new groupings are formed automatically, with a rather equal share of the population automatically assigned to one of these new political parties right from the big day of the big announcement on the 17th of December 2024 (our month one). Then all these citizens are allowed, for a charge equivalent to two US dollars, to enrol into the party for a ten-year period. Alternatively, for a charge of the equivalent of 0.25 US dollars, a person can opt to become independent of all political groupings until further notice, not being charged anything further, and thereby losing the chance to stand for election and also to vote in the primaries. Or, for a charge of 0.15 US dollars a month charged in each of three consecutive months, a person can opt to change his or her party affiliation, leaving their default party of birth and joining any other party instead.

In China, year of the dragon, year of the ox, year of the rooster, year of the snake, year of the tiger, year of the horse, etc both describes every person's default affiliation, and it also describes the name, or a part of the name of each new party competing for your vote. In other countries, we go by the month or year of birth, with most countries using a five-team set-up.

If, for example, you were born in the years 1951, 1961, 1971, 1981, 1991, 2001, 1956, 1966, 1976, 1986, 1996, 2006, or in any other year that ends in a 1 or that ends in a 6, you are automatically signed up as a member of the new People's Party (aka Party A) from the moment you become old enough to vote. Likewise, every person, man or woman, who was born or has ever lived in the country and who was born in the year 1952, 1962, 1972, 1982, 1992, 2002, 1957, 1967, 1977, 1987, 1997, 2007, or in any other year that ends in a 2 or that ends in a 7 is automatically signed up as a member of the new Freedom Party (aka the Communist Party B). If your year of birth ends in a 3 or an 8 you are automatically signed up as a member of the new Logic and Reason Party (aka the Communist Party C). If your year of birth ends in a 4 or a 9 you are automatically signed up as a member of the new Progress Party (aka the Communist Party D). If your year of birth ends in a 5 or a 0 you are automatically signed up as a member of the new Improvement Party (aka the Communist Party E). These initial default party names can and will be changed within any province at any point in time, as long as the party's leadership and the party's membership agree to the change, no name that is already taken is used and a full month's notice is given before the change takes effect.

These five new parties, who all come into being within the wider family in with the ruling governing incumbent party family of ruling parties will all be fully independent of each other, each one with its own leadership, key post holders, budget, payroll and election process team. Only one of these five can win a contest for the governor of a province or for the national head of government. And those who lose the elections will miss out on some lucrative jobs as a result of their election loss, but none of them will ever end up with less than 18% of the overall campaigning budget plus ten compulsory newspaper page rights, thus ensuring that each of the five groupings will always be able to get its key messages out in an effective way, never fading into obscurity. Every person in the country can join any of these five parties and can end up, if elected both by the party and also by the national electorate, as that party's candidate for prime minister of the country. We now know that multiparty democracy, albeit in a unique format that does not legalise any of the opposition and fringe movements who have been illegally existing as enemies of the communist party, will flourish in both China and in North Korea.

You will remain a member of your default political party, as determined by your year of birth, for the rest of your life, unless you firmly and consistently decide you wish to leave and to change over to one of the other parties, or to no longer be a member of any of them. If you stay firm in this conviction for ten months in a row, having to log this intention to reaffiliate in a central register on a monthly basis, both verbally and in writing, for ten consecutive months, with each of the last five of these also having to be accompanied by repeat-consistent central log register note of which other party you wish to join, or you can decide to leave all parties if you prefer. There will never be a sixth party, well not for the first 105 years in China and the first 183 years in North Korea, other than the five core people's parties, and these will compete against each other for each major decision that will need to be made.

So what proposal, what kind of democratisation, what format could we possibly have had? What kind of elections would the tyrants who run these countries possibly allow? Would it even be a proper democracy that they are all about to transition to? What's the catch? Give us the pros and cons and also the bottom line real-world expected outcome, please!

The **five-stage transition plan** applies to all the countries involved in this process. It is central to the whole move to bring new democratic freedoms to countries that have been lacking them for a long time.

Timeline: The first-ever provincial elections are held on the 23rd of May 2039 in all the chosen provinces, and so the campaigning has to work to this date. There are five (in all other countries) or twelve (in China) parties on the ballot, each one representing a newly created splinter-group component faction of the ruling party. Each of these newly created parties runs an "interselection process" to choose its decision-making leaders in February and March 2039, ending no later than the 25th of March 2039.

35 paid "oversight process delegates" in each transitioning country are to work hard to choose the 8 best system options to present to the voters. They must share an open letterbox that all ideas and analyses of options can be submitted into, and between them they must prove that they have read and discussed at least 50 of these submissions

thoroughly each, within their three-month "study and analysis phase", including especially the contributions from the leading experts in this field of political analysis. In case of a disagreement, they hold a debate and a vote between the 35 oversight process delegates. The winners of the vote get to announce the chosen provinces for the wave one action.

How does an interselection process work?

The candidates and the participants of each party's interselection event are each allocated a phase one group that is local or convenient to them in a random selection process. Each phase one group contains 15 – 18 people and each group is allocated a different location, in which to hold the first and last get-togethers in the upcoming two-day process. Every participant is entered as a candidate and each group has two whole days of speaking to all other members of the group, in which to learn enough about the other candidates in all-assembled and in one-to-one and smaller roaming group casual questionings, and with enough time, in which to explain enough about themselves to allow the scoring to reflect what qualities, intentions, skills and ideas each participant feels the party needs in its leadership. At the designated time near the end of the second day of the process, each participant must score each other participant in his or her group with points out of 100 (or else they must be withdrawn from the process). There must be at least three candidates scoring 80 or higher, at least three candidates scoring below 50 and at least three candidates scoring 50 to 80.

Once all the scores that each candidate has received are added up, we now have our top two, who progress into the phase two scoring round which takes place on day 4 and day 5 in one of the towns or villages all around the province. Each phase two group has 19 or 20 candidates who finished in the top two in their phase one group participating in it, and a random drawing determines, which village's phase two group each candidate participates in. At the end of day 5, each phase two group has a full vote at the designated time near the end of the day. Here, each participant must score each other participant in his or her group out of 100 (or else they must be withdrawn from the process). There must be at least five candidates scoring 80 or higher, at least two candidates scoring below 50 and at least two candidates scoring 50 to 80 on each participating voter's scoresheet. The votes are submitted anonymously and in secret, so nobody can know who voted against them and this will avoid the risk of abusive language and angry outbursts once the outcome scores are revealed.

The number of candidates and participants in an interselection process can vary greatly, and a very detailed rulebook specifies exactly how many phases the process has in response to each number of entrants from 2 up to 40,000. In most cases, two to four phases will suffice, for the party's leaders to be chosen. For example, if there are 843 entrants, the phase one groupings contain (this number 843 divided by 17 = 49.5882 rounded up or down to the nearest number) = 50 phase one groups of 16 or 17 people each, and phase two contains the 100 participants who ended up finishing first or second place in their group now . Then there are (100 / 19.5 = 5.12821 rounds to 5) five-phase two groups, and the top two from each of these progresses through to the phase three groups, where the ultimate winners and party chosen leaders and candidates emerge for the upcoming five-year term. At the end of the interselection process we have the winners, the chosen representatives of the grouping or party they are chosen from.

In the 2039 interselection process, each new party ends up with an employed, funded, firmly chosen official 15-person leadership party-ruling governing group, consisting of the top 15 scorers in the final phase of voting. These can be new to politics or they can be existing figures of authority, or any mixture. In the above 843-candidate example, the 2039 process ends at the end of phase two, with each phase two group electing 3 of the 15 party-ruling leadership team. There are five new splinter-group parties to pick leaders for in each province in every other country, apart from China, where there are twelve new parties, each one based on one the 12 Chinese new year cycle of animals (year of the ox, year of the rooster, year of the dragon, etc), so every person's year of birth, not their membership, rank, income or job, determines their initial affiliation. The parties all undergo the same process, one after the other, with the dates and the order chosen at random and with one party entering its phase one group stage on each consecutive Saturday starting on the first Saturday in February. Due to the deadline of 25th of March 2039 for each party to have chosen its new leaders in a multi-stage interselection process, we will be starting the process of stage one interselection groups on the first Saturday in February. During the course of the 8 Saturdays of February and March and 3 Wednesdays in February we will end up having obtained all the rosters of new splinter party leaders in on time, and we will also have held the first two-week-long sitting of each party, where matters of policy, problem-solving, budgeting, priorities, employees and election strategy will be discussed. Democracy is a team sport, and so each party will need to try to get a more convincing message out than all the others do.

In the event of a tie-score within any of the interselection process groupings, a head-to-head count-back is held. It checks to see which of the tied candidates scored better with a greater number of the group's participant voters. If there is still a tie, and the tie is between the crucial second and third place in the group (or between a top 15 finish and 16th place), the person with a better school graduation test overall mark wins. If this is also equal, or deemed incomparably different, an IQ test is held one hour after the end of vote-count, with the higher IQ score winning. These in-built tie-breakers of last resort seek to bring in the better mind and the better talent. If these IQ scores are also tied, the person who finished his or her IQ test first (faster) wins. This system works in producing a clear winner, who goes on to the next stage or who succeeds in clinching the leadership role job.

Due to the fact that the long-term leadership jobs within each new political party faction grouping is being chosen in the first year of the system operating in this province, which can make for fame, power and good pay, it is anticipated that a large number of people will apply as candidates within each new party. For this reason, we will do a second example, with 7,913 participants signing up for the interselection process of one newly forming political party. Not one of them is excluded (unless they are deemed to be a resident of another jurisdiction area or a member of another political party's remit (year of birth) and having missed the deadline for switching affiliation to another party): The maths is like this: 7913 divided by 17 (average intended stage one group size) = 465.4706. This rounds to 465. The 465 phase one groups each contain at least 17 of the candidates, allocated in a lottery, and 8 of these phase one groups each contain 18 applicant participants. Whenever we have more than 2,000 participants, we only let one winner from each phase one group go on to phase two. The 465 phase one group winners are then each allocated to a phase two group somewhere in the province at random. As 465 / 19.5 (average intended stage two group size) = 23.8462, which rounds to 24, we have 24 phase two groups, each with 19 or 20 stage one group winners in it. A drawing is held with the 465 names on it and the first name pulled out goes into group one, the second one into group two, the third one into group three, and so on until each group is ready for its second, third, 4th and subsequent members to be allocated.

The top two vote-point-receivers off the other group members from each of these phase two groups then makes it into the phase three groups. 48 people are assigned to three phase three groups, each containing 16 participants. In year one, where 15 winners are chosen, each phase three group in this scenario gets to elect five winners onto the party's leadership decision-making epicentre.

These party leadership decision-making epicentres are full-time paid jobs, so the successful candidate is given a week to give notice on his current job, or risk foregoing the post to the next-highest-scoring applicant. If having to give a month's notice or more, the person can appoint a temp to cover for him until he is able to fulfil his post.

These 15 leaders of the political party will work closely together in formulating each of the party's policies, nominations, votes, actions, intended actions and proposals. There is a rotating presidency of one week per member in determining the running order of tasks for the day within the grouping, though a person can opt to give his rotating presidency turn, or left over bits of it, over to another one of the 15 if he or she so wishes, and specialisations into different realms of government departments and ministries will emerge over time, with the backing of the 15-member party leadership as a whole supporting the one who represents them in this quest.

This is long-term job, but not a job for life. The system requires that each 15-person party-leadership in every province must run a further interselection event every time a vacancy arises, regardless of whether the vacancy arose through a resignation, a retirement, the prolonged absence of one of them or a sacking. In addition, once every three years one of the party's longest-serving 5 and one of the newer ten must be voted off by an interselection vote of the 15 party rulers at the time. This rule is pre-stipulated accordingly in the early years, so that if there are more than 10 party leaders with equally long terms in office, any 13 of the 15 can be interselected to stay on and any two of them can lose their job in this end-of-year-three interselection vote, in which each party leader must give at least five of the other 14 party leaders 90 points or more and the remainder may not all be given the same exact score, in an anonymous deadline-made 15-person scoring round.

This party leadership seat expiration vote results in two vacancies, which are filled through a new multi-phase interselection event, similar to the above. No advantage is given to those who made it through to the later stages last time or to those who have served in any particular role in the past. All applicants are equal, in that they all go into a phase one group first, only by winning the group (or by clinching qualification to the next phase) and then winning any number of later progression groups too, can they progress to the crucial final phase. There are no primaries and no interview rounds, as the interselection process takes care of the full process of party leaders selection for each province.

A similar vote is held once every two years to determine the party leader and its candidate for head of province or head of government, with the 15 party leaders allowed to nominate themselves or another person of their choosing, as long as they come under the party's membership. The voters are entitled to know who each party's candidate for the main leadership role is, and these are all determined somewhere between one and six months before the election occurs.

The final phase interselection group will contain anything from 6 to 24 candidates, who have successfully progressed from the previous interselection round(s) of groups, and these finalists spend three full days examining one another and explaining their skills, stances and ideas to each other before they all vote on each other's capabilities, evaluating each other group member once again in terms of who would make the best party leadership epicentre contributor, who has the most to offer the party and the world, and who represents my stances, opinions, budgetary inclinations and worries best.

Of course, this is not the perfect system. It is a good and a truly democratic tournament contest system, but maybe not the perfect system. Of course, other people will come up with better ideas than this, over the years. The beauty of the system we are rolling out is that every society gets to rewrite its ground-rules every 50 years, as a new group of 35 oversight process delegates will be assembled every 50 years in every province, tasked with formulating the 7 best other options apart from the current system, for the voters to choose between. And the electorate chooses among these 8 ways forward, picking a winner for each quarter-final, semi-final and finalist options pairing, with the chosen way coming into force, for a 50-year period, within 24 hours of being chosen. This allows new improvements to be brough in, or change-reversing steps to be taken by the voters, depending on what they pick. More on this in a few pages' time.

Can a person change his or her party?

Yes. There are two ways a person can change which party he or she is affiliates to, in most participating countries, in the initial default system: Each party within each province may pick one of the applicants every year to bring into their party as a party leader. When they do so, they go over to the new party and if they accept, this person must renounce his or her old party membership. This results in a 16th person entering the party leadership, skipping the usual mass-interselection process. When the next party members' term expiration occurs, all but 12 of the party's leaders must be voted off, including at least one of the five longest-serving and at least two of the ten longest-serving. The other way to change party is to submit an intention to switch parties to the centrally registered board, which is acknowledged with a reply, and which has to be followed up with at least three more letters indicating this same intended change, not having changed one's mind, before it takes effect. Any person can switch to any other party, or they can step out of all parties if they wish to, which requires only two such letters in any two months. The numbers of people who can change affiliation per year is unrestricted in most countries, though there is one province in Cuba where each party may only let a maximum of ten new joiner applicants a year in.

So does this mean we no longer have a one party state in power?

The newly formed political parties primarily operate independently of one another, and at the province level. Each one is funded equally at first, though one third of the available overall party leaders' funding will later be readjusted according to the percentage of all votes won in the election. Each one makes its own suggestions, without any other body or department of state intervening in any way. These new parties compete with each other for power, for leadership posts and for a bigger say in the provincial, local and national legislatures. They are almost enemies. But only by working together respectfully and with good listening skills can they flourish.

Due to the system, under which everybody is allocated a default party to automatically belong to right from the beginning, we expect each party to start out with the same mix of left and right instinct tendencies. They will drift apart a little over the years, due to people defecting over to other parties where their personal views are better accommodated, but we do not expect to ever end up with anywhere near the polarisation that we saw in Europe in the 19th century, Asia, Africa and Latin America in the 20th century or in USA in the 2010s and 2020s, all of which were extreme polarisations way beyond what voters would ever want. The constant automatic feeding in of new young and immigrant members into all the parties will do much to reduce the polarising drift-apart forces. Instead, we will have a system that results in more agreement and less disagreement between the parties, with each one primarily located very close to the centre of the left-right scale.

Power over funding is split in such a way, in most affected countries, that 60% of all public sector spending is under the control of the provinces, free to allocate this much out among its various programmes as it chooses. A further 30% is allocated out at the national or federal level, and 10% at the town, borough or village level. This means that all the different kinds of taxes and other forms of state revenue are eternally split in this way, until a change to this split is brought in one day by a new act of law or through a change of constitution. Most revenue types' local and provincial 60% stay in the province where they were collected or paid, with only 1% of it being transferred from the richest to the poorest province per capita. Some countries are going with a slightly different split, but such changes are only possible with the full and well-informed agreement of the voters.

Powers of the legislature: Legal issues and budgetary issues are discussed in the legislature, with three biggest parties each getting one Tuesday in three, on which to submit a new proposal that then goes up for vote in front of the legislature. If the other parties all reject the matter and if the party has less than 50% of the overall voters, which usually applies to all five parties in all provinces, the suggestion in its original form is dead, but the next stage of the process then opens the bill up for improvements, amendments and alterations. There is also the possibility that a party will decide to use up its one token it gets every 25 years for a mini-referendum of the voters, in which case the voters decide whether to overturn the legislature's rejection of the idea, proposal and legislative bill or not.

Not only the largest party gets to introduce suggestions into the legislature. A special system gives each party a turn, followed by the biggest party getting five turns and then the next-biggest two parties get a turn, before each party a turn again. A turn means a full day's legislative agenda, which may only encompass one issue per day.

Whenever a party opens a new debate on a new suggestion up in the provincial or in the national legislature, its new suggestion is allowed to splinter, based on the feedback it receives from the other parties in the legislative debate, into several amended and non-amended forms of the proposal and idea, all of whom will go up against each other in the final vote, where the current way and the non-amended idea go up against all the changed versions of the idea that each other party adds into the mix. If there are more than three possible ways by the end of the period of debate, including the suggestion in its original form and the current way the law sets this matter, then the possible alternatives submitted by all the other political parties, all of whom must be fully formulated, finalised and submitted within three hours of the debate commencing, are all added into the tournament of ideas on this topic, with a series of qualifying round head-to-heads and then either a quarter-final and semi-final and final vote-off, or three triangular semi-finals of competing solution options and variations, all held within 25 minutes of each other, at the end of the day, culminating in one chosen best way winning out in the end.

The current way, the suggestion of the day and the largest party's amended version all enter at the semi-final stage, with all other amended versions all entering at the quarter-final stage. The votes are all held during the final hour of the day's session of the legislature, and each defeated option is eliminated until only one wording remains, which then becomes law. Most legislatures will not have an absolute voting majority for any one party. These will need to work on common ground and on deals they have struck to win the votes.

If a legislature does have an absolute voting majority for any one party, the constitution, assuming the annual referendums and the mini-referendums haven't changed it out, guarantees that the five biggest citizens' petitions every year will go to mini-referendums, which in the event of succeeding in two such mini-referendums in a row, the first one at a scale of 1% of voting locations and the second at 25%, then automatically overturns the legislature and becomes law. This way the people, rather than the government, will always get to set the main limits and parameters of power. They can take power back, limit politicians' pay and remove dogmatic prescriptions from applying to all if they are only widely accepted within the largest political party.

When it comes to budgetary matters, age limits involving the use of some number, and other legal and financial acts of government involving some amount of money in it, it is not unusual in this brilliant new world, to see different parties submitting differently scaled alternatives to the vote. In these cases, if the differences end up being the size of the budget, rather than the wording of the law or policy around it, we hold a "median numbers vote" instead, where the lowest and the highest numbers submitted are taken out until the winning middle is found. If the action of the day involves an increased funding commitment for anything, then the matter is not over until a stage two vote then decides what percentage of this new spending commitment that has just been decided upon through a median numbers vote is to come from tax hikes, spending decreases elsewhere, specifying where exactly, quantitative easing, a mixture, or other revenue routes (specify them). They must also specify whether to repeat at the same funding level in later years, uplift, expire, phase out, or let the budget-setting leader on the day decide.

Local level elections

All national and local-level bodies are determined in provincial elections; and all mayors and national posts are nominated by the provincial party leaders, with the electorate in this location voting the new appointments in. Given that not all provinces hold their elections on the same date, this means that there are no dates where the entire country is holding an election, as each province's portion of the national legislature is all that expires and is renewed in any one province's elections. Well, this and all the provincial leadership, provincial legislature and local mayoral, district and borough posts.

When there is a need for temporary maternity leave or sickness leave cover in a legislative assembly, the person who will be absent for a while is allowed to choose who fills the post in their absence, with the recent interselection contest contact info made available to her every time. This person is known as an "appointed empowered cover temp". The usual person holding the post must give at least three weeks' notice when they are ready to return to their post before resuming it, and they do not have to give any notice before picking an appointed empowered cover temp to cover for them with immediate effect. This three week rule is there to help the appointed empowered cover temp to do an orderly handover and to plan his or her next career move better.

In the event that an appointed empowered cover temp wishes to appoint another appointed empowered cover temp to cover them, they may do so, but the original and substantive postholder may of course put a replacement of his or her choosing in to replace this person, or indeed to replace the appointed empowered cover temp they appointed initially. They are, after all, only there to represent the person who is missing, and while doing so, they are gaining valuable experience that may serve them well in the next interselection event the party holds.

In later years, the party leadership seat expiration vote continues to result in three vacancies every three years in every party in every province, in addition to the otherwise occurring vacancies from people stepping down, going missing or being thrown out, so new opportunities to sign up for an interselection event keep on arising, year after year open-ended. One of these expiring mandates has to be one of the five longest-serving members of the 15-member leadership panel and one further member of the ten longer-serving members is also voted off. This rule is important in ensuring that no party keeps on shooting all newcomers down just because they are newcomers. Renewal and youth is important in any well-functioning unit, just as access to wisdom and experience are too.

The person being voted off should either have views that are not the same as the majority's, have less skill, mind-power, commitment, popularity or ability, a worse reputation, contribute less than others do to the wellbeing of the country, or has said or done things to make him- or herself unpopular with the party. There is also a system-in-built rule that each party leadership who plans to throw one of their own out must do so in two 15 party leaders' votes, occurring at least one week apart, just in case a press headline panic on one day has turned out to be a no infringement or someone else did it situation, by the time of the second party leaders' vote on the matter.

The **five-stage transition plan** applies to all the countries involved in this process. It is central to the whole move to bring new democratic freedoms to countries that have been lacking them for a long time. Here is how it unfolds:

Step 1) The ruling regime chooses three of its provinces in China (a land of 33 entities, made up 22 provinces, 5 supposedly autonomous regions, 4 self-governing municipalities and 2 special administrative regions) and nine in Afghanistan (a land of 34) and two entity areas in most of the other countries (places with less than 20 and more than 5 provinces, like North Korea and Saudi Arabia) to serve as the forerunners of change and as the test cases in the transition process. The two or three chosen 'wave one provinces or special entities' are announced on the 19th January 2039 by the heads of state and government jointly, in each of the world's 37 least democratic countries. It is urged to let public opinion polls among the smaller population half of provinces guide each state in making this selection on which provinces (such as Hong Kong, Macao and either Tibet or Xinjiang Uyguria in terms of China's best round one selection options) to send into transition first, and to let the locals who live in these areas, as selected through a lottery that picks just 35 paid "oversight process delegates" from five age band quotas, five regions and ten profession groups, to serve in each province to be in charge of the transition process locally.

These 35 paid "oversight process delegates" are to work hard to choose **the 8 best system options** to present to the voters. They must share an open letterbox that all ideas and analyses of options can be submitted into, and between them they must prove that they have read and discussed at least 50 of these submissions thoroughly each, within their three-month "study and analysis phase", including especially the contributions from the leading experts in this field of political analysis. In case of a disagreement, they hold a debate and a vote between the 35 oversight process delegates. The winners of the vote get to announce the chosen provinces for the wave one action. Any threatening or abusive contributions will be reported for police action.

Step 2) The ruling regime chooses five more provinces in China and in Afghanistan and one more province in countries with fewer provinces overall like North Korea and Cuba, exactly one year later, on the 19th January 2039, or within the three weeks just before this date, to send into the same kind of transition process toward a five party system, though each province's 35 paid "oversight process delegates" may, if two thirds of them agree, make additional caveats, rules, notes and stipulations to improve the quality of the process and the quality of the options the voters of the province will soon have. Now we have newly improved systems going live in a second wave of provinces and regions, with real power to decide attached to all resulting outcomes.

Step 3) On the 19th January 2041, or within the three weeks just before this date, the ruling regime chooses five provinces (Chn & Afg or just one province in all other countries) to keep under the old system for another ten years, while all other provinces will now undergo the transition into the main five party electoral system, where the split into five is based on the last digit in your year if birth, pairing 1s and 6s up in one team. 2s and 7s in another, and so on. In countries with less than 20 provinces overall but with more than ten, only two provinces are kept out of the transition process at this stage. In countries with ten provinces or less: only one province is kept out of the transition process, for now. The "keep out of the process" provinces (aka exempt hold-backs for established incumbents only) are chosen on the basis of where has the largest support for the government of the country at the time. The provinces with the biggest support for the regime government are gifted as areas it gets to keep for a few more years, during which time these provinces will be presented by their 35 lottery-picked oversight process delegates with a number of structural and system options that they could pick or reject.

This transition process not only brings in new options and choices for the voters and a new multi-party legislative system, but it also gives them a feel for how things become under this sort of constitutional set-up. Notice that step 4 is all about letting each province choose for itself what sort of society it wishes to be and what sort of government regime it wishes to have. The default way does not have to be kept, if other ways are deemed preferable. By the end of June 2042, each of the step three transition process provinces are to have held their first five-party elections.

Step 4) Each of the provinces holds a mini-referendum, held in three stages, so that the winning proposal between eight good option models of transition, two of which represent a return away from the year-of-birth based multiparty politics to the "old way" and to rule by just one party in government, three more options are different unique new forms of panel-15 change as described in brilliant detail this book, and the other three options are a devotion to three chosen other countries whose well-functioning and well-structured system is to be copied.

Of these 8 options, the chose ones will have won a quarter-final involving 1% of the province's eligible voters, a semi-final involving 3% of the province's eligible voters and final vote involving 100% of the province's eligible voters. By letting the people of each province "shop around" and choose the best system solution for them, we are democratising not just the battle for the big decision-making posts, but also the very ground rules, the framework, the structure, the rulebook, and overall set-up within which all else happens to a marvellous extent, thus surpassing through the introduction of constitutional alternative options anything that any other more established democracy has ever had. It is such a good thing to have, it truly beats all other routes to democracy the world has ever seen. It also allows the voters to ditch the main initial plan of transition to democracy and to go with a different solution instead, if it chooses one that is destined to deliver a better outcome. None of the 8 options in these votes are just there as a formality or are just there to be an automatic loser. Each of the 8 will have things going for it and reasons to support it that are disclosed openly to the voters by the 35 organising delegates.

This important all-deciding referendum is to be held once every 50 years in each province. The step one provinces are to hold this vote on the first such vote in the beginning (QF), middle (SF) and end (final) of January 2040: 4 Quarter-Final vote-offs, all held on the 1st day of the month at 1% of the polling stations in the province), two semi-finals, each held at 3% of the polling locations on the 11th day of the month and the crucial final to be held on the 31st of January 2040 at all 100% of polling locations in the province. The step two transition process provinces are to hold this same 8-destination-options menu vote in May 2041. The step three provinces are to hold this vote in the beginning, middle and end of January 2040. The step two transition process provinces are to hold this vote in June 2029. The final exempt hold-back provinces are to hold this vote on the first such vote in the beginning, middle and end of January 2043. The step two transition process provinces are to hold the vote in March 2037, not having rolled out any multi-party elections until then. These votes are all held again, with eight newly chosen options, carefully prepared by a new 35-man panel of organising delegates 50 years later, starting in January 2076, so no province is made to remain stuck with a choice it regrets forever.

This is an achievement that surpasses anything any other democracy on earth has ever given its voters, just like the way no other country on earth has ever been given 8 decent constitutional set-ups to choose between before, so the system of multiparty democracy or other democracy or one-party rule will be fully self-imposed and subject to later systemic and rulebook improvements, which is the most optimistically positive future imaginable, so we are deeply grateful to the Malaysian delegation for suggesting it and to the Chinese Communist party for being brave, strong, open-minded, good and kind-hearted enough to agree it in this final version that took two and a half years of negotiation, ending on the 17th of December 2024 to agree.

A lottery drawing is held to determine which 1% (for QFs) and which 3% of polling stations (for SFs) to activate in each of the preliminary rounds, with the affected voters notified with two weeks' notice to make their decision carefully, plus a lottery drawing also determines each option's opponent and its position in overall the 8-option overall tournament of systemic menu options. The 8 options the voters have in this process (A to H) are basically summarised as: one recent year of the way the nation was set up is chosen and defined as one kind of destination the province could go back to if it chooses to abandon the five-party process and the multiparty democracy idea and to return to the "old way" (G).

Option B gives the power to choose a different outcome in legal, financial, tax and spend and policy decisions to the towns, villages, workers' councils, communes and districts above the provinces, decentralising the final say on most questions, limiting the national budget to a maximum 6.1% of GDP. These two options, A & B are also different from each other in that A places the power to overrule others and to decide, impose and harmonise in the provincial and in the national centre, while the other, B empowers the locality to make its own decisions.

Three of the 8 constitutional ballot options (C, D & E) are three different unique new forms of change and speeds of change toward multiparty democracy, as described in this book: one (C) intends to keep the province in a five party system forever, one (D) intends to allow ten specially created other people's parties (be they a collection of companies, NGOs, individuals chosen by interselection, by lottery or by IQ tests) to function and compete within it too, and a fifth option (E) intends to allow all other independent and oppositional movements to go onto the ballot too, gradually opening the doors to hundreds of possible new challenger parties, groupings, movements and one-man bands who may decide to try and emerge, grow and win, and three of the eight ballot options (F, G & H) are devoted to three chosen other countries whose system is to be copied as closely as possible. These three countries are chosen by the 35 paid "oversight process delegates" among the 200 nations of the earth now or among any past set-up that any country has ever had.

The international advisers have added a recommendation to the 35 organising delegates to please make sure that one of the chosen options (F) should use proportional representation (with or without a qualifying cut-off threshold and with or without regionalised seat compartments) at the legislative level. One of the other options should be to use single seat constituencies (G), and one (H) should use round-robin votes (with or without a split into the top few and a qualifying bracket) or a single transferrable vote system. Any one of the 35 delegates may submit a suggested formulation for each of the 8 ballot options, while the full 35 delegate assembly then has a week to study each of the submissions and to choose the best one of the suggested option wordings for each of the 8 ballot options A to H. This process is run in the month that is two before the month when the three-stage mass vote between these 8 options is held. In choosing the final 8 options to take to the voters, each of the 35 can back any two of the ideas with a 500-point backer vote and a 200-point backer each, while also scoring all the other entries from 00 to 10. In the event that the sum of all these votes from all 35 delegates still results in a tie between two of the proposals, some provinces will hold a special 1% mini-referendum heat to choose the winning proposal that goes through to the final 8, while other, poorer nations will hold tie-breaking head-to-head votes conducted by the 35 delegates.

Step 5) On the 19th January 2034, the old ruling regime of China, Cuba, Vietnam, Afghanistan, Syria, Iran, UAE, Indonesia, DRC, Morocco, all the stans and Saudi Arabia each chooses one province among the fewe it had chosen to keep away from all the changes in its decision on the 19th January 2041, in which to carry on the old way for another 15 years, while all the other provinces move into stage B, opening up the process to whichever of the eight menu options its people pick in the three-stage process as the new system rules to play by in this province for the next 50 years. The one kept province does not hold its first 8-option systemic vote until these final 15 years are over, in the month of January 2049, while the other four (stage five democratisation provinces) all hold their already in the month of March 2037. such is the gradual nature of transition, negotiated in to ensure that the outgoing regime is not handing over too much power and too much of the work of governing too quickly, which would be accompanied by an armed fight-back, which this more civilised and more amicable "carry on in your province until you retire" method, which wisely avoids the need for war, after centuries of humankind getting it wrong and descending into winner takes all duels to the death that should never have been allowed to happen.

So, to recap, this important all-deciding referendum is to be held once every 50 years in each province. The step one provinces are to hold their second such vote in the beginning (QF), middle (SF) and end (final) of January 2076: 4 Quarter-Final vote-offs, all held on the 1st day of the month at 1% of the polling stations in the province), two semi-finals, each held at 3% of the polling locations on the 21th day of the month and the crucial final to be held on the 17st day of the following month, at all of polling locations in the province. The same dates of the month are generally used in all other systemic votes too.

The step two transition process provinces are to hold this same 8-destination-options menu vote in May 2041 and in June 2057. The step three provinces are to hold this vote in the beginning, middle and end of January 2040 and Feb 2076. The step four transition process provinces are to hold this vote in June 2029 and in July 2079. The final five provinces are to hold the first such vote in the beginning, middle and end of January 2040 and the second one in Feb 2076. The step five transition process provinces are to hold the vote in March 2037, not having rolled out any multi-party elections until then and in April 2087.

These votes are all held again, with eight newly, carefully and expertly chosen options, carefully prepared by a new 35-man panel of organising delegates. Another 50 years later, starting in March 2126, so no province is made to remain stuck with a choice it regrets forever. This is an achievement that surpasses anything any other democracy on earth has ever given its voters, just like the way no other country's people on earth has ever been given 8 good or even decent constitutional set-ups to choose between before, so the system of multiparty democracy or other democracy or one-party rule or other system will be fully self-imposed and subject to later systemic and rulebook improvements, which is the most optimistically positive future imaginable, so we are deeply grateful to the Malaysian delegation for suggesting it on the 27th June 2022 and to the Chinese Communist party for being brave, strong, open-minded, good and kind-hearted enough to agree it in this final version that took two and a half years of negotiation, ending on the 17th of December 2024 to agree to undergo this "process of letting the people select possible systemic improvements".

The rest of the book from here on in will need to differentiate, depending which of the 8 options the voters of the province have chosen. We do not know what they will choose, or indeed how the options will be defined on the ballots, so we need to be specific about all 8 of them. We can be quite sure that not all areas will pick the same exact combination of how it allocates powers, what the rules of the game are and how much of the power over spending is going to be held back for the provinces to decide. We also anticipate that a province's options and its final selection will sometimes vary from one year to the next vote 50 years later, so the future reality of China and of all other countries accepting this brilliant transition deal, some of which will be long-established semi-democracies and others will be emerging out of authoritarian and dictatorial set-ups is going to be a fascinating mixture between the 8 paths on offer here.

The five party affiliations by year of birth method is a wonderful starting point in bringing about a system where there are five competent, trustworthy, realistic and well-informed contenders for the top head of government posts. This is why we do strongly hope that it is used in all countries at first, while the people get used to living in a society where people can criticise the head and can make alternative suggestions without being taken away by the ruling regime anymore. That's when your have crossed the gateway into a democratic and free society. It's a big step to take and one that the ruling regime will be reluctant about, but they must rest assured that this change is not about destroying the previous rulers. It is about ensuring that the big decisions made next must better reflect the will of the people than any system until now has allowed or achieved.

By the year 2047, it is hoped, suggested, stipulated and expected that each and every province of every country on earth will have given its people an 8-option menu of where to go in terms of the systemic rules of the game. This does not require countries like USA, Canada, the UK, France and Germany to throw all its decades of popular constitutional evolution into the bin. Not at all. But some aspect of the way things are currently set up in these countries can go up against a number of new ideas from near and far, potentially improving something about the constitution of the land, be it a rephrasing of the rights of man to gradually clear away all guns and deadly blades not held by the police one state at a time, or maybe finding something brilliant about how something specific about the health system or the election funding system works in one other country and offering the chance to build this into our system.

The 35 proposal formulators (aka "oversight proposal delegates") do not change the constitution. They just pick seven particularly good ideas to present to voters alongside the way things currently are, and once all the voting is over, one of the seven particularly good ideas OR the way things currently are wins and these then determine how these people will live for the next 50 years, when the process repeats itself, allowing new better ideas to be considered, including ideas that the biggest political party in the land would never have raised, for a variety of sinister and corrupt reasons. Any improvement this brings about is a good thing, a better world to live in.

By applying this principle at a "each province chooses its own bets system and its own best future" level, we make it probable that different parts of a country will end up with a different system for a while, but in the long run, once all the evaluations, the data, the migration and economy figures are in, if rational thought still exists in the world in 150 years from now, we would expect the truly best systems to have been identified, found and adopted more or less everywhere by then, and for the 7 other options, in this point in the future, to either be rejected or to be representing a slight improving, empowering, limiting, partnering up, refocussing or reframing tweak that further ensures that no one person or one organisation ever ends up with too much wealth, power or market share, so that the many can flourish too, and so that a bigger majority can own their own home. It will take a long time to reach perfection, but we can expect big strides in this direction to have been made by then.

Part 12B - Long-established democracies

For long-established democracies, option G will mean no change is what the voters choose to pick; option A will be to move to the five parties by five years of birth groupings system with round-robin head-to-head on-ballot votes; option B is to grant more powers to one of the local, provincial, county, town or state levels, with the suggested grown remit and the percentage of all tax revenues going to this local level of government specified very clearly on the ballot paper; option C will always be offering a selected form of proportional representation or a move away from the current proportional representation system toward single seat constituencies if the country has PR in use at present; option D aims to bring in special parties whose decision-making leadership is determined either by, individuals chosen by interselection, by ransel lottery method, by IQ tests or by assembling on its central leadership board a collection of companies, NGOs, politicians, special interest groups, local authority areas, or something similar.

Option E chooses something good about how some other country functions to introduce here, which could be a policy, a payment system a criminal treatment system or a structural update. Option F chooses something good about what one 'submission from the public' suggests is introduced here, to improve something about our health, education, infrastructure, crime, forestry, agriculture, flood-protection, waste-management, renewably energy use or transport system. Or option F might introduce an idea on how to cut the crime rate, or something related to crime, violence and conflict. option G will mean no change is what the voters choose to pick. And option H brings in a citizen's letter idea on how to improve the voting system, the lobbying system, the legislature, the court system, the central bank and currency, the police, the military, or the campaign funding system, making sure that not just one political grouping benefits from what the legal system can offer them.

A specially held drawing of lots places each finalised oversight proposal delegates formulated option somewhere in the formation of four quarter-finals or into the heats for a place in the QF. The first round of mini-referendums, held at 1% of the voting precinct wards, chosen at random in that same specially held drawing of lots, for each one of the four quarter-finals, chooses the better one among each pairing of suggested ways, choosing which best systemic ideas to put into the semi-finals round. In the semi-finals round, 5% of the voting precinct wards vote between each of the two semi-finals round options it is presented with. And the best winning ideas then meet in the final, which is voted on by all the voters in all the wards of the county, state or province the vote is being held in.

In the end, one of the 8 options has been picked in the mini-referendums and the in the mass vote final, resulting, in most cases, in one very specific system improvement going live within one month of the vote having been held. Voila presto! We proudly present: a better here and now and a better tomorrow in a much-improved world!!!! Instant success!!!! There is no way the government or any coalition of narrow interests can prevent the true will of the people from going live, from replacing what has been there until now with the changes that were chosen in the once every 50 years in each province super referendum final.

Option D has a lot of possibilities in it, many of which we feel deserve further explaining here:

Ransel explained: Instead of using the interselection process, a lottery among all the applicants might be held to determine who the finalist candidates should be and who the deciding voters to pick between them should be. This is known as the ransel principle, as the lottery operates on a random selection principle. Compared to the interselection process, it greatly reduces the number of people who need to travel, take time off to support their application and to physically assemble for whole days at time. It can also be loaded with any number of relevant quotas applied, such as ones that ensure that people from various age groups, from both genders, from various professions, ethnic groups, income quintiles, backgrounds, and from the towns and villages of the north, south, east, west and centre of the province will all end up on the party's leadership board. Ransel can instead choose the members of a province's party leadership team, ensuring that the required quotas are upheld, while also giving people who take longer to befriend and to persuade and convince people, ordinary people like you and I, are given a chance to get into government too.

The 35 proposal formulators may instead decide to let the party leaders interview applicants, or for an IQ test, along with some kind of quota to ensure that various forms of knowledge are brought in to decide a shortlist of candidates to then be interviewed. It could even use all of the above methods as it gradually reduces the number of applicants who are still in the running to the 15 who will win a place on a party leadership board in the end.

Or maybe it wants there to be several parties, each one with a different selection method in use. There could be a party made up of auction winning delegates. Or a party of long-term unemployed, or pensioners, famers, construction workers, factory workers, teachers, lawyers, office workers, or housewives. It may alternatively allow the party activists who have volunteered the most effort to help the party be considered. But this risks the party evolving into a narrow fringe clique or a succession-choosing power-grab-and keep monarchy of eternal rulers. Holding primaries, or auctioning off posts on a party's board may be a financially lucrative method idea that a cash-strapped society may think of allowing in the party leaders selection process, but it too has severe disadvantages.

The idea of assembling a collection of companies, NGOs, politicians, special interest groups, local authority areas, or other entities, groupings or beliefs into one political explained: Let's start with the idea of a political party that is made up of a collection of 15 people who have been nominated by 15 specially selected companies. Firstly, the leadership of this political party is made up of 15 people who each have an equal voting say on the party's main decisions. This line-up of 15 is split into five categories, each of whom get 3 of these 15 seats in the party's leadership. So three voting leadership roles is reserved only for companies with less than 10 employees and members (A); three are only for companies with 10 to 40 employees (B), three are reserved for companies with 41 to 200 employees (C), three are for the three biggest employer companies in the state or province (D) and three are for the other companies in the state or province who employ over 200 people (E). By allocating the segments out in this way, and by potentially giving all 15 a potential veto over the main policy lines, we ensure that the big, small and middle-sized companies have to listen to each other and to work together, never working to harm each other in the party's dealings. We could allow 15 companies to choose a delegate each and have done with it, but instead we are allowing 25 locally active companies (5-6 from each company each segment, chosen in a lottery among all confirmed applicant companies) to nominate a candidate each, and these 25 candidates are then screened, examined, questioned and scored by each of the 25 companies (interselection scoring or eurovision system), with the top three from each company size segment then winning a seat in the party's leadership epicentre.

Similarly, a political party might use ransel, interselection, or appointment by a figure of authority to assemble a permanent representative of each of the 15 largest faith groups in the country, or the top 15 in the province as one moralistic and wise new political party. Alternatively, by instead assembling representatives of the 15 biggest membership groupings in the country, from the automobile association to the nature-lovers WWF, from trade unions to the stage actors' guild, the chartered accountants and the legal profession, we would be assembling a good cross-section of the society the party is here to represent. Giving such a party a special push through constitutional privileges would put it into the running to win elections to form the government of the land.

Instead of the biggest 15, it could be the biggest five only, plus five of all the others on rotation, in an order determined by a lottery-style drawing. And this could be companies, NGOs, lobby groups, ethnicities, hobby groups, special interests, religions, trade unions, or just a gathering of individuals who were picked in a lottery to represent their age range, gender, region, income bracket and profession. We list so many options here, but what the 35 will put onto one of the 8 systemic voters options will be much more specific and chosen to be the best   from this list only. The creators of the system must examine all the possibilities and the probable outcomes and must invent and boost whatever set up would work best in their province. They could launch three such parties of the grassroots and might reserve maybe 60% of the seats in the legislature for these parties, to ensure they have the desired level of influence. This quota might then be reduced by 1% every time there is a new election cycle until one day the quota is no longer what is keeping these groupings in the mix and involved in the debates that shape the agenda of the politics of the province or state on the day.

Part 13A - Can the Extinction of Mankind Still Be avoided?

View 1, Keith: "Was it avoidable? Of course it bleedin well was! The yanks fucked up by going in to invade Iran. The Chinese fucked up by accepting a 800 trillion dollar deal to supply Iran with so many nukes, and got found out by the CIA. All three nations leaders missed their chances to back down and to stop shooting down each other's war ships and planes, and as for the 70,000 nuclear rockets, well these should never have been used. They should never have been an option. Now we have two days left to live, and then it's game over. For all of us."

View 2, Sara: "I still don't fully believe it. Or I wish I didn't. The shops are closed. The buses aren't running. There are people preparing for war, and people going over the top, already now, in a bid to join or invade and conquer the secret army bunker project on Hayham Hill. It's mad. I'm just glad I at least know that this bunker exists, as this place might give me, if I make it there, some chance of surviving."

View 3, Greg: "None of this makes any sense to me. The world has gone completely mad. I was perfectly happy, and my life was just coming together, and now this happens! My girlfriend has gone god knows where. I guess my only chance of surviving this next week is if I somehow manage to get recognition for being the guy who joined the army, worked his way up in 2 days of madness. And protected the prime minister, a visiting president, the queen's favourite princess, or the head of a global company, and did it so well that I got picked to join him or her in the bunker."

View 4, Ollie: "Life is full of tough decisions, but the toughest one anyone has ever had to make is here with me now: Do I try to fight with the government, Like Greg, or with the local farmer's militia? If I get this one wrong, I'm toast. If I get it right, I may have a slim chance."

View 5, Kate: "Ollie is right. So is Keith. And Sara too. Not sure about Greg, and no idea why he ditched me for this missing girl? We do all talk, you know. We don't know what each other is putting in the diary, except for me. I have privileged access, as I have the job of collating the entries. We do get together to speak, and to sound out each other's thoughts, as we do all live on the same street in Weybridge Abbey. If we can help each other survive the hell that is this terrible apocalypse, we might actually make it."

The voice that knows: The above was in the evening of the day of the missile strikes, nuclear missile strikes! It was the 17th of May 2023, and it was total mass-nuclear-obliteration. Had they used ballistic missiles, the fall-out would have been manageable, but no. The US used up all the nuclear warheads they had been building up to annihilate all the strategic targets in Iran and in China, and both countries gave as good as they got hit, with more strikes taking out more targets all over the US. Everything was taken out. And the nuclear fall-out was now hitting the air currents and spreading all over the planet. The below statements were collected in the morning of the following day:

Keith: "I can see that the sky has changed, the blue sky is gone forever, and I feel my body filling up with crazy levels of radioactivity already. I don't know how much more of this I really even want to witness. If things get ultra-super-painful long-term, I don't wish to be a part of it"

Sara: "Everyone with half a brain understands that the radioactivity will be lethal to all, except maybe if you are in a tightly sealed bunker." But it all happened so suddenly that none of the big new state-of-the-art bunkers are ready yet, and how long will their stocks need to last? "I hear the only bunkers that could contain any humans who might live to have offspring in the distant future will need to be sealed up already today or tomorrow morning, and to remain fully sealed for up for 35 years, due to the radiation levels that are coming our way. I sure hope they have enough supplies!

Greg: "The tellie is no longer showing anything but repeats, and no adverts, no hosts, no news updates, and no commentary. Most radio stations have shut down. Most shops too. The roads are clogged. The lights have stopped working. The police no longer exists, at least not here in Weybridge Abbey. And the papers have come out with one final farewell edition, which I am going to read carefully now, in case there is any kind of clue in there about how to survive, or, if not, how best to go, …"

Ollie: "Seeing as how the government is definitely intending to put long-established VIPs, leaders and their top-ranking life-long career soldiers only into that survival bunker up on Hayham Hill, my only hope now is to get them lot and these farmer militia boys to shoot each other into oblivion, and only if the farmer boys, my lads, win, and decide to include me and keep me in the bunker with them, can I make it. I am off to join the militia, and to do my all to become indispensable for them. Bye"

Kate: I have always loved Ollie, and my dream is to end up in the bunker with him, giving birth to the two babies who will one day repopulate the world, Adam and Eve, with him and me cuddled together for 35 sweet slow loving years …. If the supplies run short, all the others in the bunker will have to die in order so Ollie and I, or maybe, in those final years, just pregnant me alone(?) may live!

The voice that knows: Needless to say, the scene is similar all over the world. People are preparing to go to war in a desperate last-ditch effort to get themselves into a survival bunker, one of the thousands of such bunkers that are now being hastily dug, engineered, constructed and reinforced. Each country has hastily launched some sort of competition or a points system that supposedly gives the top five or ten winners a place in the bunker. The points system has been devised in such a way that people are encouraged and rewarded with crucial points for helping each other out, for getting the backing of other people, and for supporting the government's efforts to transition smoothly into bunker life.

If the points race winners have much hope, these can only go into bunkers that are built and loaded with supplies in time and are then hidden away or defended, and sealed up successfully, and then the troops who got them in may have the final say and trump card when there isn't room for everybody in these bunkers after all.

What none of them knows, is that no bunker on earth is going to be equipped, so quickly, with enough food and water, a safe, hygienic and functioning system of dealing with sewage waste and with enough anti-radiation medicine to survive. Without each of these, all humans will die of the radiation that is soon to be inside them. Something sufficient might have been built if humanity had had more notice, more time, more focus, and more collaboration. But the way it came, no human is going to survive. But not all of the planet's creatures and plants will be lost and extinct, fortunately. There were 17 space rocket missions in 2022 and in 2023 bringing plant seeds to the Jupiter-moon Europa, where melting ice means that abundant life will soon flourish there. A small number of small fury mammals were also sent, in those last three missions (15 to 17), and they will make it, long-term, but we humans won't.

I hate to be the one to tell you this, throwing a spoiler so early on, as none of our five will have much longer to live. Be pre-warned and prepare yourself. Do not build up too much affinity with them, and try not to think about your loves one, your friends, family or pets either, as this may never happen in real life. Not if this collated diary turns out to be fiction.

Well, dear reader, have you guessed yet, which one of these neighbours from Weybridge Abbey will be the last one left? I won't reveal this now, but I can tell you that only one of them has much more than 48 hours left to live at this point, on the 18th of May 2023. This is known for sure. The final human colony to perish, two years in, in March 2025 to be precise will be a Japanese troop cave-dwelling of dwarfs on a small island near Okinawa, who run out of supplies and open the hatch too early for survival to be possible. They knew this was their biggest risk, and that they could not last another week in their bunker with no food left at this point. The last UK colony, dwindling and going a few months before this, on 19th January 2025, is the one containing the specially chosen points-winning TV beauties.

Everyone from the state, military and official offices died knowing that all hope was now invested in these seven girls and one boy.

What they did not know was that the bunker, though adequately stocked, was slowly letting the deadly radiation in through the same pipes that were giving them fresh water and taking all their waste away. I hope you can forgive us for throwing the last big reveal in so early. We miniature guinea-capibarras of Europa are not very good at keeping secrets.

Now back to the excitement:

In the evening of the first full day after the bomb blasts:

Keith: "The sky has now vanished forever under a huge wall of grey clouds. No crops can grow any more. I have been thinking about how I will choose to die. I have also been indulging in my meat, cannabis and alcohol stocks with Greg, who told me about a fun way of making an exit that the government (or the press) supposedly recommends and supports. This will also be my one last chance to finally meet that pretty celebrity TV show hostess who I have always fantasized about, and who I adore so incredibly much."

Sara: The government has admitted that it is about to seal off its bunkers. According to the last ever newspapers to be printed, it will wait nine days before it seals the last one of them off for a 35 year period. It has launched a new system of letting people all score each other to see who goes into it: Each person gets to give out 10, 5, 3, 2 and 1 points per day to the five people who they feel have behaved the best, and a further 10, 5, 3, 2 and 1 points to whoever they feel looks strongest, healthiest and prettiest and who would be best to be kept for repopulating the world in 35 years' time, but the app prevents people from giving any one individual both kinds of points on the same day. I have just been on the website and have installed the app, and I see that there are people with over 90 points already, so it will not be easy for any of us to 'win on points' but it is being presented as the only way to be in with a chance.

Greg: "I have seen some lovely ideas in the paper on how best to go, for a single guy of my age: One suggested method is to go to this creepy prison up Elm Hill, which has been converted into a safe house for celebrities. I don't know what they've done with the inmates who used to live there? Maybe made some sort of cargo carrying unit to support the army as it defends our princess, our prime minister and the points leaders? There, at the Palace of Pleasures, which is occupying the very spot where the Elm Hill Penetentiary was, we get to choose the two most beautiful celebrity women, and well, this is hard to say out loud, so I will whisper it: You get to choose a pretty leggy bird to have her legs around your throat and a cute curvy gal with a nice ass to sit on your face and while the two ladies you choose finish you off, you do your bit to save these heavenly women, as they get 295 points each from your ultimate sacrifice, as long as they are of the most fertile, healthy, young and strong category (or 45 points if gifting yourself to your own girlfriend, daughter or wife or to anyone who comes under some other category)"

Ollie: Gosh, things move quickly these days. The militia boys have already given me my weapon and most of my training (no uniform, as we go incognito!), and we will burst our way into that survival bunker on Hayham Hill at 0500 tomorrow morning, occupy it, kill all outsiders, take their bodies away, then get our supplies in, plant land mines all around us, in keeping with our secret map for when re-emergence day comes all those years later, and will then seal it up. Job done. I will be there, though I hope to somehow manage to end up somewhere other than the firing line at the very front when it all kicks off. It's the only way I'm going to make it in one piece.

Kate:" I too have been given my weapon and my training, but I think I will lurk near the back and say 'it's ok guys, don't worry about me, I am protecting our flank from attacks from behind'. My gamble is that Ollie and I will be away from the deadliest bits of gunfire, but close enough to get in when the bunker is taken. There are also some boxes of supplies hidden away in some houses, but I don't yet know how I am going to get all this stuff into the bunker? …. Ooh, I know, I'll get us a van! And then we could do multiple trips and really shift those supplies quickly!"

In the morning of the 2nd day, the 20th January 2025:

Keith: "The bad news is that I now know that today is the day I am going to die. The good news? Well, I am going to meet, and not just meet but even have an intimate life-saving (for her) encounter with the woman of my dreams, yes that ultra-gorgeous TV show presenter slash weather girl slash shampoo model slash twitter star, panel show contestant and my does she look great in the newspapers and in the magazines. She's the one that I have the really biggest hardest fullest crush on! She's the one I want to save!"

Sara: "Sh. Don't tell the others. I have decided to build my own bunker, and I will fill it with all the things I like to read, eat and do. It's going to be hard work, but I've bought a 20-ton digger and I've already started making the cave, deep in a nearby large abandoned field. This will be my salvation. I just hope my prince charming turns up. Oh I just know he will, I won't settle for any old passing male. I will pick one with potential" (giggles).

Greg: "Me and Keith have both signed up to the thing up at the prison. This way, even though we will not make it ourselves, we can die in an arousing position of pleasure, under some famous leggy curvy TV goddesses, and we can go to eternal sleep in the belief that these fabulous girls will make it, using the points they earn from having us go there and choose them. First we given them some immediate pleasure, and then we save them long-term. That's how a true valiant knight goes out".

Ollie: "The battle began at 0520, just a little behind schedule. We were well equipped and we had a good plan. It was all go. Our surge of improvised explosives took out the entire government and military contingent, we think. Though we did lose many brave fighters in the skirmish, we seem to have won the bunker, fortunately. And we hope we haven't damaged it. This means we will be saved. But first we need to figure out how to open the damn thing up, and how to get all the supplies that our boys and girls have brought inside?"

Kate: "I have found us a working van, and have loaded it full of supplies, twice so far. Now I am guarding it and that second load of goods carefully, while the militia boys are out in the town, preparing the boxes of goods to fill it up a third time – there are lots of scary looking people around, and the boys have been gone for a long while. I'm now just waiting for word when the bunker is opened up, so we can get our supplies and ourselves safely inside. Maybe if I move the van to be completely hidden and camouflaged, these creepy weirdos will stop eyeing up my precious stockpiles."

Around midday:

Keith: "Well, I am now third in the queue, and then it will be my turn. I can now confirm that these lethal ladies are definitely the very celebs I fancy most. I have seen them coming out to grab their next donor. I am giving them all the points I can, in the hope that some of these amazingly talented beauties will survive. There are my two daily allocations of 10,5,3,2,1 to give out, there's the 295 each for doing the ultimate deed on me, and then, the menu chart on the wall over there says: There are also some 5 point, 10 point and 20 point gifts I can give by also sacrificing my ears, toes, and balls just before the final erotic choke begins. Tough one. …. Well, seeing as it is my one supreme dream girl, who I am giving these to, I think I will say yes to the loss of my ears and both my balls. I am not going to be needing them in those eight minutes I'll have left to live. But my toes? I didn't choose this option, as I could not bear the needless suffering. I hope they'll understand."

Sara: "After these two unknown girls and a bloke turned up unexpectedly, the bunker-building project on the farm sped up nicely. My next worry is: where are we going to find a door that can seal us in? And do we have enough supplies for the four of us?"

Greg: "I only ended up signing up for the loss of my ears and the squashing of one of my balls today, as a points donor, which will happen in a few minutes from now. I am right after Keith in the queue. He's doing a 295, and will not going to be coming home. My choice went to a different bird than Keith's, as he's into skimpy blondes and I'm into curvy brunettes and redheads. I will go home afterward and will finish off the last of my booze, meat and drugs, before coming back here tomorrow for my final deed. That's if I don't find a bunker I can survive in by then. I still hold out some faint hope that maybe fortune will save me."

Ollie: "Can't speak now, hard at work." Grunt. "We're digging our way around the bunker door, as we can only open the flippin' door from the inside … Damn, this is hard, but we must hurry. We can rest once we're sealed inside."

Kate crying, sobbing intensely: "I tried so hard to fight them off, but the van and the supplies are gone, my face is a bloody mess, and I fear Ollie and the guys won't want me in this condition. Crap! I should've driven off before they got close enough to open the van door. They had a road-blocking pole and heavy stand structure, blocking the road off, but I should've crashed into it as hard as I could, and maybe I'd have got through. I nearly did, but then I fell for their we're on your side spiel. Now they'll hate me, and will send me out to go get it back. Shit."

Then Ollie and the boys give the signal that the door is finally open! But they have the shock of their lives, when they find that there are people inside the bunker already, and among them are none other than the British royal family! "What?"

Part 13B - In the evening:

The finger of the one he longed for most waved Keith in. His turn had come at last. The waiting was over. It was time to make the ultimate sacrifice, so his biggest crush might live.

Sara is now bringing all the supplies she can find into her brand new mini bunker – apart from the medication to keep the radiation in check, which she has not found much of, it's looking good … maybe she will find another way of getting more of it … Let's hope she has found a way of dealing with sewage waste …

Greg is now back home, having donated a high-heel flattened ball to one tall, attractive cutie, and his ears to another. He is now finishing off the last of the booze in his home. There is no point in wasting any time on sleep tonight. Greg will have plenty of time for this after tomorrow, when he is done in, so there's actually time to watch his favourite movie one final time, properly, while smoking the last of the weed, gulping gin by the gallon and enjoying some intense one-ball self-arousal time, for old-times' sake.

Ollie and the farmer's militia have managed to get the door open and have gotten themselves into a deadly skirmish shoot-out with the queen of England's entourage inside the bunker. The beautiful, pregnant and not long out of breast-feeding royal princess and her royal delegation had been in the bunker, all sealed away, with 35 years' worth of treats, or so they thought. Well, neither side had much ammo on them now that anyone could locate in such haste, and so it turned into a jiu jitsu mass brawl inside the bunker, while another militia that neither side knew about, made up of teachers, coppers, shopworkers and lorry drivers, was lurking outside, about to make its daring move on this same bunker.

The voice that knows: With complete human extinction now imminent, all our five subjects were triangulating: Ollie and Kate were busy triangulating a soft spot on their opponents that they could target and so take them out. Sara was zooming in on all the pharmacies in the area. And Greg was trying to convince himself he was going to go out with the biggest pleasure anyone has ever had, when he goes back to the Palace of Sins one more time. Now back to the excitement:

Our Weybridge Abbey Kate is in a hair-pulling and eye-gouging brawl with the Dutchess, the one who is meant to give birth to the future king, and also with her butler: all three are taking quite a beating, and Kate has used a bottle strike to take out one butler already, and has, in full flow, deployed a deadly karate move on another, which took him out instantly.

Sara had done one round of triangulating to choose a good place in a quiet field for her bunker and then another round of dazzling triangulation to find all the supplies, which now that all the shops were only open for ten minutes a day was an act of near-miracle and of much breaking and entering. The medicinal anti-radiation supplies were, in the end, not found in shops, but in the vehicles of the soldiers who had died in the recent skirmishes. Taking them without making any noises was not easy.

Greg was zooming in on his favourite woman's best body parts, which is where he longed to spend the last of his moments: He wanted to go out with his tongue in the vagina of his favourite TV personality, and he was pleased that his last glances before he went down and under her were filled with the sight of a warm, soft, girly, attractive woman who could enjoy receiving the affection and final joke-telling of a man who devoted himself to her.

Sara is now defending her bunker from an unwanted intruder. She has hit him with a shovel, eight times, but he has kept on coming at her, so desperate to climb into the bunker with her, and there just isn't room for five in her tiny little bunker! She sees the chance to stick the shovel in his throat, and put him out of his misery, but does she do it? Is she the killing type?

Keith went out with a smile on his face – his last thoughts were: she's quite a big lady down under, and a little bit hairy too … so lucky to be allowed to do this … in goes the tongue … it's sticky in there … blimey, that's a tight grip! I never knew her legs were this strong … and nice … oh crap, can't breathe. Is that some sort of sumo giantess with her foot on my head, stopping me from lifting me 'ead … dying … dying … what can I do? May as well try to let her cum … it's really her. My angel, the goddess of the TV world, and my, can she squeeze hard with them legs of hers … going faint … fading … sleep time? …out.

Greg made his final visit to the former prison and chose a woman who he wanted to make a 295 point donation to. He even got to look at her pretty face as she fired the gun, six times, that ended his run (and extended hers, but only by an extra week). It wasn't working, and nor did the rope she had tried to strangle him with, so she had to finish him off with a knife and with four spears. He was still so drunk that he never fully knew what hit him. But his manners were such that he helped his woman out all the way, even when it was time to give her the throat and the chest and then the throat again.

As the girls all got together for their lunch break, they had a chance to admire each other's outfits, while also giggling about the experiences they've just had as the glambabes who were active being angels of death at the Elm Hill Palace of Pleasures today. All of them were looking superb, just like they have just stepped out of a shampoo advert. They were clothed in sensual lingerie, swimwear or just underwear, which the majority of the girls were wearing today. These extra-stunning four girls wore very short red skirts that barely covered all their "charms".

Intricate patterns of pink thread in their skirts, which if one sees them from up close spell out "to die for" worked well as patterns that were woven into these skirts. The girls' socks were clean, soft and pink.

Their hair was long, well-grouped and wavy; and these girls' tops were white, with plenty of skin-reveal holes and slits in-built in the design, helping to turn some already super-sexy young women into irresistibly gorgeous killers, who no man could ever say no to. In today's world, their clothes resemble an abbreviated tennis dress, enhanced with beautiful pink girly designs. In their stunning looks, they really were, as their skirts implied, to die for!

Sophie was determined to get herself an equally striking skirt for next time, so more of the men would choose her, and if it means she will do better in terms of her kill count, it will win her more points too, giving her a better chance of making it into the best bunker.

The floor in front of the tightly packed try-out area viewers rows in the conference room had become a deadly chamber of kills. All the girls who had come to try out and to show they were good enough to become a smothering glambabe angel of death were busy demonstrating their killing techniques, as a panel of judges made notes on a clipboard.

It was like that throughout the whole glambabe palace. According to Rachael, this was the way things were going to be until the end of the following month. The people in power had fifteen weeks ago decisively and defeated several archenemies and were now in custody of all the survival bunkers as well as all the military units and there were millions upon millions of prisoners, who were now surplus to requirements and no longer needed to be kept alive. The government has started to reward their glambabes angels of death smothering cooperative for their good work by being given them bonus death sentence prisoners free-of-charge, each of whom was worth 4,000 survival points.

Many of the suitably instinctively overly submissive men had been brought in to work in the glambabes' palace as special house prisoners, until such time as their time to "go under" comes. It was useful to have them around, as they could bring out clean sheets every so often, prepare the food and take away all the freshly smothered to the disposal site. But if any of these house prisoners did not behave and work, or if they failed to obey a single command, the girl cop rulers of the site, the authorities, and ultimately, the glambabes would get them and would take them out.

Nicola, her three daughters and the maids had a GREAT home life together,
living in the glambabes angels of death smothering cooperative, smothering two to seven men per evening each in their girls' room, while reading girly magazines. It wasn't an uncommon sight to see a mother, astride a victim, while she breastfed her newborn. Giving life and taking life, all within the same cycle.

The oldest daughter, Elle, was likely to be squeezing another male to death at the same time, right across from her, in the very same room. Both of them would enjoy the pleasures that come with their work. And the second-oldest daughter would alternate between the two, providing the legs around the throat assistance that goes with the standard finish. They were a happy family and they worked well as a team. No male ever lasted more than 25 minutes in their room with them.

Everything had gone along so wonderfully. All the women had even adjusted to the frantic pace of 'taking men out' now demanded of them. Sophie found she could easily put away 5 to 6 males every 60 minutes without feeling exhausted. Due to this constant pace, Sophie and the other glambabes were now in an almost continuous state of action, and they loved it.

Life was now so beautiful to Sophie. She didn't feel the least bit remorseful taking so many victims out. She, and the rest of the glambabes, were sparing them a slow horrible death from radiation poisoning in the cells or out in the streets. They were playing an important role, and giving the boys a pleasant enjoyable and meaningful exit, in her presence. That's how they looked at it.

Sophie couldn't finish off any victims at all if they cried and begged for mercy. Each victim, without exception, had to gladly submit to the gentle, purposeful death the glambabes offered. Most of them did. If ever one of them did cry, struggle and beg for mercy, which was rare, Sophie's partner in their angel of death work, Céline, would have to jump in and finish the male off, using her tight lethal legs around his throat, until he was no more, no longer posing a moral dilemma for Sophie. Céline also had a knife, in case it ever became necessary.

One such occasion arose in the morning session, right after returning to their designated room after delivering a "how to finish-em off" demonstration to a visiting crowd in the conference room. A man in his 20s who has been reluctant all along, started to fight when he was in position. Céline tightened the grip that her legs had around his throat, determined not to let him get out, and she waved her left hand frantically, signalling to Sophie that she needed her knife.

Sophie hesitated, but seeing the grip of the legs be subject to round house thumps and a lot of leg-flick jerks designed to break her hold, she ended up giving Céline her knife.

And Céline plunged it deep into the male's heart so quickly that she must have been holding the knife for less than one second before plunging it in his chest. This worked, and did the trick. The male's violent fights were over, and now Céline's legs were able to choke him out.

Seeing that he was defeated and on the way out, the male glanced longingly up at Sophie, who saw this and knew what it meant. The man was now ready to kiss her and to die while giving Sophie the satisfaction of another successful finish. Sophie sighed. She would have wanted to spare the male, or at least to spend some time with him for a bit longer. But it was time to move on to the next victim, who was sitting outside and reading a girly magazine, ready to enter the moment he is called, just like you would see in a doctor's surgery.

Then, while he enters, the assistants drag the newly departed out and sling him onto a trolley for further removal and disposal. This one was way more compliant and gentle, and Sophie was able to ride his face to a cacophony of orgasms, which more than made up for what the previous guy's offerings were lacking. This sense of euphoria spread, and the dying man and Céline all managed to clap for Sophie's performance, in the middle of the angels of death kill throes.

The girls had time to engage in chitchat.
"Oh, that one was so much better! I've just got to get one of these sexy little outfits you're wearing,

Céline." Sophie stated. "I love the way it accentuates your curves, your tummy, your hips, abs, ass, cleavage, and your legs, all at the same time! It's perfect!"

"No problem, we know just the shop," replied Céline. "It's no longer open, but we can gain entry through a broken window in the rear. We'll go there tonight!" They exchanged compliments around how well their lip stick matches their skirt and also around how dazzling their eyes had been made to look, and then they gossiped about the men who were sitting outside and waiting in the queue, speculating on how far they might go on a date with them under pre-apocalypse circumstances. Does all this seem familiar? The madness of the end of world battles seems to make repeating conversations seem normal. It just doesn't matter, in the bigger context. What do a few lives of the doomed ever matter really, when they have no hope of survival at all, and their words, of course, matter even less so.

The twins had the room next door. They worked for their points, and were amassing up to 14 kills a day, between them. They were among the most successful of all the girls who were employed here as glambabes, as their poster on the entrance hall wall makes them look so dazzling, in their carefully staged wavy long hair and their curvy short-cut sexy outfit, making them look so nice and so desirable in this pose. This invites many of the men who are not sure when they first arrive which girl they will give themselves to, to make the decision to pick them.

Many of the girls also benefit from having a very good picture up in the entrance hall. By getting picked more often, a girl can really soar up the rankings, clocking one lot of 395 survival points after another, or 4,000 survival points at a time, in later dates, after the big scoring revision. This often continues all day long. It's hard work, being so damn pretty and cute!

 As the next two men, a bunch of convicted crooks who had been sent here to be finished off made their way to the glambabes that awaited them, Sophie thought of those poor dirty convicts being led into their cells, not for being paedophiles, thieves or violent, but for being with an opposition party. Perhaps she might be made to do away with some of them today.

Or maybe these two who are coming in now are nothing better than a bunch of stalkers, rapists, killers and robbers. The thought cheered her up immensely. Sophie's recollection of her life before coming to the glambabe palace of Elm Hill was no longer very clear. She did remember much about going to school, getting a house, getting a job, moving in with a boyfriend who later left her.

All her memories were now more recent: of betting going on in the stands about her precise kill time, of Céline wrestling down and killing those who squirm too much, quickly and violently, and of those blissful moments of pleasure, as a handsome and cute compliant visitor, one of many that day, gave himself over completely to her deadly vaginal pleasures on his face.

A new male visitor to her parlour, the kind who wanted to sit and chat, rather than go straight into the required position, would be quickly brought down by Céline's marvellous legs sweeping his legs out from under him, as she crept up from behind him while he was facing Sophie, and her grabbing hands controlled the angle she wanted his head to be in as he fell. He would then be finished off by Céline, while Sophie had to take her turn on leg chokes duty.

This was the usual way to welcome a new visitor into her room, into her angelic chamber parlour of death. No man would last more than 14 minutes max in there on a busy day, when these two girls, Sophie and Céline, working as a team, had more than 20 bookings to get through. Sophie surmised that her style of finishing them off would offer a more refined, relaxed, sophisticated and fulfilling finish than some of the other glambabe girls in the palace, who were a bit rougher with their men, provide, as they lack that air of trustable, divine, gentle control that makes most men surrender themselves fully to Sophie the moment they meet and fall for this angel of elegant glambabe doom.

This difference is very much apparent in the try-outs, which were once again going on at the end of the corridor in the conference room. There, victim after victim was being smothered to death by so many aspiring applicant girls, performing to the cheers of the crowd while being tested and assessed.

But only very few of them had that aura about them that made the men they were putting out surrender themselves fully, gently and willingly to the girl who was taking them to death. This difference was being noted, and it was going to make the difference between getting the position on offer or not for quite a few of the women in the audition.

One of our five main characters at the start of the story, Sara, was among the many women trying out here today. She was not just here to explore the only way of surviving the next 30 years. She was also interested in smothering, having thought, dreamt and fantasized about being a smother girl angel of death many times.

But she comes here without much coaching, training, experience or advice. For this reason, she is unlikely to win the contest here today. But she and all the other girls are sure to get one kill under their belts during the try-out, which may be very enjoyable for the girls, as it involves using her pussy on a dying man's face and tongue.

As the man has been allocated to her, rather than choosing her, the girl taking him to death in these try-outs will only get 1000 points today, while the woman he picks as the cutest and best-looking, the one he would have wanted to 'go under' most, wins no less than 3500 points from this, as long as one of the try-out girls is picked, which not only improves her survivability score. It also helps her greatly, in the battle of the many try-out contenders.

The glambabe palace is spacious and lush, with an inner courtyard, a neat and lovely garden of plants and flowers and a fountain. In the garden, the birds were tweeting and some children were playing, obliviously unaware of the fact that hundreds of men were being brought to their deaths inside the building right now.

While the girls in the garden, wearing tiara crowns of daisies, were chasing and playfully catching some smaller and younger boys repeatedly, giggling as they went, the grown ups inside were not able to rise again. The kids were happily at play, unaware that while mummy was busy putting some man to death, daddy was already dead, a victim of a take out move applied by an ambitious and sassy girl in the first group of try-out girls in the conference room today. The fabric of society was changing fast, and the population figure was dropping fast.

Inside the conference room, the many try-out participant applicant women and girls are arranged in a pattern of positions along its main central floor, reminiscent of a tile pattern from Spain, while the spectators, mostly made up of supportive friends and family of the applicant girls and of women who were studying the technique and were hoping to be in the next try-out the following week, are lined up along its perimeter.

Quite a few of the male supportive friends and family who had come to be spectators, cheering their girl on as she fought her way through the try-outs, have themselves been claimed by one of the other participant girls from the try-outs, with a yellow soft silk belt placed around a man's neck to denote her choice. None of these chosen men will be alive by the end of these try-outs today, as each participating woman is entitled to complete her kill and to go for a good score from the judges. Sadly, this means the end of many good boyfriends, husbands, dads, uncles and brothers in there today.

A raven-haired beauty such as Sara could earn incredible pay as an angel of death smothering glambabe, with looks "to die for" as one of the sponsor's slogans up on the back wall reads. Sara understood the humour of the message, and she grinned, as she saw the last of the dead male victims from the second try-out group being lifted onto trolleys and taken away.

Sara glanced around and noticed women of a select young range of ages, the third group, now all astride their victims. Some of the girls were quite young. They may be lacking in her killer instinct skills, but presumably they get extra points for the fact that they could still be of child-bearing age in the distant post-lock-down future, when it is finally time to emerge from the bunkers. Well, if the menopause is usually at 51 and we subtract 35 for the number of years the lucky few will be in those bunkers, this requires some seriously young girls to be picked and brought in. Hopefully the selectors will have thought of this.

Sara wondered how could the lighter and smaller applicants ever even make a kill of a male who is sometimes nearly twice their size, or significantly stronger than she is. Then she noticed one young thin girl, possibly 18 and not very tall, atop a male. She was frantically pumping hard on him, smothering him with her ass as part of the try-out. That answered Sara's question.

Having been here to see the previous round of try-outs performed here moments ago, in which there were numerous smothers of various techniques, Sara was now familiar with the positions the women were using. The common straddle smother, reverse straddle smother, full body smother or "69", upper thigh head scissors, squat smother (forward and reverse, with and without tongue) and the ass in face cosy sit smother. Sara saw every one of these positions being used and among these were a few new positions she'd never thought of. As expected, most of the male victims were laying still and hardly resisting. They didn't even need to be bound. But they had all been bound, as a procedural precaution.

Sara's group is up next, how exciting. Younger girls and boys, stadium attendants, were busy removing bodies and directing fresh victims to the various rooms. They normally get a nice and slow pace of work in the palace of pleasures, as there are so many of them to share the work between, but during a try-out there is always an awful lot of bodies to remove and a lot of people to shift, which makes the try-out days by far their hardest shift to work.

They are also the most perilous, as those thin yellow soft silk scarves can be placed around any male's neck to denote a smothering woman's choice, and it is not unusual to see a bunch of helpers 'go under' after being thus picked for smothering in these massive try-outs. Very often, it's the newest male recruits among the team of helpers, who had not known how the try-out girls' selection system operates, who end up with a soft silk yellow scarf placed around a man's neck to denote her choice, which means the male has less than half an hour left to live, and he will have to spend it all in positions of worship of the woman who has chosen him!

Pay for the helpers is poor, but the lunches could sometimes be quite generous and after a full week on the job, a special package of perks, vouchers and survival points was to be earned. For the lucky few who do end up becoming glamourbabe smothering angels of death, there is a mountain of survival points, potentially thousands of them to be earned, a guarantee that every court case will go her way, and an automatic exemption from all low-scoring citizens' duties to give themselves over for smothering.

Sara was pleasantly surprised about this revelation. Glamourbabe status is not easy to attain. You have to earn it through mastery of the walk, the dress, the pout, `the look', the takedown, the squat, and so on.

When Sara's try-out group was invited to start selecting their target males, which was after a line-up of men, all tied together in one long train, had been brought out, they leapt into action. Most of the girls quickly returned with a cute male claimed through the yellow silk scarf method. But there were more girls in this group than boys in that train of tied men, and so, after missing the dash to claim the last one of them, as they had already run out of specially brought in men to use, Sara was left without a man. Sara sighed despondently.

Then she remembered that all males in the room and beyond were choose-able targets. Luckily, there was a handsome helper close by, who had just finished piling up three of the dead onto his trolley. In a haste, Sara slung her soft yellow scarf around his neck, narrowly beating two other girls, who were now left having to claim one of the for men in the spectators rows each who had been left to last because they were sitting there and holding hands with a woman they love. Sorry, guys, but you know the house rules? Well, here's a copy of them on a card for your girlfriends, while our female helpers are helping the choosers bring the last of the chosen males to their positions.

Everyone ready? Go! While most of the chosen males were already kneeling and kissing the hips of the girl who had chosen them anyway, and these males were easy to push over onto their backs, there was also the ones who were still on their feet. This included the three puzzled males who were picked last. In keeping with the house rules, these three stayed near the women who had chosen them and they were all spectacularly swept off their feet by some very determined and attractive females, who now had all the men on their backs and ready for mounting.

Sara's chosen helper boy made an audible gasp when he was skilfully thrown onto his back by Sara. He looked up to her, admiring every inch of the sensually curved body of Sara bathed in the bright spotlights from the conference room ceiling. Her eyes felt like they contained a mood hue of moonlight that was making him want to stay down and await her leggy areas shortly descending down on him. Without saying a word, he lay down at her feet.

Sara then clamped her legs in around his head, her skirt going all around his head like a curtain. She began carefully applying the squeeze move. The feeling was so overwhelmingly delicious to have a victim's helpless head pressed hard between her powerful determined legs and his heaving chest pressed tight to her body as she had let her long, lovely legs descend down onto the rest of his body, without thinking about it. This showed a natural instinct, which the judges will like.

She then began a slow deep grinding circular pumping on the male's throat. It was not long before her clothing grew moist with sweat, so much so in fact that driplets of sweat were seen running down her face. Sara was a little embarassed by this, but again the judges looked pleased and were giving her some good points, or so it looked.

We were now in the final try-out group of the contest for a place in the angels of death palace, and everywhere around the floor, girls were now astride their victims, making short work of their targets, while also trying to look like credible pro angels of death, whatever that looks like.

The applicant glambabes managed as best they could to seal off all male abilities to breathe, using just their pink leggy legs alone. As there were so many girls here chasing so few winning posts today, it was not surprising that the judges never gave all those who they had already marked down in the first move a second glance. It was not so important for them to get the race for 29th place to 108th place right. What mattered today was that they were well enough informed about the top few that they can then choose between them.

Some might say, come on! if some of the girls are already out of the running before they have made the kill, maybe they should be tapped on the shoulder and sent home, thus sparing the male for other, more vital and points-giving uses. Well, this is a discussion that may have been different under other circumstances, but given how none of these people will live to go in a bunker anyway, you might as well give them all the thrill of the kill and let the girls think they are still in with a chance, while letting the boys go out with a positive feeling about their demise.

Sara was lucky enough to be one of the twelve girls who made it through to heat five, the finals. She did very well to get this far, but only two of the girls will get the official state-backed angels of death job here in Elm Hill today, so the fight is not over. Sara was looking around for her supportive x-boyfriend, her uncle, her brother and her dad. But unfortunately they had all become a part of the game, and were now either lifeless bodies being loaded onto the trollies to be taken away, or they had been claimed already by another one of the finalists for the next round. Only Sara's sister was still there to cheer for her.

As usual, another row of known convicts with their number and their crime on them, was brought out, and Sara was able to pick a comparatively nice looking guy for her next kill, leaving the fiendishly ugly brutes for the other two girls from the 4th heat. All the other girls now had to sit the rest of this one out, but they were free to stay and watch, applaud and cheer the girls on.

In a rare, funny, incident, one of these girls, Kelly, accidentally killed a man who had "exempt" written on his chest. He had paid a fortune to be exempt and was the general manager of the site. But nobody noticed this in the moment, when he was protesting at her yellow scarf being round his neck and it was too late when the helpers realised what it said on this corpse.

On occasion, one of the women would receive a kick from somebody's victim in his death throws, but in the orgasmic heat of the moment, his vain resistance was not noticed by her at the time.
Besides, he was under another girl and he now belonged to her alone.

Back in the main entrance area, more new arrivals were now enjoying a catwalk parade of girls they were able to choose among. They had nine minutes to make their choice, and if they had not decided in that time, the staff would give them to a girl who had not been fully booked with men who chose her yet.

They would then be marked up, by the staff, or sometimes by chosen glambabe angels of death themselves, with a big red marker pen, writing clearly, on the mens' chests, in large letters, who he was now assigned to, with each fast-choosing male getting the names of the upto three ladies he had chosen for her looks in the catwalk show written upon them. As it
was clear that, in this instance, an honest mistake had occurred, and
the crowd was chanting "honest mistake", it was agreed to dock
Shelly only 0.1 point for her mistake, and to award Suzy this kill.

Now only eleven of the 80 men remained in the queue. It was starting
to look like some of them might still be alive when the gong goes.
The rules state that any who are in mid-smother at the time of the
gong, may continue with their smother until the male's ultimate sweet surrender, the time of the final capitulation being crucial where two glambabes have the same number of kills, and if there are any left in the queue at this time, they are to be awarded one to the winner, then, if there are any more, one to the second-placed girl, one to the third, … as a `victory lap' celebration.

Handsome Stan the rodeo star and car salesman (swindler) was
pleasantly surprised by the sudden and unexpected kiss from a magnificently beautiful glambabe. She had come to collect him. Looking forward to an encounter with such a vivacious and laughy chick, he was easily felled and soon he too was in his final throws of useless struggles.

Eventually Sophie got into the swing of things, but she never made it
out of the bottom three in this event. She sat on another one's
face, a burglar, and her rear made passionate love to his bottomly
compressed face, while her leggy partner Céline was busy compressing his throat his her 10 out of 10 lovely legs. Other crooks would just walk along in silence, sharing a burning passion for the beautiful glambabes that were about to smother them. Bertram proved to be no match for Nicola's ass, which truly was everything he had ever dreamed of in an all-devouring butt. The deadly legs of her partner

Elle were also a wet dream come true in action.

The crowd, mostly made up of officials, tier two pretty women hoping for a turn tomorrow, and local men who were awaiting their turn to go under tomorrow, was chanting "kiss that ass, kiss that ass!" – They were well into the excitement and the heat of the moment now.

Obeying did not spare anyone's life, but supposedly it will win him a better start in the female-dominated after-life. This is what it said on the leaflets and on the posters at the entrance. Most of the offerings had no problem with that.

Quite pleased with herself as she finished him off, Sophie and Céline were soon done with finishing off the pilot, and they moved on to their final victim of this game, a career thief, specialising in being a car radios snatcher.

In the final minute of the game, all the women were frantically working their lethal legs and their deadly butts, trying to finish one more man off and to move onto to another. In the final 15 seconds, three more glambabes managed to finish one off, have the kill confirmed and to go up for another crook to take out.

Two of these criminals were quickly snatched by an eager for points female who wrestled him down, in partnership with her co-angel, onto his back and went to work on finishing him off right away. It was little Rachel and the blonde bombshell Brittany, who were now joint leaders with Sarah-Jane and her partner.

Then, just ahead of the buzzer, sweet Suzy, who had just run out of men with her name on them and who had already clinched 4th place came and took one of the open selection men back to her spot, where she and terrible Tara threw him over and descended on him. Within seconds, they had him in the desired spot, his face under the sweet bottom of sweet Suzy and the terrible legs of Tara pressing down on his throat. His air supply was cut off. This gruesome twosome was about to kill him off, and to earn some valuable points.

When the time finally ran out, just two of the males remained unclaimed when the gong sounded, and hence they were going to be victory laps for the top two finishers, which turned out to be Brittany and little Rachel, ahead of Samantha and Amber in this event, mostly because of Sarah-Jane's costly slip-off, which gave her final target costly extra minutes through one last bonus breather.

When the final standings were read out, and the top two planted a victorious foot on their prizes' faces, while the others planted a foot on their last victims' already surrendered faces, the crowd cheered ALL the glambabes well, and chanted "super babes, super babes" every chance they got and some chanted "that's a good innings".

Lovely curly lethal ladies wearing black evening dresses were dragging the smothered out males out

of the arena and over the edge of a nearby cliff into an empty outdoor swimming pool. More and more defeated males were being chucked off the edge and were piling up inside the empty pool. Sophie was amazed at the
huge heap of seemingly dead men (but surely most were merely
unconscious? or maybe pretending?) already, and the night was young yet.

The crowd euphorically chanted "You go, girls!" and when it was over, the glambabes' own remix of the Spice Girls' Classic Hit " I really, really, REALLY wanna sit-a-sit-ah! " was played through the sound system, while all the bodies were taken away, presumably to be turned into a variety of nifty uses, from gastronomic delicacies, to beauty products like skin cremes and shampoos, to stuffed sex toys and trophies for walls, to food for crocodiles who were being bred and raised for the women to eat when they were ready for the butchers.

But the loudest cheer of all so far, topping many a really big, loud
cheer already so far, came when the ring announceress pointed out
that there were still nine more events to come, adding how many more men still awaited smothering here tonight.

The chosen glambabes' names are written on the whitebaord in big red letters, just after the deliberating at the end of the competition.

The names are Kate and Millie, who will form a new partnership, taking over the new smothering chamber boudoir that was once known as the broom closet instead. Sara and the many other girls who came close but missed out were then sent home, their heads hanging in shame. Their contact details were taken, in case a smothering opportunity were to arise in any of the smaller locations in the area.

Then the two victory-lap-boys were slowly and pleasurefully being
smothered, kindly and mercifully given a couple of sit-up breaths
before the final sit and leg squeeze combo, in which all nine pairs of glambabes were allowed to sit on the chests and legs of the prizes, while Brittany and Lil' Rachel sat on their faces.

The competition was over. Everybody came out of the conference room, apart from those who had been smothered to death in the finals. They were not about to get up and go anywhere.

444 the Mattress Men
use   and lastly, the Mass Elimination. So we were in for a lot of
treats still to come.

We now break for lunch and then we return to each of the smothering chamber rooms to see what each of our killer girl pairings is up to this afternoon.

the In the Team Grab and Capture, four teams of four girls each were
going to use their rodeo ropes to chase and catch as many of the 100
men as possible, with bonus points available for certain maneuvres,
submissions and three-on-one positions. In the first half of the
Punch & Stuff, the most horrible, dangerous and evil, least worthy of
any proximity to girls' asses men were simply to be turned into human
punchbags, hanging well tied up first upside down from the arena
roof, then the right way up and by their arms. Each girl and boy in
this event was to have five punching opponents, with points given for
severity, style control, grace and damage done, then these failed
humans were to be stuffed into trash bins with only a leg and an arm
exposed and beaten with sticks, then each was to be taken to the
ladies restrooms and put through special head-inserts, where each was
going to be covered with girly urine and poo until they were no more.

Then the timed Precision Smother, which was a test not only of beauty
and style for the competing glambabes, but also of their abilities to
guesstimate how long they have been sitting on their victims for.
Each glambabe would have a 15 minute and a 20-minute smother boy, and
the total combined end-of-smother to end of target time differences
would be converted into points that helped decide the finishing
order. There were so many events, and so much prize money went to
the `other best placed glambabes in each event that overall, after
the whole evening, the winnings were going to be quite similar for
all glambabes.

In addition to the glambabes, there were the ironfisted Honeybabes,
who did quite well out of the Punch and Stuff and the Crush, Wind &
Log in which all the GlamFemmes Fatales also took part, and which got
rid of the worst of the crooks in a less dignified and more punitive
manner. In the latter event, as the name suggests, the emphasis was
more on its core elements, the crushing of testicles, the multiple
passing of wind onto their humiliated victims' faces, and their
ultimate demise in the special head inserts of the ladies toilets.

In The Pageant, each male chooses his top five picks from among the
girls during a lingerie catwalk show, and is guaranteed to get one of
his picks, so the more often a girl is chosen, the better are her
chances of scoring the most from her smothers, after all more men to
smother means more points potential.

Then the MultiSit awaits, which will involve getting ALL the many
birthday girls from the audience involved in a game of multiple girls
sitting on each victim at the same time. A roll of the dice decides
which woman sits on or gets off her victim for 60 seconds, and a `6'
means all bounce up and down in him. Then in the BBWs' Megasit, the
sheer size of the special SSBBW's asses accounts for a very different
style of event, with victims typically outweighed by four-to-one
ratios by their kiss of death sweet surrender girls.

The SmotherTeens `Girls' Adventure' would allow the younger ones to get
some experience in, and its rules forced them to be conscious of
their looks, style, control, elegance, technique and such elements,
allowing all the basics to be practiced and refined (while at the
same time taking a good load of crooks out).

Then in the Mattress Men game, men walk around with mattresses
strapped to their backs, and women, including the glambabes, the
Honeybabes and the GlamFemmes-Fatales, fell them with splendid high
kicks and in the ensuing smother sit, the mattress makes for a very
comfortable kiss of death for all. A very popular event, accounting
for over 200 sweet surrenders tonight, with the replays of the high
kicks deciding most of the points. So we were in for A LOT of treats
still to come.

And lastly, which was not due for over two more hours yet, given all
the action that was about to unleash a lot of FemFury onto deserving
convicts' faces, the Mass Elimination, would unleash a further 340
men, and the full participation of all the women in the audience
would mean that each man would have to endure dozens and dozens of
sittings at the hands of the ordinary members of the viewing public
before their final relief would come. When the music stops, the girls
swap over seats, with sitters moving over to the next queue, the next
few in the queue already allowed to stand on their victim's body,
awaiting their turn on his face, and the front one taking her seat of
honour on his face. When the Spice Girls' "I really really really
wanna Sit-a-sit-Aaah! " comes on, whoever is lucky enough to be
sitting on a man at the time gets to finish him off, and all the
others in that queue get to pile up sitting on top of him too.

Young Carlos waited patiently for him to be led in by one of the cute
attendants. It had been a long and difficult journey for the youth.
He was a Hispanic, born and raised by an indifferent peasant family
along the lake's coast. His father was a brute that drank up the
families small income, for which he had to be sentenced in court. His
mother took to drink herself and left he and his 11 brothers and
sisters to fend for themselves. Her only diversion from drinking was
smothering. In one of her rages she smothered one of his younger
brothers. It didn't seem to bother her in the slightest that she was
smothering one of her own children.

One day a buyer came to town and young Carlos, along with two other
brothers, was sold for a few loaves of bread. He remembers how happy
and gleeful his mother was as she tucked the loaves under her arm and
ran back to her dilapidated cottage. She was accompanied by a swarm
of begging street urchins. Just as she entered the cottage she
grabbed one of the boys and pulled him inside. So far nothing of
young Carlos's life had been fun. His
only joy was to look out onto the vast expanse of the blue lake and

imagine
himself as a brave sea captain rescuing beautiful women from evil
pirates.

Now he faced a slow, painful death in the ass of some woman, and he
longed for that ass. All of the prisoners were sullen and resigned to
their fate. It was as if they were already dead and just their body
hadn't gotten the message yet. After being fed a horrible tasting
gruel they were loaded on a large cargo lorry. Being prisoners they
were stuffed into the black cramped depths of stinking cargo unit. At
least the gentle vibrations of the journey had had a soothing effect
on him for he, as with most of the prisoners, and they soon arrived
at the arena.

Carlos's mind went blank. When put in a position such as this, beaten
down, unloved and forgotten by the world you turn inward. His young
mind was virtually blank. All thoughts of escape were laughable. The
prisoners were barely alive and defenseless. How could they overcome
well armed and perfectly healthy BBW guards. He was jarred awake when
the slavers opened the hatches. Bright sunlight, like a searing
intense beam penetrated into their lair.

All chained together at the ankle, they slowly filled into the
waiting cells. A big fat red-haired wabbly brute of a BBW looked them
over one at a time. Every so often she would select a slave and one
of her assistants would unchain the slave and make him stand in a
separate group. Finally it came Carlos's turn. All she said was "This
one goes in the next event" to his assistant and moved down the line.
Carlos found himself separated from the main body of prisoners.

There were perhaps 50 of them chained together, separate from the
rest. All of them were quite young and many of them small boys,
obviously unfit for the life. Carlos didn't get his hopes up for the
lot of prisoners was a very cruel one and any unspeakable fate could
await. Much to his surprise they were loaded into a cozy living room
area, furnished with comfortable settees. Much to Carlos's surprise
it was clean. They were even fed a decent meal.

Hundreds of other young prisoners were already in the waiting cells.
For the first time in his life he felt a spark of enthusiasm. Then he
heard the word "glambabe" whispered from slave to slave. "glambabe" -
he was to be smothered. His spirits soared. No slow death in the
mines or a dog like existence in some dirty hot dry slave pen. The
prisoners began to talk amongst themselves. They were all excited,
elated in fact. True they would die, ah, but such a death for a young
male. A slow sensual smother by beautiful women was not such an awful
fate. They all were happily looking forward to it even more so since
it would be performed by some golden haired American beauty.

After docking they were unchained and led in large groups to a bath.

This was the first time young Carlos could ever remember such a warm relaxing bath. A stern matronly like women checked each boy to see if he was clean enough and many were sent back. After the bath attendants handed out new cloths. It was nothing more than a white cloth that went around their waist. Then they were fed and what a feast.

Carlos had never seen such a display of food. A long table covered with the most delicious food his mind could ever imagine stretched out before him. The young lads ate like wild animals and Carlos was no exception. They all knew this food and decent treatment would end in their smother but they welcomed it. It would be the crowning moment of a fantastic dream. A majestic smother would tie it all together into one beautiful package.

Carlos and several hundred companions were led through the clean and neat alleys of the arena. Prisoners being led to a glambabe House was a normal everyday sight and the American citizens showed no interest in them at all. None of the lads were chained and there were occasions when a slave could have made a break for it. This was the furthest from their thoughts. They welcomed the sensual deadly embrace of the glambabe.

The column stopped momentarily when a Wisconsian housewife indicated to the guards she and her two teenage daughters wanted to look over the lads and select victims. The women, though in her early 30's and their mid teens, were very beautiful. Her beauty was also enhanced by the fact she was wearing Victorias Secret underwear only. Both her daughters, also wearing this, had immaculate bodies any lad would gladly go under. She and her daughters briefly looked over the prisoners and made their selections. Then six one dollar notes changed hands. Carlos passed the door of the women's home when one of the boys, the women's captive, turned and smiled. He was obviously pleased to have been selected and was evidently looking forward to the smother.

The large group of prisoners was further broken down into groups of two to three hundred and led off either to the various glambabe Houses throughout the city, or the waiting cells of the Smotherpalooza arena. Now and then, the column would be halted by an Illinois housewife or young maiden so she could select a victim for her smother. In most instances, the selected youth would turn and waive to his companions.

Carlos, through all the confusion, had lost sight of his pals. He had hoped to perhaps catch sight of them before the smother. Once again the column shuffled to a halt as two young women looked over the victims. A tall sexy blonde pulled his pal Markus from the line. His young face was radiant. Carlos felt a strong tinge of jealousy especially when she and her companion turned to lead the youths away.

Both young women had the most magnificent and
perfectly formed posteriors you could imagine. As Carlos passed, he called to
his pal. Markus turned and smiled. The women seemed nice and patted Markus
affectionately on the head. Markus waived and shouted "good luck!" The column
moved on and soon the young women and their victims passed from sight.

At last they arrived at their destination. Carlos didn't get to see
much of the building. An attendant came around and offered them water
or fresh fruit. Young Carlos had never at any point in his brief life
known such kindness. He knew that he would pay for this with his life
but that was of no consequence. He thought it was much better to be
smothered by some majestic beauty than to suffer for years as a
nameless slave. One attendant, a young
girl, was making her way amongst the prisoners, putting a light coat
of fragrance on
their noses. Over the next few hours an older women or young
attendant would
come in and select a few victims to be distributed to the glambabes.
At last it
was Carlos's turn. His short journey through life would come to an
end.

He was led down a long Sorority House hallway. Along the hall were a
number of rooms, or
rather more like open stalls. He looked inside and saw some intense
smothering
going on. Many of the women were being quite loud about it and
moaning in
pleasure as orgasm after orgasm swept over their bodies. Attendants
were frantically dragging body after body away. "Here" the women said
pointing to a stall.

Carlos's breath was taken away when he saw her. She was a tall beauty
with long black hair. In-shape and retaining all of her feminine
charms. "Over here, lay down here" she said impatiently. The youth
regained his senses and obediently lay where indicated. He placed is
head on a large soft pink pillow. She then lowered herself down over
his face for a "69" position. This raven haired goddess had a
glistening thick mat of jet black pubic hair. She
was well lubricated probably from the "excitement" of all of the
kills she'd performed so far that day. He had watched in almost slow
motion as she lowered herself onto him. He felt her gently wiggle her hips,
working his nose deep inside her.

Next she spread her legs wide and began a slow circular hip grinding.
He could see out from under her just a tiny bit. Carlos wanted to

giggle for her soft pubic hair was rubbing against his face tickling
him.

Gradually her pumping and grinding was making him dizzy even though he was
desperately trying to remain conscious. With a precision of a glambabe Master
she worked his nose around inside her. Then he could feel it, the often talked
about ethereal bonding between a woman and her victim. It was beautiful - they
were uniting as one. It was like some warm hot erotic sensual bath. He
couldn't believe it. Young Carlos had never experienced such beauty
in his life. Wave after wave of savage passion swept over both of them.

With each wave they rose to a new level. Then, at the height of the most intense
emotional experience of his young life young Carlos died. He surrendered
willingly. Sophie, well satisfied, climbed off his inert body. A young attendant
quickly drug his body away. When dragging away Carlos's body she had
noticed a slight smile on his face. She had seen the same smile on many such
victims.

After her first month of work Shelly had accumulated a large number
of kills. She would still have a long way to go to even get near the
2,300 or more that the quadruplets had each accumulated or the 1,600 that their mother had accounted
for. Even some of the youngest glambabes
had accounted for several thousand victims already.

The quadruplets recounted that they had made their first kills as very young girls
and that the victims had been fully grown men. Hard to believe but
Sophie had seen some of these young glambabes in action. One mere wisp of a girl,
ictoria, was incredibly aggressive and would take on any male. Some
of them
would even go so far as to laugh at the antics of such a small girl,
but within half an hour an attendant would be seen dragging his inert
body away.

Tradition called for the girls to stand spread legged over their
first victim's face until given the OK to begin. The adjudictrixes
occupied a mat at the front of the arena and all the glambabes stood
ready positioned over a young male.

"Well girls, you know what you have to do so let's get it on!" She
said
excitedly.

Sophie closed her eyes and slowly lowered herself onto her victims
face for a
reverse squat smother. She gasped when she felt his warm nose press
deep into
her butt. Shelly chose a standard straddle smother with her victims
nose pressed

deep up her wet vagina. Instinctively they all began to pump and grind down on
their victims. This constant pumping served two purposes. First it felt
delicious, working the victims nose all around inside. Second, the pumping
tended to put the victim in a stupor or dazed state and made it much easier to
complete the kill without a lot of struggling.

Nicole pressed down hard with her hip, smothering her helpless captive.
Poor Thomas, he had been her victim since they had left the Neo-Amazon home
world two months ago, now he would have to die. All of the other girls were
hard at work each finishing off their respective victims prior to disembarking.

For the long trip from the Neo-Amazon home world each budding warrior
women was assigned a victim to practice smothering during the boring
flight. Nicole was assigned Thomas, a handsome lad about her own age. He,
as well as, the other captives accepted their fate and were most
cooperative. Nicole had grown to like Thomas quit a lot. Many of the other
girls had also made the same attachments with their own victims. A loud cry
of victory resounded from the next cubicle. Chantelle had claimed her handsome
captive.

Chantelle was a tall well-developed young warrior. She had long blonde
hair, unusual for a Neo-Amazon, that was usually kept tied up in a bun. Her
Neo-Amazon forehead bone structure was very pronounced giving her a menacing
wild barbarian look. She often acted the part and could best all of the
girls in wrestling. Her favorite preoccupation was the kill. She deeply
enjoyed every one of the 4,000 practice kills she made while in training.

Another cry of victory rang out. It was TorTur. TorTur was one of
those girls you love to hate. Tall, sexy, long legs; she drew

attention
from males wherever she went. TorTur was no dumb beauty though. She
had a
quick mind and was an outstanding scholar. She was quite and shy and
very
withdrawn; preferring to keep to herself.

Her victim had been young Martin, a cute lad and the youngest captive
of
the lot. During the flight TorTur and Martin had become quite close.
Like a
big sister and little brother friendship. She had done her duty
though and
smothered her captive according to the ancient traditions of the Neo-
Amazon
warrior women.

Torris was glad to be out of the cramped quarters of the spacecraft.
The bunks were low and long and not designed to allow for many creative kill positions. Usually you
were limited to the full body smother laying on the victims face, facing his feet with your legs spread
wide for balance.

You would keep up a constant pumping grinding on him for days at a time. He was
only let up too relieve himself or to eat. None of the captives were
bound
and each was given a tour of the craft. Young martin was thrilled when
allowed to sit in the captain's chair. Thomas was intrigued by the
engineering room. His goal had been to be a Star Fleet officer.

Torris could tell by the various moans and groans that many of the
girls
were reaching the ethereal and most spiritual climaxing moment of the kill.

This was the Kill Ecstasy phase; A bonding union of the warrior women
and
her captive. Your spirit would be set free of its body to create a
bonding
and union with that of your victim. This was a quite intimate moment
for
any Neo-Amazon warrior women and one to be savored whenever possible.

Torris could feel the rising kill ecstasy filling her body like a red
hot
flame. Every muscle was now tuned to the kill. Then it hit her. It
was
overwhelming wave of passion, sex, violence and spiritual bonding all
swirling around together. The kill ecstasy could only be maintained
for a

short period but those brief minutes could leave a young Neo-Amazon
warrior
women in an emotional high for days. Thomas gave a slight twitch then
lay
still. Torris had claimed her 4,001st victim.

Nicole arched her back and let out a wild scream that mingled with
that of
the other girls all proclaiming their kills. This was a particularly
important point in their young lives. Once they left the shuttle and
set
foot on the surface below their whole Neo-Amazon heritage and
tradition walked
with them. If they failed their whole family would live in shame.
Millions
of young Neo-Amazon women had gone before, endured four years of
hardship, to
achieve the title of Neo-Amazon Warrior Women. The girls' screams were
especially loud. Each one was distinctive and there last for the next
four
years. They now had to hone the fine skills of stealth, stalking,
sudden
attacks, and violent smothers. Loud screams of victory would just
give away
their position.

Nicole didn't give Keith a second glance as she pulled her large
backpack down from an overhead bin. Soon all 12 girls and the Nest Master were assembled in the
cargo bay. They were all nude. There was nothing new to this. The Neo-Amazon culture had few
prudish hang-ups about clothing.

They had not worn any clothing during most of their six month training. It was especially important
that the not wear any clothing while on the hunt. The obvious reason was for the purposes of the
smother. Another was because of the TX shots.

TX was a chemical that, when injected, would slowly, over a few hours, allow your skin to take on
the shade and pattern of whatever environment you were in. For instance on a sandy desert like planet
you would be almost indistinguishable from the surrounding sand. This condition could only be
reversed when given an antidote. Nicole planet of assignment was hot and jungle like. She wondered
how she'd look with a leaf pattern body.

The Teams Grab and Capture Event was now underway. Half of the men
were frantically trying to run away from the 4 teams of 4 gorgeous,
elegant and skillful lassooists. It was a hopeless task. The other

half were soon to be released into the arena too, in three smaller batches when most of the early ones had been caught and sat on, a sweet surrender awaited them all. The smothering was habit forming and it did not stop during a women's period. Sophie found she now had an enormous wet patch, hers was not period-related, unlike that of Angelina.

At last in addition to the long-established individual events, team events were beginning to take place. This one was a free-run with lassoes. Young victims were turned loose in the open area to try to run from the predatory glambabe's. One by one, they were caught and smothered. After they were smothered, the women had to drag the body to a collection point. The team of women with the most kills generally won. The Illinoians seemed to excel in this as their long legs gave them an advantage in running. Laughter erupted in the stands when one small lad managed to outwit his pursuer, a tall and powerfully build Ohian. She had a lot
of rage and could have crushed her victims skull between her thighs - if she could catch him. She was angrier and angrier by the minute and even stopped long enough to shake a fist at the laughing onlookers. At last she caught him and pulled the lad down for a deep-ass smother. Finally the body of her first and not last but possibly least victim was dragged out.

With a loud shout more victims were released. The adolescent males ran frantically in all directions like small fish scattering from a predator. Seconds later the women had already caught all of them in their lassoes. It was a thrilling and exciting moment as the women whooped and yelled triumphantly. Victim after victim was being brought down all around her. Sophie concentrated on one particular youth. Finally she caught him and was about to pull him down when a young teenage girl, a true Amazon, pulled him down. She quickly tucked him under her in a squat smother.

Just at that second a young lad, fleeing a pursuer, ran headlong into Sophie. She then brought him down in a reverse squat smother. The young Amazon shrugged her shoulders about grabbing Sophie's victim. "Don't worry Sophie said" its such a mess out here it was bound to happen." Sophie said while keeping up a steady stroking on her victim. It was too early in the smothering for a kill to have taken place so the women could relax a bit while they smothered. Many of them spent their time smothering and talking to whomever was
near them.

"What's your name?" the young Amazon asked. "Sophie, what's yours?" she replied.
"Gabrielle." It was a nice pleasant name. Somehow the pretty Amazon looked familiar, it was as it they had known or would know each other. She was a nice pleasant girl with an expert and well developed

squat smother technique. "Kill many victims?" Sophie asked. "Tens of
thousands, that's all we do between and during events." Then the girl
made a curious statement. "Do I know you? Somehow I think I know you.
It's weird." Sophie was surprised by this question especially when
she was about to ask the same thing. Their pleasant visit came to a
conclusion when the girl's young male expired. Sophie hurried to
complete her
kill as well. Frantically she half drug and carried the body of her
victim to the collection point.

Young males were swarming all around when Sophie reached for one. She
caught him
by the hair and spun him to the ground. He landed with a thud, the
wind knocked out of him. Just then a tall blonde Ohian laid down on
his face in a "69" working his nose up tight into her. She looked up
at Sophie and laughed. Sophie was furious at this blonde giant, she
was contemplating knocking her for a good one but this was the
glambabe Olympics and she had to maintain her composure.

There was no time to stand around and argue so she made a dive for
another small youth. She caught him by the wrist and pulled him down.
She then mounted him in a "69". She was behind the blonde barbarian
and got a close up view as the women furiously pumped hard on her
captive. She was a big powerful women with a strong grinding hip
motion. Very little was visible of her victim's head. She had all but
consumed his small head up into her body. Just then Sophie heard a
familiar voice, the young Amazon Gabrielle, she had a victim and was
preparing to mount him in a straddle smother. "She's the
reigning "69" champion." Indicating to the giant blonde
barbarian. "I'm scheduled for that event," Sophie said. "Well good
luck, you'll need it, she's a terror. Champion 3 times in a row. Not
even any of my sister Amazons are as good." The young girl replied
while she worked her victims nose deep inside her.

Sophie asked the girl what events she was scheduled for and would
make an effort to watch out for her. Gabrielle was very proud of her
squat and reverse squat smother and had entered most of the events.
Their conversation was interrupted when the blonde giantess completed
her kill. She casually tucked the body of her victim under her arm
and walked over to the collection point. She flung him on top of the
pile like he was a rag doll.

Before long, 17 of the men had already been caught and thoroughly
tied up with lassoo rope, and found that they were having some of the
most divine asses in human history pressed down over their faces.

With a slow patient voice Sophie began to explain. "My name is Sophie
and I was thinking, you would have made such a nice husband and
father - ah but in bed women sometimes cannot hold back on their wild
uncontrolled passion. Would you be up to it?" Sophie forced herself

to listen to his words but he could not speak through her anchored in place ass, and soon, like the others, he too was no more.

Everything was thrown into turmoil. Victims were now being smothered "artistically" . A victims nose that casually might slip out of a women's body was now a major mistake. Nicola was very upset when this happened to two of her victims. The judging was very specific, a simple everyday occurrence like that might cost them valuable points. Sophie, while pumping away on a young lad, also felt his nose slip out of place. Quickly she reacted to correct the error. She had always felt pride in her smothering techniques and now some twerp of a judge was to watch closely for flaws.

The very successful glambabe Sarah-Jane was about to mount a lassooed young victim in a squat smother when he cried out "Sarah-Jane" . "Sarah-Jane, do you remember me, Chris Lewis, from your school." Sarah-Jane thought for a second and remembered a small obnoxious boy that used to throw stones. "Well you've grown up," she said kneeling next to his head. They talked briefly, even laughed over the ridiculous pompous mayor, the antics of the village drunk and other amusing things of their past. Though she knew the young male laying at her feet she also knew she had to smother him. His love for Sarah-Jane was very intense and hadn't wavered. This secret, as best Sophie could guess, involved his position as a pilot or perhaps involved her curvy beauty itsself.

Samantha was nearby, astride a victim and asked if Sarah-Jane wanted to switch with her so she wouldn't have to smother Chris. "No please, I will get my revenge on this turnip, and as for his friend, Sophie will you please do it. I couldn't think a more beautiful death than to be smothered by you." Young Matt, Chris's friend started looking up at her. "All right Chris, but I'm not going to work on you for a long time. You'll be a short-term victim."

Long-term victims were just that. Sometimes a glambabe would come across a particularly handsome victim and they would send them off the cliff unconscious, then come back for him later on, take him home with her, and smother them when not otherwise on another victim. Long-term victims could last for months. Chris's handsome brown eyes came alive with excitement at the prospect of having Sophie's beautiful body continuously astride him. One hard and fast rule of the glambabes was No Mercy On Victims! Sophie firmly stated this to Chris right away so he would know right where they stood, not that what she said would matter two minutes from now anyway, but laying down the ground rules was a principle that mattered to the babes. She also casually informed him that she would smother him to death, and that at home, she has an ample supply of prisoners to smother whenever she felt like it. It could be tomorrow,

next week or two months from now that one of them meets their
ultimate capitulation.

Chris seemed content with her entitlement to such an ample supply.
Looking over one of the cute attendants Chris whispered to
Sophie. "Does that no mercy rule apply to the attendants?" Sophie
smiled and whispered "No" to the mischievous Chris. "But the
attendants only prepare the doomed, and right now none are as doomed
as you," with that she pressed down hard and permanently on his face.

Events such as this were not measured solely on how many victims
could be smothered but also on how expertly it was accomplished. She
would a number of victims and the chance to show her skills. The
first kill went off without a hitch and she received a high score.
Next a pretty Wisconsinian glambabe did a magnificent straddle
smother on her victim. Many other fine glambabes racked up impressive
scores.

Sophie was stroking hard on her prone victim with a judge watching
intently then
tragedy struck, kinda. Sophie felt his nose slip out from inside her.
The judges frowned and made a note. Sophie was allowed to complete
the kill but she knew she'd screwed up big time. "penalty points" in
big letters was posted next to her team's name on the Master Listing.

The smothering continued furiously for nearly the next two hours. It
was exhausting but nobody was relieved when a trumpet sounded to
cease the event, as the final male had finally been done. When the
final tally was made, the Ohio girls had won the event. They were so
tired they hardly had the energy to celebrate.

The rescue of crooks' trapped souls went on for hours, and the
audience was getting the full benefit of this. Whenever the
glambabes' houses emptied of victims, the glambabes would go to the
local jail to pick up their next batch immediately, they never liked
to skip a day,
as they lustfully contributed to the decriminalization of the region.
And the prisons were never half-empty, as the courtrooms turned a
large volume of males to the smothering cells each hour.

Sophie couldn't help but notice that each victim kind of embraced the
ass that sits on him in appreciation and worship, a gesture that
means more than a pat on the back to the appreciative glambabes. A
mans lips always seemed, while women were getting comfortable, about
to get in the position to cause a man's demise, stuck and pressed
close to the particular glambabe that was in the process of
smothering them. A little appreciation went a long way.

Mid way through the BBWs' Megasit the youths that had been up first
lay dead or dying under the Megawomen. Some were already on their

third victim, and there were hundreds more victims queuing to be
next. Then suddenly, a male came leaping out of the audience,
screaming "I admit it, it was me – that guy over there did not do
what he was sentenced for." "Is this true?" asked one of the
MegaGoddesses of the next in line "yes, but I too have sinned this
year" – "Well, then, you shall have your choice of SSBBWs to be
megasat on, while the man who waited until now to reveal the truth
will have no choice but be sat on by the biggest woman of all, the
574 pound Mount Patty, right now. And so, once again, justice had
been served, and there was more and more room in the prisons for new
cases to be tried and more men to be sentenced.

Just then, as both men were being smothered, the young noses still
glistening from the
lubricating juice that came out of the BBWs cracks, the strangest
thing happened. Three more men came out and volunteered to be next,
and all three were duly put to the front of the queue and smothered.
The first confessed to also having taken part in the robbery of a
convenience store, taking part in the same incident ass the above.
The second admitted to stealing from the fridge of a SSBBW sorority
and not having been caught, and the third was sent there by his wife,
who had no tolerance or understanding for him forgetting their second
wedding anniversary.

All these intrusions meant that the men that were waiting in the
queue to be Megasat and smothered by the SSBBWs now needed additional
stroking from the lithe attendees who had led them out into this
queue. A big custard pie was generously applied to one who complained
out loud, however, and really rubbed in. Complaints were not
tolerated, and there were to be no last wishes either.

Some of the SSBBWs liked to wear their victims around the ring, their
faces having been inserted under their expandable lycra trousers,
their bodies tucked into their bras, and when they finally sat down,
the most massive and womanly of asses in the world came down on the
men. Just minutes ago Suzy, a cutesie large woman, had had his nose
pressed deep into the depths of her body, now she sat heavily on him,
slowly killing him. Now there were SSBBWs pinning men down by sitting
on their chests, while others, even biggest still, slibed up the
stairs to a podium, and jumped from there onto the helpless men,
landing with their asses on the crooks' faces AND upper bodies, and
killing them instantly from the impact.

Some of the doomed men still made a valiant effort to bring joy to
the ladies, giving them roses and compliments before being put under
the most massive of asses. It was these men who were spared the
humiliation of multiple stand-up-and- drop-with- speed-onto- male-faces
moves, winning the BBWs affections instead and thus being given a
gentle and loving demise.

Sophie, having the untapped qualities of a leader, stood out as the most valiant attendee. With
a long queue of young victims to maintain, and may more just arriving at the back of the queue, it was her sweet whispers that not only kept them calm and compliant, but truly got them into the mood as well. So when it came their turn to be shown where to lie facing up, all the men were ready to go out with a compliment, a gentlemanly gesture and a kind embrace of the ass that was on them.

An official finally ordered the ex-head of the 20th century Republicans to comply as he was to be inserted into a lycra-clad big beauty. Once he was in, she had the chance to do some walking and showboating, enjoying the press against her back and ass and her victim had the chance to take a rest before she sat down. Naked, sweaty and covered in pink pen marks, he was being carried around upside down, tucked into her clothing. The crowd cheered again and as she came crashing down on his face, white dust that had come off him, went flying in both directions as she sat down on top of him, while her youthful attendant helper dragged away her previous toy.

During the competition the attendants were very busy clearing away defeated males. Everyone of the glambabes had a quick bath and something to eat before these women, in the next event, resumed where they had left off, with the very pleasurable Mattress Men event, a true favourite with the crowd, the glambabes and all.

After applying a fresh coating of Ultralashes, Sophie quickly kicked over and laid down on the face of her first victim and inserted his nose back into place. He had shown such
bravery during the flower giving and finger kissing that she decided to give him the full smothering treatment and worked him in every position imaginable. The youth loved it and
cooperated as best he could while she furiously worked him.

Her young victim couldn't hold out much longer. Sophie was preparing to go for
the kill when another volunteer arrived. "My queen" shouted another male escapee from the audience, "here we go again" thought Sophie. Sophie was deeply engrossed in the process of killing her victim when she had to suddenly stop. Her young male lay still for several minutes while he caught his breath. He sat up and looked around curiously. Once again a most delicious smother had been interrupted and she wasn't happy. For Sophie was mad at being deprived of a kill, or rather at being interrupted.

"I have twice failed to give a waitress a tip." screamed the sudden volunteer. Both Sophie and Amber reacted with shock. "The ruling royalty of this land is your women, and you cannot withhold their rightful rewards. I am saddened that there are still women in this land so shy that they do not report vermin like you, and for what you

have done you must now go to the end of the queue and await your
sweet demise" ordered the experience Amber, "and make sure the
attendants write the words `needs brutal ballcrushing during smother'
on his chest". added Sophie, who had finally made the transition from
rookie to pro with this action.

Sophie thought of the queen of the country, permanent head of the
ruling `Prisoners for All' party Keira Church. She had a reputation
for smothering tens of thousands of victims in one weekend Girls
Night In Party. Though not officially as a glambabe she, as with most
women, she loved nothing more than a good long relaxing smother, and
to prove it, she was watching from the VIP booth in the front row,
while sitting on a member of her staff's face. He was clearly a temp.

Many women, be they glambabes, SmotherTeens or ordinary women, often enjoyed a
good smother. Sophie remembered one of her young friends while growing up back
in her village, a cute lad, being led away to be smothered. It was just an
accepted way of life, one of those hazards a young lad has to get through.
Though the women leading him away was Sophie's own mother. Sophie recalled the
constant creaking the floorboards made as she worked him. Sometimes Sophie would
hear a long gasp or moaning then silence, seconds later the constant squeaking
would resume. Not having the luxury of a bedroom all of the smothering was
done on the cottage floor, usually in front of the fireplace. It did bother
Sophie a bit to watch as her mother slowly smothered her friend. Sophie would miss
him, but then again this was a normal everyday hazard of any young
male, and Sophie learned soon that the best way to cheer up was to
fantasize about her own next smother, a fantasy that never waited
long to become reality.

One day the victim's mother came calling. She was a pleasant lady that didn't
seem the slightest bit disturbed that Sophie's mother was working her
son. And why would she be, she had herself smothered out at least
three of Sophie's elder brothers.
Sophie's mother directed Sophie to mount him while they visited. Though the lad
had been her friend, the thought of mounting her first victim was exciting.
Sophie pumped hard and fast on him while the women visited and reluctantly

turned him back over to her mother when the guest left. Eventually Sophie's
mother made her kill and days later selected a young lad from a large
destitute family that was travelling through. The destitute family was glad to get rid of
him, one less mouth to feed, and no more toilet seats left up in
their house.

Sophie's college was no different from hundreds or thousands of
others throughout the modern world. Young victims were constantly
being smothered day and night by the rich and poor. Even the queen
herself and every member of the Government had an unsatisfied hunger
for victims.

It seemed that whenever a large family or even stray street urchins wondered
into town, the women of the suburbs would be out looking them over, deciding
which ones would make a good smother. Sophie's neighbour, Simone, had an
insatiable appetite for victims. She was always hard at work pumping away on a
young male. Sophie liked her and would often visit while she furiously worked a
chosen young lad. The lady was tall and rather thin with a lot of gymnastic
energy. She was in her early 30's and had several rowdy children, all girls. Her husband
had been killed in one of the innumerable arguments with the ladies. For her
services at the prison and at the court, she received a widows
pension. This pension allowed her to concentrate on her true passion -
smothering!

Her favourite position was the "69" which was, while Sophie thought
about it, now her favourite, because you could kick your victim in
the balls while sitting on their face. Several incidents occurred
that stuck in Sophie's memory. Once, while Sophie and
Simone were talking, they heard the voice of a local woman calling
for her son.
Her son, at that particular moment, had his nose pressed deep into Simone's
body. The lad, upon hearing his name, put his hands on the women's
hips, and gave them a light tap.

Simone ignored him and continued her pumping. She then called to the
women outside in the market pace and informed them she was smothering
her son. The women didn't act upset about it and replied in a joking
light hearted manner, "That's two of my sons you've
smothered so far. You've nearly reached your quota!" She then

added "when are you
going to kill him so I can plan for his funeral?" Simone momentarily
stopped
her pumping and thought for a moment. "Not anytime soon, I'd like to
work him
for at least a month but I don't think he's going to hold out that
long." No
doubt the poor victim was quite upset to hear of his death to be so
casually
discussed.

Sophie remembered how brave her mother had been. One day some rich
high official
was travelling through and stopped in their small village to get fuel
and a coffee.
There the family sat, in all their wedding curled hair and surrounded
by a cordon of
soldiers who were protecting this official. Then Sophie's mother's
eyes lit up - a victim. He was a cute young lad, sitting high in the
coach. Sophie tried to talk her mother out of it but to no avail.
Somehow, she made it through the cordon of soldiers and boldly told
the
lad's mother she wanted her son for a smother. The women looked down
at her in
disbelief " You smother my son" she thought for a moment. It was
universally
accepted that any young lad was "up for grabs" so to speak - even a
high
official's son. Besides this women had probably smothered countless
young
victims herself. She immediately informed her husband. He seemed
shaken by the
matter, as they had promised the boy to a close friend of his
mother's, but he was well aware of a women's right to select a young
male as her victim, no matter how rich or powerful. To go against
such a basic right might even cause a riot and much more dire
consequences greater than loosing a son.

The lad was shocked when his mother ordered him out of the cart. He
was even
amazed more when he was led away. The village women cheered and
congratulated
Sophie's mother for her determination and bravery. Once back at the
cottage
Sophie's mother directed the lad to remove his shirt and lay flat on
the sofa.
She then slipped out of her clothes, apart from some lace underwear
that emphasized her pert breasts and her ass. The lad was completely
terrified, as she slowly squatted down onto his face in a reverse
squat smother, tracking his nose deep up her posterior. She'd hardly

started on him when the village women came in, one by one, or in small groups,
to visit and complement her on such a fine catch. A number of women marvelled
at his fine clothes, still others looked at his trembling callous
free hands, and all of these women had casually grabbed a soldier on
her way in. They had never seen such a finely dressed or delicious
victim as the boy. Eventually the parade of well wishers trickled off
to their various homes, happily pulling their catches with them and
throwing them on sofas when they got in. Now Sophie's mother could
concentrate on her handsome captive.

He proved to be a rather nice adolescent male and tried to cooperate
in any
way possible. A bonding began to grow between Sophie's mother and the
victim.
They would sometimes play little jokes on each other. He knew she was
going to
eventually kill him and she knew she would kill him - this was a
given fact.
But, none-the-less, a close friendship did flourish, and the boy was
kind to both the mother and the daughter. She was continuously
sitting on him in one position or another working his nose around
inside her. He would tap her on the side of the leg in some little
secret code known only to them. While squat smothering him, he would
pass out and when he awoke, she was sitting on his chest and she
would look down into his bright blue eyes. When being furiously
smothered and his view obscured by a thick mat of pubic hair, he
would somehow manage to wink up at her with his tongue. One day,
Sophie could tell by the way she climbed on top of him that this was
going to be his last time. Sophie cried as she saw his final
struggles die down. They drug his body out into the cold dark night.
A grave
had been prepared for him and they solemnly lowered his still form
into the
ground. So many memories.

Meanwhile, in the Precision Sitting event, one of the victims proved
to be a rather sturdy lad and lasted much longer than most other
victims. The other 19 first-rounders had all got done in within two
minutes of the target time of 15 minutes, 20 minutes for the second
round of smother-men, and Brittany has won with a time of 14 minutes
and 59 seconds. But poor old Lil' Rachel was still trying to end
round one when Round Two got under way, and she was signalling to the
attendees that she required another weight belt.

In spite of the time pressure, Sophie was having a very relaxing
evening. The quadruplets were now totally nude except for their bras,
straddle smothering men in front of a roaring, enthusiastic audience.
Sometimes they would ask each other if they wanted to swap victims or

to change to a different position.

It was nearing the end of the 20 minute period now, and they could
all sense it. One of those relaxing smotherings was getting more
frantic, as the 20 pairs of girls butt-cheeks were starting to
squeeze harder, many smothered their victims while at the height of a
massive orgasm. Some came too early, wrecking their chance of a top
ten finish in this event, as these intense orgasms inevitably took
their victims out with them. A particularly big cheer came from the
crowd when Lil' Rachael finally climed off a lifeless victim.
Although now inelligible for the second round, she gave a happy smirk
and raised her arms in triumph while planting her foot on the
vanquished male, to the cheer of the whole stadium.

It has to be noted here that the sight of the the Queen and her
cabinet members totally naked and smothering away on a helpless
victim was quite common place on TV. In fact, huge
numbers of posters of them astride a young victim now adorned many a
young male
and females dorm or bedroom wall. Posters of the Minister of Woman
Affairs' beautiful daughter furiously smothering a young male or the
younger sister of the Minister of Justice sitting on a heap of
defeated males were also just as common.

The boys who judges and were later smothered by the contestants of
The Pageant were in some sort of scout uniform and being smothered in
full public view on the beautifully manicured female members of their
families. The camera then went in for an extreme close up of the
minister of Facesitting Affairs's victim in the VIP booth of the
audience and his wet nose being worked furiously in and out of her
perfect body. The next scene was the president and her beautiful
daughter Chlessa astride the second young male. This boy was
struggling, though vainly, and kicking his feet madly about. Again a
close up of the victims nose being violently massaged in and out of
beautiful Chlessa. Eventually Chlessa's victim stopped kicking about
and lay still.

Sabrina noticed President Gabrielle and her daughter were quite pleased
with the camera attention and not the least embarrassed of close-ups
of them deeply engrossed in victim
smothering. Several pre-teen girls were busily snapping pictures
while a half dozen
BBW security guards were busy keeping them from getting too close,
and keeping the next dozen VIPs' victims ready for use whenever they
were needed.

One close up zoomed in for a view of the lads face pressed tight to
the presidents crotch. Suddenly the president gasped. To an untrained
observer it might seem she was approaching a natural orgasm but in
reality it was the Viagragirl taking effect. President Gabrielle's eye

were wide in amazement. The effects of ViagraGirl tend to overwhelm
the female body. Like having 100 massive orgasms all at once. In the
background you could hear Chlessa call out "something's wrong mother.
I feel no resistance, I think I've killed another one." Security
guards immediately rushed forward and the camera crew had to vacate
the area quickly, while her next victim was inserted under her ass.

glambabe after glambabe now demonstrated to the judges their
expertise in the "69". Some did very well but Sophie knew she was the
best. Finally it came down to Sophie versus the blonde Brittany.
Sophie, gathering all her inner strength, won the coveted Gold Medal!
The blonde giant gave Sophie a hug and congratulated her. She didn't
turn out to be such a brute after all.
The president's daughter was, later on that night, as a special treat
for being so cute, going to start the final event off, the event that
opens the smothering to all in the arena. Meanwhile, the Queen
herself was going to crown the overall winner. The women of Sophie's
glambabe House celebrated as one. Chants of "WOMEN POWER!" rang
through the night. This was perhaps the high point of her life. To
have so many warm and caring friends yet they were
so different and diverse from each other.

Tears streamed from her eyes as she stood on the podium and the gold
medal was hung around her neck. The memory of that moment would be
savoured forever. She vowed to never, as long as she lived, forget
the friends she'd made or the glory of the arena. At last Sophie felt
an inner peace, she could accomplish anything now. A young woman had
died at that moment and a valiant brave warrior princess was born.

Though it was hard to come down from such a high, the everyday task
of smothering victims had to continue. Sophie's love affair was
turning to marriage. At home, Sophie now wanted a bed large enough to
accommodate multiple victims. Sophie was out there again, squat
smothering a young male, receiving particular support and approval
from the millions of spectators.

In the final event, the women of Nebraska and the surrounding region,
all beautiful, feminine, lusty, and very deservant of some action
resumed the smothering. While atop a squirming adolescent male,
Sophie's friend Emma wondered what it must be like for the victim.
True, her constant and sometimes violent pumping would put the victim
into a dazed or even euphoric state, but she was afraid she might be
hurting them. She could never smother any victim if she knew that he
was suffering.

Rejoicing at the chance to have a bit of girl triumph too, Sophie's
sister Keira stated plainly her intention to one of the final-
eventers. "I want to kill you, boy. I want to sit on you
and smother you to death. I want you to feel the triumphant
superpower of a superior woman taking you out." The youth looked up

at the tall beauty. Perhaps he had guessed at Sophie's sister's
intentions all along. Sophie was aware that there seemed to be some
unspoken connection or mutual mind link between a women and her
intended victim. He shrugged his shoulders and sighed. A queue of 30
women had now formed behind her, all waiting for their turn to sit on
this face.

She led him not far off his seat to a small patch of carpet. He
immediately laid flat on his back to await Sophie's suster's smother.
He didn't have long to wait. Keira stood over his upturned face then
slowly settled down on him in a squat smother. She closed her eyes as
the familiar pleasure of his nose rose deep into her body. The
exquisite feeling of his young nose resting tight inside her reminded
her of the glambabe's elegant style. She took him, slowly at
first then building to an overwhelming orgasm. He had been a most
cooperative victim so far, so, with great restraint, Sophie's sister
had to climb off him when the music changed to allow the next girl to
sit on him, hoping to be able to get a kill in that night, Keira
joined the shortest queue in the vicinity. She, with great
reluctance, climbed off him.

The youth laid still for a moment in a dazed state. Then his chest
heaved deeply as he gasped for air. Being under Keira's pumping hips
for over two hours had all but exhausted him. He was quit surprised
to discover that he was still alive. In fact, he seemed anxious for
Sophie's sister to remount him. The lad seemed happy to hear that
Keira was going to save him for a long relaxing smother later that
evening.

The women shot a bored glance in his direction "He's a fantastic
victim. I've been smother'en the hell out'a him for the last few
minutes and it made me feel great, so enjoy!"

The thoroughly exhausted boy turned toward a girl called Kylie. He
was in a very bad way. No doubt the constant smothering by all the
girls was having a devastating effect on his
frail body. He tried to sit up but couldn't and just slumped back
down moaning and taking in air in small raspy gulps. Sophie noticed
that he was especially young for a victim. But then this was not
Geneva. American women couldn't be choosy. They had to take what was
available and be thankful at that. Sophie's mother, as with the rest
of the women of her village, had no hesitation to smother a young
boy. Many a time she had seen her mother stretched out atop a small
male. Sophie had made only 23 kills as a young girl. They were mostly
young village boys. This was normal and expected of a young girl.
Some of the
more aggressive girls of the village accounted for hundreds of
smothers. You
might expect that with all the smothering going on a shortage of
young males

might develop. The peasants bread like rats, each family might have 12 or more
children and there was never any danger of a shortage.

Sophie remembered one time while out playing with her friends she looked at one
of her playmates. He was a young boy several years younger than her. She had
only made a few kills so far so and smothering was a new adventure for her. He
had always been a playmate, now it suddenly dawned on her that he would make a
nice smother. They wrestled playfully for a few minutes then Sophie pinned him
to the ground. She remembered the surprised look on his face as she carefully
hiked her dress up and slid over his face. It took her four hours of hard
work, including a lot of grunting and groaning, before she made her kill.

Sophie thanked L'Oreal and Hermes for their support but explained she
wanted to put a particular prisoner's face behind her before dark.
She tried to pay for the drink but L'Oreal and Hermes wouldn't accept
any money. Young Claire paused at the door and looked around. He knew
he wouldn't ever be coming back. Sophie could tell that the ladies
from L'Oreal and Hermes were anxious to start again on their victim.
As Sophie prepared to leave, the girls from L'Oreal and Hermes pulled
up their skirts and sat firmly on her victims face in a reverse
straddle smother. They then smoothed the dress around themselves so only the boy's
small feet protruded out from under her.

While walking toward the main road Sophie asked Claire if her mother did much
smothering. Yes, a lot, she was always sitting on a victim. All of the women
seemed to have a young lad in their bed. The nights were long and lonely,
their men were often gone to work or to prison so a relaxing smother was a nice
reward after a hard day's work.

Sophie's long powerful legs were no match for her victim, nor were Claire's.
Claire then lay down on his face, spread her legs wide and wiggled her hips
around, working his nose deep into place. Once satisfied she pulled a blanket
over both of them so they would be protected from the sight of the

adjudicatrixes and attendants. They then began a deep pumping circular hip grinding. A flood of warm erotic sensuality swept over her almost immediately. She rode him like a ship riding a violent flowing sea. She travelled to new heights of orgasm, time and time again her body
trembled as she was swept away in the sweat embrace of passion. She hadn't put
any spit on the youths face, but she was giving him a very wet ride none the
less. She violently worked him long into the night, then, at the height of a
majestic orgasm, he died.

Sophie then saw some of the chicks from her school. Given half a chance at a smothering, these bitches wouldn't have hesitated for a second. Sophie's own mother would
have had any man under in no time. The possibility of taking him for a smother
intrigued Sophie's sister Keira. She would look him over, talk to him while sitting on his face and perhaps build up her courage to mount him.

Her current conquest was very cute with jet black hair and a small round face. His name was
Barry or something like that for he slurred his sentences and ran words together. According to the lad he had been abandoned by his parents a few days ago and he'd been living on apples since. While they were talking Keira carefully took note of the tall warm grassy field behind them which would make a good location for a long smother. She sat down next to the lad and brushed the hair out of face. He had big round dark eyes. She gently pushed him flat to the warm grass a swung a leg across his chest. Sophie was contemplating which
position to use on him when another woman approached.

She was one of those "colorful people" or an eccentric. Her ragged cloths was nothing more than various patches of brightly colored cloth sewn together. She had a big colorful floppy hat that made her whole appearance comical. She was tall and very fat with a rugged weather-beaten face. "Well sister, ya gon'na plant your bare butt on his face or not." She said, getting right to the point.

"Keira ran her fingers across his small bare chest and said thoughtfully "maybe.
Do you want him?" "Damn right I do, I ain't had a nose up the old puss for over a week." Sophie hadn't quite gathered up the courage to sit on the boy - perhaps, she thought, theirs a victim more to her choosing right around the next corner. Besides, this poor chubby lady had gone for a week without a smother.

"Take him if you want, he's a little too young for my appetite."
Sophie said
sitting up. "Well thank you. Names Jenny" she said extending a hand.
She
then stood over the boys head, hiked up her skirt and lowered down on
him in a
straddle smother. She spread her legs really wide and began to slide
slowly
over his head. The lad arched his head back and looked out on the
world for
the last time. He had a frightened look in his eye. "Come on little
one,
cooperate with Jenny" she said as she held his head straight. She then
slid over him and his nose slowly disappeared into a dark mat of
pubic hair.
All that was now visible of the boy was a small wisp of his black
hair now
mingling with Jenny's dark brown pubic hair. Satisfied he was firmly
in place, she began working his nose around inside her.

"Ah, oh, this feel SOOO damn good. You shouldn't be so damn fussy. Ya
got'ta
take your smothers were you find 'em. I've had many a young nose up
my butt.
Hell, a lot a them younger than this." Jenny stated as she smoothed
her dress around herself.

Sophie and the eccentric old lady talked for sometime. It seemed that
a band of
Amazon raiders had recently swept through the farmland up ahead. They
didn't
do much damage but concentrated on smothering every young male they
could
find. Even small babies were not exempt from their smothering frenzy.
By
stripping certain areas bare of young males they reduced the prospect
of them
becoming warriors when they grew up, warriors that the Amazons would
then face
in battle. By keeping the male population down to a more manageable
level they
ensured their own survival.

Sophie then excused herself and wished the old lady a good smother
and moved on.
The thought of a whole vast area stripped clear of victims was
frightening. It
was about mid noon when she came across two women arguing over a
small boy.
Both of them were claiming him. It was quit a heated exchange that

might
eventually lead to a fight. The women of this area, deprived of
victims, would
soon get desperate - who knows what would happen then.

Sophie then observed a tall 17-year-old typical piano student type
girl rounding her bend, she almost stumbled onto a young boy, before
carefully sitting down on his face. He was even younger than Jenny's
victim. It seemed like in no time at all she was sitting on his face,
stroking his nose up her butt in a reverse straddle smother. With
each stroke she began to
feel her female needs satisfied. Aside from being young he was also
very
frail. Sophie had to be careful and not get carried away. With choice
victims in
short supply she wanted this one to last a bit, to get the most out
of him.
After two hours she decided to climb off the lad and look over just
what she'd
captured.

He gasped for breath and coughed. His soft blonde curly hair was all
matted
down. "Sorry about his." Sophie said apolitically. He didn't say much
then
looked up at her.

"You an Amazon? He asked rubbing his nose. He was terrified of them.
He had
been playing with his brothers and sisters when the Amazons swept in.
They
wore frightening masks, feathers and held long swords. Somehow he
managed to
dive into a pile of hay. The boy watched from safety as they
smothered his
brothers to death. Some of them then went into his house and drug out
his
mother's victim to smother as well. She was begging and pleading to
spare the
boy but they ignored her. Now, well satisfied, they grabbed his
sisters to
take them away and raise them as Amazons. His mother tried to fight
them but
was instantly killed by a sword thrust. He was now alone and
subsisting as
best he could.

"Well you'll have a new home of sorts deep inside me." Sophie said
gently
stroking his hair. Holding back tears he nodded in agreement. About

that time
a farm girl approached. Sophie asked if she fancied a ride. With the
exchange of a few warm and graetful glances Keita departed from her
fresh victim and handed him over to this farm girl. Sophie
immediately noticed the body of a very young victim stretched out
underneath an old lady.

Sophie then directed the farmgirl's young victim to lay down in the
same position so she
could sit on his face while the queue forms behind her. The old lady
handed Sophie a large blanket. "Better cover him up good" she said
pointing to Sophie's victim. "Them's scarce around her and lot'sa
women gonna get REAL excited over a cute one like that." She said.

The old lady then raised up slightly off her victim. "You want water
or something honey?" she asked looking down at him. The victim, as
much as Sophie could see of him, had light brown hair and was about
the same age as Sophie's captive. A small weak voice replied "no
thank you." "Suit yourself," replied the old woman sitting back on
his face. With Sophie's victim safely concealed under a blanket she
sat securely on his face. The old madam made a lurch and moved
forward. The motion of her ass constantly massaged the victims nose's
up inside the woman, creating a most pleasing sensation.

After a few minutes later, Sophie saw a woman in her 30's wearing
red, a necklace and large circular earrings thank the woman in front
of her and help her off an exhausted victim. The lad was in a bad way
so this vixen decided to kill him. She led his nose to a spot at the
end of her crack and mounted him. The smother didn't take long and
soon she was back on the protl for another victim.

Not far ahead five ordinary looking men blocked a path, with dozens
of women sitting or standing on them. They didn't look threatening or
particularly dangerous. The men didn't have a chance. With so many
women simultaneously sitting on or tredding or stomping on their
chest, it was all over in seconds. Sophie never gave them a second
thought and resumed her
journey.

Man after man lay stretched out in boring repetition. Then she perked
up when she noticed many delicious young males about. At first just a
few then more and more. She was now out of the devastated area. While
walking along she noticed the bodies of three freshly smothered young
males on the side of the road. A women in her mid 40's was struggling
with a heavy pack. She was nude except for a black dress skirt. A
tall blonde with her hair piled high on her head - an Nebraskan! She
had two girls with her, they were also nude apart from a skirt and in
their early teens. Evidently they had just completed kills and were
resuming their journey. Sophie approached and said "Hi." They looked
at her with warmth

Perhaps they could make a living as a glambabe, they wondered. The
young girls were especially excited over such a prospect. Piles of
men lay before them, and when they saw more living ones, a whole new
adventure was about to unfold.

ENSIGN NICOLE - THE EARLY YEARS
By Mike
Nicole pressed down hard with her hip, smothering her helpless
captive ...

The Neo-Amazons, above all the known races in the universe, were the
most
fascinating to the human race. Perhaps it is because the Neo-Amazons
are akin
to our own historical roots such as the ancient Vikings or the brave
Massi
warriors. Women of the Neo-Amazon Empire are particularly intriguing.
The
thought of wild, uncontrolled warrior women, rejecting the norms and
conventions of "polite" society and becoming virtual free spirits
makes all
of us envious. This is a story of the development and training of one
such
free spirit - Ensign Nicole.

The situation of illegal human settlements infringing on the
Neo-Amazon
Empire was an old one. The Federation detested these illegal
settlements.
They were built on greed. Some rare mineral was rumored to be on one,
perhaps a new crystal, and thousands upon thousands of fortune seekers
would flock there. The planet would end up as an ecological disaster,
the
local natives all killed off and a few robber barons would get rich;
not
unlike the development of our west. Any logical person might indicate
all
that was needed was for everyone to sit down at a table and talk over
their
differences and everyone would walk away satisfied. Reality was
something
else, especially when dealing with enormous amounts of money.

The Neo-Amazons, for hundreds of years had used these illegal human settlements as a testing
ground for young warrior women.

Promising

young
teenage girls, after six months of training would be deposited near a
large
human settlement. Through attrition they would eliminate as many young
males as possible. To attack the settlements directly would require a
major
military operation. Besides the Neo-Amazons usually were engaged in
mortal
combat with some foe such as the Romulans and they didn't have the
resources to attack and conquer all of the settlements. Thus the
destruction of the settlements would be done quietly and without fuss.

Young men were the heart and soul of these settlements. They
provided
the new blood for huge families and overpopulation. Break this one
chain in
the link and the settlement would eventually dry up. The settlements
never
really went away though. Depopulate the young males in one and another
would crop up somewhere else. In reality the Neo-Amazons found the
settlements
useful to train their warrior women and as political leverage against
the
Federation.

The young warrior women were organized into groups of 12 with an
adult warrior women as the Nests Master (Neo-Amazons always have had a
fascination with birds and long ago began this naming convention).
After
six months of extensive training the Nest Master and her young charges
would be clandestinely dropped off near a large settlement. For three
to
four years they would hunt and stalk their prey, killing as many young
males as possible.

The Neo-Amazons are very physical people and the young females
preferred
to make their kills as intimate and personal as possible. They chose
to
wrestle their young victims down then sit on them and slowly smother
them
to death. Once they completed their warrior women training they were
insured a daily supply of victims for the rest of their life.

The Federation, ever mindful of the sensitivity of Neo-Amazon
traditions
and culture, were reluctant to criticize their actions. Moreover they
cooperated in many aspects to discourage the establishment of illegal
settlements. One aspect of this cooperation was that Neo-Amazon
warrior women

assigned to Federation starships would be guaranteed a steady supply
of
victims, though they would have to be supplied through Neo-Amazon
channels. A
Federation starship might take on several hundred victims prior to a
long
voyage and keep them in cryogenic suspension until needed.

A similar system has also been up and running for women to go and gift themselves to the country's
best-looking, best-known and most fancied men, but there is only one such site in the country, who
are also competing for selection and survival, and this is located a very long way away from
Weybridge Abbey. Some people, be they gay, lesbian, trans, bi or just huge fans of one of our
sublime and amazing deadly angel celebrities, do opt to "go under" a candidate for survival of the
same sex as they are, but none of the people heading to the Elm Hill palace of pleasures tomorrow,
when we take a closer look around, comes under this list of people.

Thousands of ordinary people have, instead, gifted themselves to their spouses (usually to the wife),
girlfriend, sister, niece, offspring or to their close friends, to a long-admired school mate beauty or to
a sorority group, in the hope that this first 450 points will help catapult this other very cherished
person into an angels of death shortlist and then on to ultimate long-term survival.

1 Chapter I

Keith went out with a smile on his face – his last thoughts were: she's quite a big lady down under,
and a little bit hairy too … so lucky to be allowed to do this … in goes the tongue … it's sticky in
there … blimey, that's a tight grip! I never knew her legs were this strong … and nice … oh crap,
can't breathe. Is that some sort of sumo giantess with her foot on my head, stopping me from lifting
me 'ead … dying … dying … what can I do? May as well try to let her cum … it's really her. My
angel, the goddess of the TV world, and my, can she squeeze hard with them legs of hers … going
faint … fading … sleep time? …out.

Keith's body was already cold and discarded. They had thrown it onto a massive pile in the back
corridor's cell blocks. He was down and out. He died in the belief that he was saving his dream girl
and giving her a treat. Greg's much messier and still warm body was now being carried away to the
same pile. Well, actually he was on a trolley, pulled along by his femme fatale. It made no difference
if he was fully dead or not. Any re-arise-ers would be shot in the routine morning sweep.

The Nest Master, Valak, ordered them to get ready to disembark. She

was
tall, powerfully built; with over 250 thousand smothered victims to her
credit. She took no guff or slackness from anyone and it seemed her only
pleasures in life was a good blood wine and a relaxing smother.

One by one the girls approached Valak to receive their TX shot. Corporal
Kamra barked out "hurry up, hurry up" to keep the girls moving along. Kamra
was a perky brown haired young girl that had tremendous energy. One thing
about her - she was human. She had been captured by Neo-Amazon raiders long
ago and raised as a Neo-Amazon. To everyone she was truly a Neo-Amazon and as fit
as the rest of the girls. Though human, she smothered her 4,001 victims
while in training as professionally as the rest. She harbored no special
affinity for her fellow humans and loathed the settlers. Neo-Amazon honor and
the title of Warrior Women meant everything to her. These illegal
settlements infuriated her. They destroyed the environment and local
inhabitants, took land away from Neo-Amazons and, in general, gave the
Federation a bad name. Nicole admired the spunk and energy of Kamra and
looked to her as a role model.

The craft grew a bit unsteady as it began to settle down. Nicole had to put
a hand against the hull of the ship to steady herself. Suddenly a green
light came on and Kamer began to shout "Go, Go". Without warning a blast of
hot humid air hit Nicole square in the face that it almost took her breath
away. She ran into the bushes and watched as the shuttle disappeared into
the depths of space. One second they were surrounded by the shine and
polish of Neo-Amazon technology and the next they were dumped into the depths
of a primitive jungle. Nicole adjusted the straps of her heavy backpack and
assembled with the others.

The Nest Master was anxious that they cover a lot of miles to the base
camp. Month's prior large supplies of food and essentials were pre
positioned throughout the jungle. These supplies would sustain them

for
along time and re-supply drops had also been coordinated. Everything was
set up so as to free the girls to concentrate only on hunting. Food
foraging trips were to be kept at a minimum.

After two hours of steady marching they pulled off the trail. The Nest
Master walking point had heard something. Two young males, their chosen
prey were approaching. With quick military precision she motioned Chantelle
and Clarissa to position themselves for the attack.

Clarissa was short, wiry and very aggressive. She loved a good fight and
often took on opponents much larger than herself. Nicole wondered why those
two were chosen to receive the honor of first kill while on a
mission. Then
she noticed both girls skin had taken on the most camouflage pattern while
her own skin had several patches of white.

Oblivious to the silent death lurking off the trail, the two young males
laughed loudly. As far as Nicole could determine the youths were a few
years younger than the girls and should make easy kills. One second they
were on the trail then the next they were drug off into the underbrush.
"What the." was all that one frightened male able to utter. All the girls
gathered around to watch.

Lance Vixen 4 was sitting on the face of her captive, facing his feet for a
reverse straddle

smother. Valak knelt down near her, giving her helpful hints. The victim
was not struggling but lay still accepting his fate. Both lads were
shirtless and Nicole watched the heaving chest of the victim positioned
firmly under Lance Vixen 4s' powerful body. She would make quick work of him, one
of the girls said softly. "Get his nose in deeper, deeper" Valak said
urgently. To emphasize the point she hit Lance Vixen 4 across the top of the
head.

Lance Vixen 4 spread her legs quite wide then pressed down viciously. Nicole

and
the other girls understood that these were not to be
relaxed "controlled"
smothers like they had done in training. Valak was satisfied with
Chantelles'
position and indicated she could begin her deep hip grinding pumping
motions on him.

The pumping grinding down on the victim was necessary to quickly put
him
into a state of atrophy where he wouldn't struggle and fight for
life. Once
he was in this disoriented state you could change positions on him
without
fear of him trying to escape or putting up a major struggle.

Valak now turned her attentions toward Meltek. Meltek held her
captive down
in the standard straddle smother. Not wanting a slap across the head
she
pulled the head of her victim tight to her body. He struggled a bit,
even
trying to push her off. Tracey Delights, a tall sexy powerful farm girl
grabbed
one of the youths hands to help hold him down. Meltek let out a low
guttural snarl, like some wild beast protecting it prey. Tracey Delights
quickly
backed off.

Valak looked over Malaks position and nodded indicating it was ok to
begin
the deadly pumping grinding motions. Soon both girls were deep in kill
ecstasy. Malaks victim showed some spunk and was resisting as much as
possible. He was no match for the aggressive Malak. She had him under
complete control at all times. A little over a half hour both victims
succumb and lay still.

The bodies were drug deeper into the bush. The jungle creatures and
insets
would soon take care of them. Valak said that probably within a few
days
nothing much would be left. Once again they resumed their torturous
journey. After a few hours the endless twists and tangles of paths and
dried up riverbeds all seemed to become a monotonous blur. It was
getting
near dark when came across a well traveled path. Dozens of settlers
were
walking up and down the path completely unaware of the presence of
Neo-Amazon
warrior women.

Their seemed to be a break in the traffic and much to the girls surprise,
three talkative young males approached. Valak was quick to set up the
attack. She, Caltur and Etar were to lead this attack.

Caltur had light red hair, a good trim figure and was an excellent athlete.
She had a deep and burning hate for settlers for they had murdered her
parents some years back. Nicole could see her virtually licking her lips in
anticipation of a kill.

Etar had long brown hair and stocky in build. Etar was quiet and very
studious. While in training you would often find her slowly smothering a
victim while deeply engrossed in a physics book. Etar enjoyed nothing more
than a nice long relaxing smother. Her creative and innovative kill
positions were the envy of all the girls. Valak, as much as she
wanted to, could hardly find fault with her method.

Caltur burst out of the dense brush and dove towards one of the
males. She had been premature and almost blown the ambush. The youth turned to
run but she grabbed him by his hair and drug him into the bushes.

Our Nest Master, Valak, a veteran of many such ambushes easily tucked
her victim under her arm and carried him off into the underbrush like a
sack of potatoes.

Etar had a more difficult task. Because of Caltur's over reaction
Etar had to chase after her male. She quickly caught up with him and pushed
him into the jungle.

Because the road was so well traveled, Valak decided that they should
all retire deeper into the jungle to perform their kills. One by one they
formed up single file and marched for a about 10 minutes. The march ceased
when they came upon a small grassy clearing, a perfect place. Three girls,
Chantelle, Clarissa and Sue-Saleek were sent out for perimeter security.

The males, though quit disoriented by their sudden capture, showed no fear.
One said softly "Neo-Amazon Warrior Women" and acted genuinely impressed by
their captors. Another youth, the youngest and Valaks' victim asked
politely if they were to be smothered. Valak smiled down at the young male
and pointed to the ground. With an audible "gulp" he laid down flat

on his back. His companions then obediently lay flat on their backs awaiting the smother.

Greg made his final visit to the former prison and chose a woman who he wanted to make a 4,000 point donation to. He even got to look at her pretty face as she fired the gun, six times, that ended his run (and extended hers, but only by an extra week). It wasn't working, and nor did the rope she had tried to strangle him with, so she had to finish him off with a knife and with four spears. He was still so drunk that he never fully knew what hit him. But his manners were such that he helped his woman out all the way, even when it was time to give her the throat and the chest and then the throat again.

Caltur knelt down and began to rip the shirt off her victim. He was trying
to help by unbuttoning it by received a hard slap for his efforts. The
youth gave a quick glance at his companions but his face soon vanished
under Calturs posterior. She had him down in a revere straddle
smother, her
favorite position.

Neo-Amazons, particularly Neo-Amazon women, have long sharp
fingernails. Caltur
had such an enduring hate of settlers that she began to rake her
victims
chest. She made stroke after stroke while he withered in pain. Soon
his
chest was all bloody; nothing but shreds. Valak made no effort to
interfere. Generally Neo-Amazon warrior women were known for their
aggressive
kills but not torture. The kills were performed in as humane manner as
possible, putting the victim almost to sleep prior to the actual kill.
Performing a good kill meant you and your victim shared in it's glory;
bonding together.
... ...

Chlessa was also presented a fresh victim as well. The boys eyes
lit
up with
 excitement when he found him positioned under the beauty Chlessa.
Every women
 has her own particular smothering position. Chlessa was well known
for her
 expert 69 whereas President Gabrielle preferred the old tried and true
straddle
 smother. Soon both women were furiously pumping away on their
respective
 victims while talking quietly. President Gabrielle then hugged her

daughter
 affectionately. It was a very beautiful sight to see the caring
loving mother
 side of President Gabrielle. All too often it was the busy president
jetting off
 to some conference. Of course there were the usual "staged" family
together at
 Christmas and such. However, it was heartening to see that the
affection
 between them was genuine. Chlessa went to hug her mother when her
victims nose
 slipped out of her. That was one of those embarrassing moments that

women
 hoped no one saw. A women was supposed to be in total control of
her victim
 and a nose slipping out of it's designated location was an awkward
unplanned
 mistake. The boys nose wasn't out long and Sabrina figured he'd
hardly had
 time for a breath of air before Chlessa reacted quickly and
reinserted it back
 into her body.

Chlessa, showing a bit of embarrassment, turned toward Sabrina.
Sabrina had
 been introduced to them previously but it had been a cordial formal
 introduction with miner small talk. "You didn't see that did you?"
Chlessa
 said looking over her shoulder smiling. "Not a thing" Sabrina said
with a
 laugh. President Gabrielle then gently reminded Chlessa to always
concentrate on
 her smothering. Nancy and Dr Sanchez were both sound asleep so
Sabrina was
 thrilled when, for the next hour or more, she got to talk to her two
 prestigious roommates. During the course of there conversation
Sabrina
 casually mentioned her "hunt" through the hospital. Much to
Sabrina's
 amazement and pleasure President Gabrielle asked if she and her
daughter
could go
 along on the next one. Hunting victims through the hospital with the
 "President and her Daughter"! almost sent Sabrina through the roof
with
 excitement. She smiled to herself when she felt her body twitch
with
a sudden
 orgasm. Her victim wiggled around a bit, evidently it was getting a

bit "wet"
 for him down there.

Several serious looking men and women now entered the room. The talked to
 President Gabrielle in hushed quiet tone. Chlessa began to sob and Sabrina heard
 her say "No mom,.you can't." Various papers were signed and they quickly left.
 Sabrina saw the red around Chlessa's eyes where she'd been crying.

Trying to break the serious mode Sabrina told them of the great
luck
she and
 her companions had had while going through the examination rooms. Sabrina then
 added "I can't wait until I tell my friends that we're going
hunting
victims
 with the president." President Rodden looked over her shoulder and corrected
 "That's Ex-President Gabrielle Rodden. Just call me Gabrielle from now on.
Sabrina
 slumped into her bed. The greatest and most loved of all presidents was
 brought down not by some rival political machine but by a damn virus.
No known
 cure for VIAGRA GIRL had been found. It was necessary that the reigns
of government be
 turned over to the capable hands of the vice president.

A woman
infected had
 to be under constant supervision and consume 20 to 30 victims per day. This
 was too much of a burden to carry. Sabrina lost her president that
 day but gained two new friends.

Poor Kate is now in a death-choke hold sleeper grip move that the
pretty royal princess herself is administering – her hands are trapped
under the side of a piano and of no use – will anyone come to her
rescue? Or is this the end of another one of our main characters?

Sara manages to finish her intruder off, and to seal her bunker. She does so with her female friends, a rope, a shoe, a sock, and lot of womanly hands pressing down on their target's mouth, for a long time. "It took 25 minutes of time and a whole lot of energy to finish him off. But he's no longer a threat now, the bastard!" concluded Sara. She looked around for other invaders, saw none, and threw some camouflage and some old junk up to make the area look like just a small patch of trees with nothing worth having under them.

Others were planning, building, arguing, battling and working to try and get into one of the bigger and better equipped bunkers. What they sensed a risk of but did not know for sure was that before long a fatal dose of radiation will, most likely, have built up inside all of them, not enough to kill them straight away, but enough to mean that 35 years of lurking in a bunker, alive, was not likely to happen, unfortunately.

Ollie tries hard to save Kate from the hold she was in, and he would have made it too, had it not been for the gun-fire of the newly arriving militia, now making their move, now that all their opponents were sitting ducks, and Ollie's back was their very first target in the lair. Just as the defeat of the royal family and their entourage was within grasping proximity, the arrival of these gunmen that nobody knew were coming was the death of Ollie, who took several bullets and fell, bleeding to death on the bunker floor. Most of the others, and all the militia men soon followed, as this other militia was now going to be replacing all these residents. They might make an exception for the pretty pregnant princess though, carrying the heir to the throne, as she will have her uses, they thought.

Soon after Ollie, Kate too was sadly shot, and so were the royals. All apart from the pretty princess, who worth keeping. The mysterious late arrivals were in such a hurry to get yet more supplies in, the dead bodies out, and to seal themselves in that they did not take time to get rid of the last two of the bodies. The following day, realising that it was going to be getting very smelly in there very soon, they decided to cook all the dead'uns for supper.

This was ok for protein and carbs, but it raised the CO levels in there, as they were cooking, and it also raised the amount of bone waste that they could not get rid of so easily now that they were sealed in. Then, another day later, they realised that the water supply system was broken or stuck, and so they had to open the hatch again, to try to fix it, while taking in all the deadly radiation they had been sheltering from. Sadly, this incident shortened their life span from years to weeks. They did all they could to nurse the royal princess back to health, and to turn her into their supreme leader, but then they all fell into rapid decline, and those last days were proper depressing like, as none of them had the strength left to nurse the others.

Sara did manage to wave goodbye to the outside world, take a deep breath, and to step inside her new home. The group of four worked together to double-check they had everything and to seal the door. From now on, they knew nothing about what is going on elsewhere. And they were all fully committed to surviving at all costs.

Two days later, Sara got so angry at the one male in there with her that he nearly died, at her unforgiving martial arts prowess-filled hands. He should have learned his lesson then, and turned into a faithful servant, but he didn't learn, and his terrible behaviour was wasting precious supplies at very unsustainable rates of consumption. He had failed to do what was expected of him, and he was of no use, the crappy excuse of a man that he had been! It was time to start keeping him tied up from now on, and to put him on minimum rations. If he struggled, she would have no choice but to KO him or worse.

Sara soon realised that her supplies were only good for a couple of years, and that her bunker might not be fully radiation-proof. So she decided to just make the most of each day she had left. She dived into her fantasy book world, while lying on her tied up man who had to keep really still. She loved these books, the world they were set in, and she analysed each line for hours, before reflecting on how to use this wisdom in raising these young'ens she had in with her. She was convinced she was pregnant, and so it was now ok to straddle squat smother her tied-up male out of existence, which happened at night. She had plans for getting rid of one or two of her other fellow co-residents as a way of making the supplies last longer. But it never came to this.

Not long thereafter, five weeks into her bunker-dwelling time, Sara started getting more and more consumed by the lack of a single living male in her 35-year den. She dreamt of stepping out and finding some fertile, handsome and not particularly strong guy nearby, who was dying like everyone else of the radiation, and of throwing him onto a car and having her way with him right out in the open, without saying a single word.

Sara was in her den for a good number of days, with the two girls who had turned up the previous day, living out their last days in girl chat, book talk, reminiscing, and dishing out as much mutual praise and encouragement as they could. But her lair was attacked several times more, and each time the girls, knowing that their door was by no means unbreakable, had to open the door, whack some half-dead sick zombified blokes into oblivion with shovels and planks of wood, maybe take one in with them if he was cute, submissive and weak enough to tie up, control and instruct (This happened twice!), and they lived out their den days in as much partnership, chatter, massages, good energy and sexual pleasure as they could possibly have, while the radiation was slowly killing them off in their sleep.

It started with these vaginal cravings and with the fantasies, including a worryingly sick fantasy to 'have some fun' with the face and body of an intruder man that the girls had just bludgeoned to death near the entrance to her cave. And it turned real when one of those who had been locked out of all the safe dens somehow arose from where he had fallen after an earlier invasion attempt and started banging frantically on the door and using a crowbar to rip it open.

This guy, and another one who turned up a week later, had their uses. Sara was lusting "after that male touch in her woman regions," and she failed to resist these urges for more than a day after she realised there were still good-looking boys alive out there, desperate for shelter, and willing and able to give her a good time in between book club chats and reminiscing sessions.

Sara always did it "her way" which involved her tying them up, just in case, with the girls nearby to help her kill them in the event of a struggle, which they knew and understood, and it involved Sara sleeping fully on top of them, both men, full weight, all night long, and then making them pleasure her with more body parts, from nose to mouth, from willy to toe to finger, and in more ways than I care to list. She never turned kind, and she never gave them a break, not even when they were covered all over the face in her juices and she was having a period and had a flatulent spell to boot. To object to whatever she wanted to do to you was to die, they thought, and they much preferred to keep on pleasuring her for now.

Half a year later, Sara and the last of the girls both faded away, all in the same night, in their sleep, in January 2027, with a let's do another book club night tomorrow last thought. They never found out about each other's similar timing. The last of her sex slaves died in the October before, of strangulation after a disagreement, and he even helped Sara get her legs around his throat so she could get rid of him when she had found that the supplies were running short, and that he had been secretly sneaking off with the forbidden snickers bars, and in his mind the women in the den were all preggers by now, and there just wasn't enough food left now so all of them could make it.

The voice that knows: The final human colony to perish, two years in, in March 2028 to be precise, will be a Japanese troop of cave-dwelling dwarfs on a small island near Okinawa, who then run out of supplies, have issues with their water supply system and are overrun with wastewater flooding and sewage waste inside their cave hideout, two years in.

They are left with no alternative but to open the hatch and hope to make it on the outside. But it is too early for survival to be possible. They knew this was their biggest risk, and that they could not last another week inside their bunker with no food left at this point.

The last UK colony, dwindling and going a few months before this, on 19th January 2028, is the one containing the specially chosen points-winning TV beauties, in a mountain cave bunker near Snowden called Noah's Ark. Its supplies are ample, but its water system was always destined to be lethal. It was bringing the lethal radiation in with it, making the residents ever more ill, until the last of them, a pretty pregnant beauty queen and model, died, peacefully in her sleep, at 3 am on the morning of the 19th January.

Everyone from the state, the military and from the main official offices of government died knowing that all hope was now invested in these seven chosen girls and one boy in the Weybridge Abbey bunker. What they did not know was that the bunker, though adequately stocked, was slowly letting the deadly radiation in through the same pipes that were giving them fresh water and taking all their waste away.

I hope you can forgive us for throwing the last big reveal in so early. We miniature guinea-pig-capibarra-cross critters of Europa, assembled by this brook to tell you this sad true story, are not very good at keeping secrets.

Various efforts in the US, Russia, China, France, Spain, Germany, Canada, Bosnia, Belarus, Kazakhstan, Peru, Nepal, Iran, Australia

and Argentina succeed in surviving the first year, but are
insufficiently sealed off from the radiation overall to avoid
succumbing in the second perilous year since the apocalypse.

So you must make the most of every day you have on earth, as it
may well be quite close to your last day alive, everyone.

Part 14 – this morning

It is now the year 2040. As I look out the window, the buds of spring
are opening up in the trees outside my window. I have had porridge
with berries for breakfast. It was nice. I had friends over in the
evening and we spoke about all that was on our minds. The first
voting ballot for provinces that have not yet had their 8 systemic
options vote is finally here. It is generally laid out simply as follows:

Each of the five new catch-all parties representing people born in the
years ending 1+6, 2+7, 3+8, 4+9, and 5+0, plus all the defectors who
have changed affiliation, each with party leadership determined by
open-to-all interselection tournament events, is listed on the ballot I
will be holding in my hand in moments from now, as I go to vote.
Next to each one of these five options, there is a box I can put my
preference order number into. The best option is to be given a 1. The
2nd best is to be given a 2. And so on.

Rather than just choosing one party and putting an X in that box,
which is also possible, each voter is allowed to put a 1 into the box
he or she agrees with most and who he or she wishes to see in office,
and a 2, a 3, a 4 and a 5 into the other boxes, representing the voter's
lower order preferences. When the votes cast are counted, each two-
party combination is updated, one at a time, with an update. If for
example a voter has chosen to give the Improvement Party her
1st preference, the Freedom Party her 2nd preference, the Logic and
Reason Party her third preference, and the Progress Party her
4th preference, the computer system is pre-programmed to
automatically give all these four parties a 1 in their head-to-head
with the 5th and lowest preference People's Party, while also
updating all other head-to-heads by her one vote, so the
Improvement Party gets a "1" in each of its battles against the other
four; the Freedom Party gets a 1 in its battle against all the parties
who this voter gave a lower preference to, the Logic and Reason
Party gets a "1" in its sum number of votes in its head-to-heads
against the parties with a 4 or a 5, while its opponents gain one on it
if they scored a 1 or a 2 thus beating the 3, and so on.

When the votes of the next voter is added, some of these head-to-
head become 1-1, while others become 2-0. It's quite simple and
logical really. And it is a million times more likely to bring a

grouping into power in the end who more than 50% of the voters like and can stand.

Each of the ten vote count battles (A against B, A vs C, A vs D, A vs E, B vc C, B vs D, B vs E, C vs D, C vs E, & D vs E) are updated thus, and the 1st preference against 5th preference head-to-head it even given a bigger push of 1.3 (not just 1.0). The other exception is that the 4th preference against the 5th preference win and the 3rd preference over 4th preference only count as 0.8 of a vote, whereas the all other head to head battles are each given a 1 for whoever gets the higher preference vote, to represent this voter's contribution to the overall count.

It is mathematically possible, though it will be extremely rare, maybe even as rare as only happening once every 4,000 years for any two or three parties to end up having defeated the same number of opponents (for example: party B defeated A; C defeated B and A defeated C in their head-to-heads, all in the same election), whereas the usual way will be to have one party who defeated all opponents and another who finished second place by having defeated all but one of the opponents in head-to-head vote counts. A special pre-written protocol determines what happens then, which basically means that the closest of the three (if party B defeated A; C defeated B and A defeated C in their head-to-heads) is deemed almost a draw, 0.6 of an overall head-to-head win, so the number of won head-to-heads may now be three point six. And if this still does not separate the pack and we still do not have an overall winner, a run-off tie-breaker election is held, in which only the voters aged 20 – 70 in one location that is chosen at random exactly one week after the original election (to represent 1% of the voters) is held, and the drawing to determine which location votes in the tie-breaking decider is held exactly one week before the rare run-off vote will get to decide. We stress again that these special run-offs are extremely rare, as a general average voter's overall preference order will 99.99999993% of the time produce clear overall winners and a clear finishing order among the competing parties on the ballot. That said, it's not a fantastic how the system works write-up if it doesn't also specify what happens in case of each and every eventuality. And once it has done so once, it can be improved further with minor changes in the future, until further improvements can no longer be found.

The campaign lasted three weeks in the lead-up. It was a fairly civilized affair, as each media outlet was required to give the top five groupings equal coverage and equal chances to get their messages across, while also allowing any ten of the section B movements equal space in its 25% of the airtime and print space devoted to the section B battles. The law requires all accusations to be substantiated, investigated and reported back, with significant enough fines for wrong-doers and for liars, so that after centuries of election campaigns that were all about destroying the credibility of the opponent, we now instead live in a time when the suggestions these people wish to make themselves, and their voting intentions on each other's suggestions, are what the voters receive as messages informing us of the differences between the options we are voting between.

There has been no name-calling, doom-mongering or microphone grabbing. Each grouping was allowed to speak, and each grouping supports some or most of what the other groupings are trying to achieve. There is mutual support and respect, a big overlap in values and in common understanding of what has been going wrong in recent years. And the different groupings are refreshingly ready to back each other's efforts to solve the problems and to improve the lives of the people they serve. They even admit it when an idea was originally proposed by someone else. None of them claims to be the only one to get it, and the only one to be in a position to do it right. How terribly confusing it must have been back in the days when all the candidates were making these claims, while dismissing all the other options as "dangerous". Luckily the era or epoque of lies is finally over, and voters are now able to choose between problem-solving approaches that are honestly compared in impartial ways by neutral observers in the media, not funded by any of the parties, whose only job is to explain the difference to us without making one option sound better than the other, which would bias the vote in a sinister way.

Rather than have to choose between two equally scary options, as has been the case for too many recent decades, one right wing and the other left wing, both of whom are terrible at some or all jobs of government and both of whom leave a big mess, a mountain of debt and of ill health and social problems, and a broken society resulting from their special-interests-funded dishonest, secretive, corrupt, inefficient, tribal ill-informed ideological and just plain destructive actions, which has been terrible for democracy all round the world for many centuries, and which has led voters to try and pick the less catastrophic of two bad options time and time again, which meant they were falling for the biggest and scariest of the lies every time, picking the most crooked candidate as their ruler, and never able to go for a central option as the big two always told everyone (successfully for them) that the central option is so far behind that it cannot win and is a wasted vote. Rather than all this, the usual way that we can all remember from not long ago, we now have a world where the truth is what informs the voters. Imagine that!

The way the vote outcomes translate into seats or overall party vote shares in the legislature varies from country to country, from state to state and from province to province. My state is not alone in applying a formula that gives the top ten parties (whereby tenth place is the winner of bracket B and not the supreme loser of the main bracket's votes) vote share allocations of 40, 25, 15, 10, 6, 5, 4, 3, 2, and 1. Others do a similar thing, translating the outcome of a ballot that works by having lots of simultaneous head-to-head battles at once into a legislature.

Having a legislature is very important, as history has shown that the legislature has always been better at reflecting the will, the concerns, the interests and the needs of the people than the courts or the heads of the executive have. If the legislature, and more specifically the legislature of the provinces has more power, a better outcome is always found. That's what the lessons of the years 1500 to 2025 have taught us. Later years may change this slightly, we'll see. But power sharing and plurality is true democracy, whereas giving one man all the power is the path toward authoritarianism and then to tyranny, each and every time!!!

Having said this, each state also needs to have judicial and executive sectors that are able to work well and to achieve well, without too much meddling, target-setting, budget-cutting, target-paradoxes or bureaucracy imposed on them. They must also have monitoring systems in place that can identify and destroy corruption in every branch of the state.

A legislature used to be a place where two or more big camps spend the whole day hurling speeches at each other, wasting weeks, months and years of their lives without ever persuading each other of anything. This does not need to be the case. Apart from the functional select and standing committees, where project work is undertaken and where a specific outcome is found in the end, there is no need to have all the members of the legislature in one room, eternally disagreeing and eternally scuppering each other's efforts. That's terribly inefficient. Instead, it may make more sense to keep the people with ideas and with solutions within their own party, working together to find the best possible outcome. Then to submit this to a vote just within the party of origin, at first. Once agreement is reached within the party, deciding to back the proposal, the democratic system should then swing into life, whereby each of the other parties is allowed to either back the new proposal, make a slightly altered new version of it, or reject it in favour of the existing way. And then the voting begins, pitting each amended form of the idea against the others in a voting tournament that ends up with four, then two, then one way chosen. This may work really well.

But it may not always be the best way. Unfortunately, in the real world, the best idea is not always voted through, as the bigger teams bully and ignore their smaller opponents, shooting down the best contributions that were on offer for the wrong reasons. This is why there also needs to be a fully impartial, neutral, unaligned and purely intellectual body of the state that finds the very best proposals that should have won and puts them up for referendums, from which the best way can still end up being implemented anyway, as these override what the legislature has chosen, once the electorate has backed the better way in a referendum, in which it went up against the option that was favoured by the bigger legislative coalition but then turned out not to be the best way after all. Such a system will not be easy to get going, but it is worth achieving in the end. It can allow the greatest minds in the world to help shape a vastly better future than what the ruling party would ever have offered. And in doing so, it's as close to utopia as we will ever come.

There is also a **Section B on the ballot**, on which all the other (currently smaller) political parties that have been registered to take part in the election compete for a place in the top ten, which will replace the top five race for power we have this time around. Among the most promising options looking good in the Section B race this year in my home state are: The ransel party, the high IQ party, the congress of trade unions, the help the poor, frail, elderly and disabled party, the cut taxes party, the make Arizona stronger movement, the gathering of all professions, and all faiths moral gathering party, the gathering of all environmentalist forces, and the create many great new companies party. I had to spend a long time thinking about which of these options to give my top five preference votes to, while other charismatic one-man movements, some independents, some liberals, conservatives or progressives, traditional parties, age-group alliances and narrow cause options also add to the crowded race for a top five finish on section B. In two days from now, when all the votes have been counted by the special machines and have been multiply spot-check verified, we will finally know which five options have won out in section B and this won a place in the main section of the ballot next time around.

There will always be a section B in future votes, and the winner of section B will always move up to the main section of the ballot, where it will go up against the top nine performing of the ten options that were there last time around. It's a system of constant promotion and renewal, and one that takes the worst option out of the mix, moving it back down into section B where the big crowd of new smaller movements are, every time. Only the ten options in the main section (A) of the ballot can win the top post of legislative and executive power. These are the top nine from last time (who control 98% of the vote in parliament between them) and the winner of section B last time around, who controls 1.8% of the vote in parliament, so that the public can get to know its views on all the matters being debated ahead of the big next election, where it will be up against the top nine parties in a battle for all the big posts in power governing the state I live in.

Immigrants, criminal convictions and young voters: These three groups of voters do not have a full vote, only a partial vote. So whereas a full voter contributes 1.0 to each of the party against party battles occurring in both sections of the ballot paper, with minor exceptions making the 1 over 5 win count more than the 4 over 5 win, there are voters who do not yet get given a full vote: Foreign and domestic migrants immigrants are not allowed to vote within their first two years of living in a new county, province, or state, and after this, their vote grows by 10% of a vote per year of living there to 0.1 in the end of their 2nd year of living there, to 0.2 in the end of their 3rd year of living there, and so on up, until they permanently have a full vote or they move away and start the process again in their new location. Similarly, **young voters** are given a 0.1 vote at the age of 10, 0.2 at the age of 11, 0.3 at the age of 12, and so on up to 0.9 at the age of 18 and the full votes package at the age of 19, assuming they have lived in the state or province all this time. People who have spent between 1 week and 1 year of their lives in prison have, for the next 20 years of their lives, lost 0.1 of their votes. This grows by a further 0.1 of a vote lost for each further year they have spent in prison in their lives. Keeping track of all this is the role of the central registration body, which also keeps track of everyone's home address, their registered doctor, their registered will, any land or other listed assets they own, any tax they have paid, their passport number, their pension and their registered migration history and criminal history.

Banned candidates: The national screening body, made up of fifteen committee members, three from each party, is allowed to ban any five candidates in all of the country each year, if they have a criminal record, or evidence of inciting hatred, and any five in each province of China (apart from the four smallest population areas of China, where 4, 3, 2 and 1 are allowed to be picked as blocked from running instead). The candidates that it finds to be the most dishonest, harsh, hateful, violent, unpeaceful and dangerous for the nation's stability are removed, early on in the process of candidacy. They can still vote, but cannot go on the ballot and into the legislature.

The national screening body, made up of crystal clean governors from all ethnic groups who have been picked after all applicant's views have been examined and all extremist and confrontational views have been scored out and removed, is not allowed to pick on anyone for their stances, their ethnicity, their political affiliations or their IQ level. They can only ban a candidate for being in some way violent, mob-affiliated, undermining of the system, or dishonest. And they may not exceed the number of people excluded maximum five. They are briefed by the secret service in being given information to work with. No violent, hateful or otherwise evil candidates are allowed.

Elected heads of provinces: Each province or state has its own governor, overseeing a separate education system and a separate social services, pensions, social security, judicial, transport and planning policy from the other areas. The provinces get to decide how 71% of all the public sector finances are spent, with only 24% decided by the national government and 5% by the town or village council. These cuts are fixed, with only mutual agreement or a full referendum able to alter these. Some countries have gone for different splits, like Singapore who has no provinces within it and Turkmenistan, Iran and North Korea who have all opted for the following split instead: Power over public sector funding in these countries is split in such a way that 60% of all public sector spending is under the control of the provinces, free to allocate this much out among its various programmes as it chooses. A further 30% is allocated out at the national or federal level, and 10% at the town, borough or village level. This means that all the different kinds of taxes and other forms of state revenue are eternally split in this way, every month and every year, until a change to this split is brought in one day by a new act of law, a mini-referendum on this issue, or through a change of constitution. Most revenue types' local and provincial 60% or 71% stay in the province where they were collected or paid, with only 1% of it being transferred from the richest to the poorest province per capita, where the public sector support services are most needed.

National legislature: Each voter's contribution to the national legislature is as follows: 5th preference gets 0; 4th preference gets 0.1; 3rd preference gets 0.3; 2nd preference gets 0.9; 1st preference gets 5.0 from the voter. The summed up overall totals for each party determine its percentage share of the overall vote, and as the legislatures only convene once a week to submit each party's vote, there is only one official delegate from each party there to register that party's votes.

Method of selection of each party's candidate for any post: There are some parties on the ballot where all semi-finalists are IQ tested and the outcome of this determines whether a candidate is among the smartest 10% of candidates who will win 12 of the 15 seats on the party's provincial governing board or the bulk bracket who vie for the other 3 seats. The election method is called in separate interselection blocks and it involves having groups of five to 12 candidates spend three whole days with each other, before each candidate then secretly submits his package of valuation verdicts on each of the other candidates in his group. He must score at least one third of them with 90s – 100s and he must also score at least one of the candidates with 85 – 89, while the rest can be given any score from 00 to 100. Only the 1 (or sometimes 2) candidates with the highest score in any such interselection group then moves on to the next interselection group. Depending on how many candidates there are, there could be anything from 1 to 9 stages of interselection, though usually 2, 3 or 4 stages of progression are required to find the party's chosen candidate for a major role. The finalists are voted on not just by each other, but also by the appointed representatives of the party leaders, or sometimes, if they choose, to, even by the existing party leader(s) themselves. Previous winners and in-office incumbents get to skip straight through to the final or to any other stage of their choosing.

This whole new set-up was first announced in May 2023, and it goes live on the 1st January 2024, with elections for various regional, local, national and provincial posts occurring in May of each year. The terms are normally five years long each and the expiration of these five-year terms is staggered in such a way that an equal number of them are up for election every year, but the May 2024 election is special, in that it counts toward all of the regional, local, national and provincial leadership posts and legislatures, all in one. Then, whichever provinces had the smallest gaps between their first and second place finishers go back to the ballot booths in 2039, while those with the biggest gaps between their first and second place finishers go back to the ballot booths in the fifth and final grouping, in 2029. Then in 2030, the 2039 group will be up again.

Initial criticism and observations:

In many countries, we have observed a strong tendency to join the party that the current leader of the country is a member of. This is observed in many provinces, especially in the home province of the top government officials and in the regions where this party has its traditional power base. A lot of people initially defect from their default party to join the country's long-established and much-loved leader, and such developments are not uncommon also in later years, under the new system, and under later leaders, as people keep on opting to join the winner of the most recent election, either out of personal conviction, or in the hope of ending up in his ruling government team.

This tendency peaks at approximately 37% of all voters doing this in year two of the new system being in place, and fortunately it is observed to have dwindled to less than 10% by year 25, as the other parties evolve to have a draw-in appeal of their own, with each party having a credible national leader and a good set of ideas to go in support of. Also, it is not a problem to have a drift of affiliated members from one party to another and to have one party be bigger than the others, as long as the others are still able to get their messages, ideas and concerns across.

Being in favour of one party's ideas does <u>not</u> mean you have to be hostile to all the ideas emanating from the other parties. The new parties are close together in terms of their place in the scale of right to left and the new similarity will bring about a new trend to agree on things, accepting what the problems are that need solving and accepting that it is better to try ten things to more fully solve this problem than to try only one.

It is hoped that a system is chosen in most provinces worldwide that reinforces and rewards the ability for the other parties to form views, visions and solutions independently of one another, and for the possibility that they all might reach the same conclusion on any topic. Running four parties' solutions to a problem in parallel is a much better way to solve a problem than only trying one party's way out, especially as the empirical data will show that variations combining more than one approach, while also having tried other ways out, will normally win in the end.

Dealing with set-backs

Of course the world might lose a few provinces to an evil military faction who decides to topple the legislature and its executive and to live under its tyrannical evil rule instead. Such is human nature. We have seen this happen thousands of times over the years and it will keep on happening. But when it does, the outside world will need to step in and do whatever it takes to guide things back to where they need to be.

Never again should the world allow a bunch of jerks with guns to overrun a functioning society and to replace it with a crazy nut-case system where the new rulers enslave and steel from all others. A superior world army should be on stand-by at all times, ready to bring the voters back into power, at all costs, which the affected people can repay later, when they are free again. It's that simple. A state is only ever free when the voters can replace all the laws they do not like and all the leaders who misbehaved. Otherwise is remains a tyranny. And tyrannies, just as mafias, warlords, extortion racquets and cartels will topple fast when there is a proper world army that can take care of them all. Don't let the badguys win, anywhere on earth! Don't let them terrorize and harm the people of their land. Take them down. Then good things can follow.

A few provinces, during the course of the 2040s, 2050s and 2060s have opted to try out a new, more devolved option for the compartmentalisation of national and provincial budgets: Only 15% of the tax revenue is now controlled by the national or federal level in these areas of the world; 75% at provincial level; 10% at village, town, district or borough level, plus all quantitative easing, all international relations and all currency, borders and military is still in the national level, for now, BUT with a planned orderly transition taking place to shift most of these powers and duties to the international bodies that are best at dealing with them. All this is only valid until it changes: when a 35 delegate constitutional committee picks 8 new good options and the voters pick the best one among them in a 50-yearly systemic vote, all allocations of funding and of power can change again.

Calling a mini-referendum: There are three routes to holding a mini-referendum. A party can either use up its one automatic call-up right per 25 years, submitting its proposal and then getting a province-wide vote on the matter two months later if the mini-referendum of 1% of the precincts supported the change move initiative in the first mini-referendum, held exactly five weeks after the submission was made. OR, if it is willing to risk 3% of its leaders' salaries for a two-year period, it can have an additional mini-referendum called on another issue that it is sure the legislature went against the will of the people on. OR a citizens' petition initiative can bring about a mini-referendum if it emerges as the biggest citizens' petition in that province in that five-year period of time.

Median number mini-referendums: When the issue is budgetary or age limits, it makes more sense to let each voter put down a number, rather than a yes or a no. By throwing out the highest 49% and the lowest 49% of answers, we find our true middle, a figure to use that will not have a majority saying it is too high or too low.

This is how the important numbers used in big new laws are arrived at nowadays.

The pay of the members of legislature must NEVER AGAIN be decided by the members of legislature themselves, as it will rise beyond and above all reason!!! Obviously!!!! Instead, a median numbers mini-referendum must be called once every ten years in every province to decide how many % the wages of the party leaders, the legislature the heads of the executive, the police, the military, the regulators, the central bank, and the judiciary is to rise (or fall) every year, letting the voters decide, rather than the people that are seeking the payment themselves. This is wonderful system, and it takes the corruption out of politics completely!

It does come with a danger that the voters might set some of these pay rates so low that the best people will no longer apply for these jobs, and there are probably 25 other dangers in this category, or in the opposite end of this judgement, where pay rates are set too high or too low, but such mistakes are unlikely, as the systematic disregarding of the top and bottom 49% of responses tends to result in an outcome that keeps the pay more or less unchanged, maybe adding 1% of an increase at a time when inflation is 2.8%. This is a stable and predictable way, and it is wise to use an outcome like this for the whole civil service too, but with the ordinary civil servants to be kept more closely in line with inflation, so as not to have a worsening of the general standard of living as caused through the ballot box. Such mature outcomes will be found under these brilliant new structural systems of democracy. You can rely on it!

In deciding the pay of the leaders and of the legislators, many provinces have already acted decisively, setting good boundary parameters that ensure that the pay of the elected legislative party leaders may never go above three times the average national wage or below one point three times the average national wage; and the heads of government, the heads of the national and provincial budgets, the heads of the national judiciary and heads of the national armed forces may not go above 5 times or below 1.8 times the average national wage. This rule and various variations of it have gone through in many provinces, but in most of them the fact that a median numbers referendum overrules the existing rules means that these formulated boundaries could be crossed, one day, if the voters decide they know better than to stick to the advice that came to them through these. Everything is possible, but nothing truly shocking is likely in a median numbers vote, so expect very little change to come from them, which is good for the system and for attracting good quality applicants into it in years to come. In times of particular shortages of money for the public sector, it is only right to make everyone share in the cuts equally and fairly; and in times of normality being restored, why not reward your leaders for making the people of your province well off by giving them a small pay rise that will keep them motivated, inspired, hard-working, devoted and proud.

Comparisons to the established western democracies

We know that there is much in this book that differs, varies and stays from the norm of the Western world in the time when you are reading this. This is intentional. While our tone of change is reformist and slow-moving and not disruptively scary and revolutionary, we do nevertheless feel the need to emphasize that there is so much that has not been achieved in any country in the world yet, which they should try hard to achieve over the next 50 years. Not one of them is perfect. And those who are closer to being perfect, which might be a not-so-well known country in Europe, Asia, the Americas or elsewhere, need to be identified and copied fast.

While all the laws, rules, systems and constitutions of the world have been written by the one ruling party, to suit themselves, and to make certain types of changes in the future be impossible, this suits them well, but it is definitely NOT the best way. By not offering the people any alternative formulations for any part of their constitution so far, we have told them accept all our rubbish or you will get nothing. This is square one in a 80,000 step way to the best of systems, and I doubt that any country on earth has made it past square 25 in this long voyage so far.

I strongly hope that by reading this book, and others like it, the world can come to realise what the problem with the current system is, and how to describe the improved way that we could seek to have instead. It won't be easy, and it will take more than one law to be passed to get there, but if there is a rational brain at work inside our leaders' heads, it's not impossible to move in the right direction and to end up, one distant day, in the utopia we would like to choose for ourselves.

By 2052, there is now talk of building a self-sufficient community of earth plants, fungi and insects on a planet, moon or space station in the near future, and this project will definitely succeed, albeit with many base layer stages requires first. Once this is up and running, they reckon, it may one day be possible to settle some mammals, fish, birds and lizards there too. It could one day serve as a survival back-stop in case life on earth ever ends, and perhaps humans are best omitted, for a while, as they cause so much trouble and eat all the other animals, or spoil their habitats. But this will require a lot of further research, and it is unlikely to be up and running, in the form of plants living and flourishing forever more outside our planet before 2058.

The Iranian Revolution, like the Taliban, Putin, Kim Young Eun, Shi Jinping and the King of Saudi, shrink their empire down gradually to five and later to only one remaining province, and trans-ind, a new regional world government task force, makes sure that no guns, mobs or weapons are involved, apart from when the protesters are being protected. After 15 years, the voters in these last provinces opt to reelect what is left of their old rulers, while the neighbouring areas opt to shake off the shackles of having a clergy-led state, a monarchy or a one-party state, and they move over to giving the multi-party legislature all the powers that one would normally see it get. The elected candidates still incorporate the main dogmatic beliefs into their manifestos, but not at the cost of excluding any progressive plans.

Britain's many little successor states, shires and boroughs all follow Norfolk's, Lambeth's and Wales' lead and decide to join trans-eur, and its commonwealth country friends also decide to stop being aloof from their regional neighbours and issues, and so trans-southaf, trans-oc, trans-ind, trans-carib and trans-east all receive lots of new members too, with the x-colonies, such as Hong Kong, Guyana, Georgia, Belize, Cayman Islands and the Falkland Islands reaffiliating across from trans-brit, which they stay honorary videoconferencing partners in to making stronger partnerships and tax-revenue-sharing schemes with their nearest neighbours be the most important thing.

In 2053 London becomes a cluster of 32 independent borough cities, each with its own government, a different immigration policy and with different health, tax, welfare, pension and governance systems, greater Manchester becomes ten independent borough states, and all other regions undergo a similar process. Westminster still hosts trans-brit, but 91% of tax-funded schemes are now 100% devolved, and so having one MP for each one of them proves to be too expensive to be necessary, and the trans-brit leadership delegates are instead chosen by five of the member nations in a lottery.

All other trans-regional bodies follow suit, realising that there are no more major transformations to argue about, and so each one can now, in especially peaceful times, shrink down in size and let other levels of decision-making flourish. This also makes for a depolarisation of the debate about the future direction of travel for the international bodies. Those continents who, like trans-eur, still wish to have additional agreements in place on top of what the current ones and the new global order provide, now do so with an a la carte menu of opt-in and opt-out initiatives, and a parliament that gives its 20 biggest parties' five-person epicentres a percentage of the vote each that corresponds with its share of the overall vote.

There is a vicious verbal hostility from the Sunni Muslims of Western Asia and also in some rural regions in South Asia and in West and East Africa toward the Shiites, Druze, Alawi, Yazidi, and sometimes also toward the Bahai, Zoroastrian, various Christian, pagan, non-religious, Jewish, Hindu, Parsi, Jain, Sikh and other belief groups and so the trans-regional bodies are given special remits by the global UN body to ensure that every person who is being marginalised because of their ethnicity is allowed to move into a nearby free and welcoming cosmopolitan city, town or province that is under the ruling control of the ethnicity (or a coalition including it) of the persecuted, and that the hostile area always ends up financially covering and facilitating all the moving and transaction costs associated with having to sell your home here and to move there plus interest.

This becomes quite a long-term drain on these (mostly ultra-radical Sunni) societies, and they undergo new efforts to tone the hostility down as a best way of winning the right to one day have lower taxes, better reputations and more development aid. Some towns, where Isis, taliban, boko haram or similar dogma and devotionist influences are strongest prefer to opt to stay hostile to other ways of life, staunchly ultra-religious and to reluctantly pay all the fines, taxes and the moving costs that come with it.

When any of these groups do extra-violent acts to adulterous women or to minorities or foreigners, though, trans-ind and trans-arab do feel the need to intervene to carry out a rescue and to make some arrests. It means that all international bodies are viewed, in these areas, with great suspicion and with dislike in some areas, and visitors permits, except for ultra-religious inward migrants, are very hard to come by in these areas. They sometimes even to reject inoculation programmes, and so many illnesses that are under control elsewhere are busy taking down thousands of religious nutters and their innocent children in some of these ultra-Islamic utopias, but the world is slowly starting to get out, as the young generation of ulema and imams themselves are seeing the need to back these programmes at last.

Afghanistan, Syria, Niger, Sudan, Yemen and Somalia are places where warlords, barons and ulema thrive, and where support for multi-party democratic systems are lower. This is why the trans-regional bodies make sure that each province of these corners of the world remains fully independent, with no one province's thugs and troops ever able to invade, pressurise, send military support to a violent militia in or to bring warfare to any other. This way, even though it is not always possible to stay in the area where you grew up, there are many opportunities to work and settle in other nearby areas where the going isn't so tough if you are the sort of person who is likely to fall foul of the ultra-strict rules that the most conservative and religious societies like to impose upon themselves.

Sharia law, in some interpretations of the quran, requires anyone who is raised to believe but then denounces Islam, and any woman who disobeys her husband or father or who has a fling with a lover to be brutally butchered. This barbaric practice presents a large problem, and a number of anonymous phone lines are websites are set up to offer assistance to young women with big problems of craving a man other than the one the father has chosen for her.

The local governments shut off all info about these rescue programmes, and so a long sequence of leaflet air-drops are necessary, with many tens of thousands of young women opting to accept the offer to disappear from these societies and to live a free life in a cosmopolitan and variety-embracing society elsewhere. This in turn leads to a terrible shortage of women in the ultra-Islamic areas, with thousands of men ending up dying either in duels over a remaining woman or in suicides after they have ended up without a wife.

Many good, caring together from different independent societies get together to discuss the possible solutions to this problem, and many ideas are trialled, including some that pair up male singletons with older female widows until such time as when the old widow dies and then a new loving wife may be sought. Even after the quran is slightly changed to make it say that a sinner must be offered the chance to leave town, repent, or will otherwise face a barbaric punishment, it still takes many years for the risk of violence toward women in these villages to sink.

Those women who find the bravery inside them to go to a multicultural society, find the shock of suddenly being without the overbearing and controlling family to be a mixed blessing at first, but fortunately there are a lot of options and a lot of loving affectionate welcoming people out there to help them blend in and to find a good life here. Some even go on to become leaders, authors or heads of social care, counselling or psychiatry once they get the hang of the way free life works, and most do end up making videoconferencing friends with people in their family and in their village of origin in the end, once both sides work out how to avoid offending the other.

Oil money is shared out widely, with trans-arab in control of the Gulf's biggest oil-extraction projects: all communities in Asia and Africa end up receiving equal shares of the profits, regardless of where the oil wells are situated. A double share is offered only by the poorer half of the 25 largest by population, and by the two poorest smaller communities, and only on a 5-year review cycle, just as the overlap between the richest 30% and the smallest 45% of communities are placed on half shares of the oil profit.

Repeated appeals, raids, legal challenges and mobs and militias seeking the take-over of a mine, an oil field, or an airport, city or industrial facility and are dealt with using inter-regional riot police resources, as many as required. It would be lovely to say that everyone agreed to share fairly right from the start, but that's where we distinguish between unrealistic utopias and the fuller recording of history we are talking about here.

Vandals, thieves and corrupt agents are painstakingly identified through a large combination of entrapment, covert surveillance and other evidence-collecting schemes. It would have been nice to bring about a good world entirely through voluntary, spontaneous and instinctively ethical actions, but in the end, there are always a few greedy or crooked opportunists who do need to be taken through a court process or two before they learn their lessons and abandon the crooked ways. In a few extreme cases people have had to be settled into prison insane asylums for life, just to prevent them from victimising any more people, and these places have to be well-resourced to stop them from victimising each other in there too.

Even in there, no bad deed goes unpunished, and no cry for help goes un-responded-to. If a person is insane enough to harm or steel, he or she clearly needs a lot of medication and a lot of complex treatment programmes compete with one another in global league tables to see which can get the best calm and civilised outcome stats. The world also receives a lot of complex treatment programme ideas competing, in massive large trials with one another in global league tables to see which can get the best calm and civilised outcome also in terms of the rehabilitation of people after their first or second offence, with new ideas constantly added to the process and with not-so-successful ideas falling out of use.

Other lucrative industries and other forms of mining are placed on similar schemes that share the proceeds out widely across entire continents. Multinational countries are, by 2097, taking over a big range of remits that were once reserved for the nation states. The wider reach the access to energy, to input from so many places, helps it to find a luscious menu of truly good advisable solutions to apply in solving each of the world's main problems.

No longer are the biggest companied and corporations in the world able to choose one wealthy tax exile country to have all their company profits taxed in. The big IT, finance, consulting, manufacturing, retail and innovative sectors are all placed into a new global regulator's remit, who ensures that the world will never be without competition and choice, and that no company ever pays its owners or its board unreasonable sums, while also diverting the revenues from sales, profit and income taxes on to the benefit of all the elected local community governments all over the world. Criminal groups and tax cheats no longer have anywhere to hide, as traceable, reversible, recorded transactions begin to replace paper cash all over the world, reducing most types of crime dramatically.

On the local level, a round-robin voting system is used to select the head of the executive body of government, and his chosen finance minister and the biggest other three parties in the legislature each get to submit rival budget plans to the voters, who pick the one that makes the most sense to them as their destination percentage split at the end of the upcoming five-year period.

Many self-governing local areas are now holding an IQ test to work out which migrants from other continents to admit, while others go purely by the level of need, the existing links to this area, the shortage category skills they bring with them, or the amount of wealth the person has. With so many different systems in simultaneous use, there is a big new demand for advice-giving agencies just to help a migrant decide which community to apply to move to. Nearly all of them admit people on a ten-year probation that fails them if they commit any form of crime, or if they end up being on unemployment benefits for more than a set percentage of the time.

Trans-brit, trans-eur, trans-oc, trans-east, trans-west, trans-sib, trans-southam, trans-carib, trans-alaskumbia and trans-mex are trialling a number of freedom to enter systems that allow people to move freely between the continents. These do not apply to people from other parts of Asia and Africa, as immigration remains a hot political issue in many areas. While there is a broad agreement allowing the people of many hundreds of areas to roam freely between all these areas, there are also areas with partial admittance and with extra clauses providing for further permits, checks, references or fees.

Nonetheless many areas continue to wish to pick and choose which applicants to admit, with most having such a system for applicants from Asia and Africa (and the top 100 or top 500 applicants per area per year are admitted), such systems are also in use for moving into the non-signatory areas from neighbouring areas and from areas elsewhere. While this is still commented on as being cruel to black Africans, it is slowly improving, from year to year, with people in Africa who have acquired a lot of knowledge about any one city in Europe generally winning the right to go there through the special selection committees route, and similar systems also help people from Asia and from Central America to move to Australia, Europe, or to North, Central or South America, or to an island somewhere that is just right for them, once they have learned a lot about their chosen favourite destination in particular and once they have memorised its taxi drivers map or become able to lecture about its history, even without falling in the special shortage skills categories.

Similarly, if an applicant has learned semi-fluent Finnish, Latvian, Welsh, Irish, Breton, Slovenian, Belarussian, Estonian, Galician, Catalan, Inuit, Lapp, Amish, Hopi, Algonquin, Blackfoot, Seminole, Cherokee, Basque, Sami, Icelandic, Norwegian, Ukrainian, Bulgarian, Albanian, Polish, Greek or Slovak before moving there, maybe through a mixture of distance learning courses, online learning and short visits with intensive courses, or has made a written commitment to learn it within a year of moving there, a five year residency and work permit all-in application that later converts into a permanent residency right is sure to succeed.

While the birth rate remains particularly high in those extra religious societies, a variety of education and birth control option giving programmes are starting to make headway, seeking to stabilise the numbers before irreparable damage is done to the environment by human overcrowding. A combination of tougher measures is also under consideration to bring the villages with the highest birth rates in the world closer to normality, though these debates remain highly controversial, difficult and heated.

For now, only six women in the whole world over the past 50 years (plus 2,600 men, most of whom were convicted rapists or cereal hit-and-run nest-flighters) have undergone forced sterilisation while they were asleep, and these were all cases where the children were destined to be poorly looked after and extremely heavily disabled and in much pain. Instead, the usual solution is to offer a special high-end elite education fees paying, family-get-together-supporting and holidays-improving allowance to people with three children that they will only get at full reward levels if they don't have any more, and this reduces by 10% with each additional child. The only unfortunate by-product of this is that the world finds a few abandoned babies who nobody owns up to, and of course the best provisions it can offer do cost a lot of money, but the alternatives are, on balance, not choose-able.

The UN, once a one-off get-together to see what all needs coordinating, and who needs the most help in getting things rolled out, soon evolves from being a mini League of Nations that meets once a year to talk about whatever is troubling them at the time to a new world government with bigger fuller solutions to bigger worldwide problems in the core of its remit. Rather than having factions, nationalities, elections, polarisations and wrangling, it is soon decided to give each trans-regional body an equal decision-making status and an equal share of the jobs at this new institution.

None should be neglected and none should ever dominate over the others. Each UN job must fully serve the interests of the people of the entire world, and the best way to select the best people to work here is to have a panel of ten top Un staffing and success-finding managers be selected in a process that begins with each trans-region submitting two good applicants into the process, and it ends when all the scores are in, and all those who chose to use their entire packet of scores to eliminate one applicant in particular have succeeded in their quest, while the ten most universally credible applicants have now won a five year term on the world government's executive board.

Pol Pot and the Khmer Rouge may only ever come to rule in one single cluster of villages, and here too not one person is ever to be harmed. When the violence breaks out, inter-malay and inter-pac send in the troops to rescue the victimised and to arrest and send to insane asylums all the culprits. Thanks to their rapid and brave intervention, what could have been a massive massacre was stopped short on the third day, and most of the intended victims managed to get to a safe province nearby, until the time came when it was safe to return home.

Idi Amin, Mobutu, Kabila, Mugabi, Qaddafi and dozens of other greedy tyrant rulers of African, Asian, American, European or Oceanian societies succeed only in attaining a maximum of four three-year terms of office in much smaller and far less militarised countries, and they end up pocketing only their government salary, as a system of checks and balances, including independent monitoring, tip-offs, trackable traceable cash and secret surveillance ensures that none of them ever manage to steal or redivert the main flows of their people's tax money.

This is more easily said than done, and it does come with its controversies, costs and with the potential that some of the people who are there to police this also end up entangled in the temptation of corruption, criminal, crooked, bribe-able, double-agents or ineffective. But through frequent rotation of staff, hidden cameras and bugging devices, along with high-tech upskilling, training, creativity, good funds traceability and frequent trap situations that test the integrity of those in positions of power, a much less corrupt and much more ethical system of government does indeed come into being, with the people who need the most help benefitting the most from these clean-up initiatives.

Iraq must never all fall into the hands of any one group, be they pro Saddam Hussein bathists, members of his earlier alliance of parties who he later the out of the governing alliance, Kurdish tigers, ISIS, centrist or leftist moderates, Shiite militia, religious or secular new or old Sunni factions or Shiite hardliners. A wise trans-arab super-body enjoys the powers to step in to make sure that each political and ethnic group has plenty of areas where it can govern, that the people in each of these differently governed areas enjoys plenty of genuine choice in their elections, and that none of these groups is ever cruelly overrun or mistreated by any of the others.

In the year 2013, a miracle happens in the great plains: Realising that they have been left out of the big discussions the world is having, the big exchanges of data and the big partnerships that genuinely do solve society's great problems, and occurring immediately after a trans-west summit of republicans, 37 of the 39 the last remaining county-size strongholds of US-republicanism who have, until now, refused to join the UN and in some cases trans-west too, situated in the remote and agricultural valleys west of the Mississippi river, now decide to join the UN.

To celebrate this bringing in of over half of the world's remaining non-participants, all in one month, a lavish and colourful new UN HQ, packed full of meaningful artwork and furniture conveying optimistic progress-seeking messages is opened in New York, making the existing HQ in Geneva take on a secondary role. The United Nations, having already been launched in 1914 as a League of Nations, now grows to have new ambitions: better coordination of information regarding the evaluation of various products, services and pilot-trial tested schemes, programmes and ideas, a new plan to create a "language for the world" and a new "currency for the world" are launched, and a set of global regulators whose role it is to bring about a fairer and better-functioning tax and spend system worldwide, including also the elimination of tax exiles, loop holes, monopolies, cartels, and the sale of unsafe and unreliable products.

The new worldwide currency comes into being on the 1st of January 2024, using a mixture of ten recent and less recent dates' exchange rates as the permanently set conversion rate and by the 31st of January 2024, every single jurisdiction all over the world has "opted in" and is now using this new currency only. The new language comes into being gradually and very slowly, but over the course of a 95-year period, from 2023 to 2118, undergoing a process of only three words at a time being replaced worldwide, once every three months, with one and the same word to be used from now on everywhere, complete universality of communication without the need for translations is truly achieved worldwide.

A panel made of government, university and dictionary master people who speak, between them, each one of the world's 100 most-spoken languages well, while also speaking English, French, Spanish, Mandarin, Russian, Hindi or Arabic. This specially assembled global people's body, known as trans-glob-lang ensures that each language has an approximately equal number of its words chosen (with double quotas given to the top 20 most widely spoken languages) as the new global word for this, while also making sure that words that sound nice, are easy to pronounce and easy to spell, and are comparatively shorter and less confusable with other global words are chosen every time.

There are, of course, more than 95 x 4 x 3 words in any language, and so the final 25 three-month periods each contain one word more than the previous, each time, and the final stage contains all the rest. The decision-making panel members spend all their time evaluating the options for the next three words, with all translations considered and evaluated using ten criteria to score them all on, in search of the best one to pick for global use. At least three of the final five options in this process is always from one of the top ten most widely spoken languages in the world, and one of the final five is always found from among the least widely spoken languages in the world, the ones who were not among the 100 languages to be on the decision-making body. This allows all sorts of indigenous people to be honoured and praised for having the world's best word for this, so good that the entire planet will one day be using it.

A simplified form of grammar is applied universally, with specially written software converting all books and news into the new global language, and the very last stage, bringing in "the rest of the dictionary" into the global language ends up being a tournament-shaped vote of the top 16 languages, competing to get voted into the quarter-finals, then semi-finals and then the final, where it ends up being English and Hindi who are put to a global vote to select the final words to make the new global language complete at last.

This eventually kills off all sorts of concepts of being different, separate, mistreated, distinct nations, and from now on there is no longer a remoteness in places that speak other languages. It means there is never again a shortage of TV programmes, cinema films, books, news and magazines to read, or people in special-interest chat rooms. The world becomes a much better and more united place.

It also ends the need for translators to exist, except, in the first few years, as a way of capturing what the elderly, who still speaks the old languages only is telling us. It makes traveling so much easier, and having global discussions about politics, the news, science, social trends, travel, cooking, work, study, research, hobbies and other topics. Schools no longer need to teach any more foreign languages, which frees them up to teach people more about the decision-making processes, advice and tools that can help them in real life.

Only three new words per three month period, over the first 70 years and then a few more words per month thereafter are "brought in" (merged into one world-wide) and dozens of widely spoken languages all around the world will each contribute equally to this new language: When the English word "peace" , the Spanish word for "friendship" and the Hindi word for "cooking" are rolled out in the first weeks of the new world language's gradual existence, all translations of this new word, in all press, book, email and internet writing are automatically "translated over" to this new word, so that by the middle of week three, even a Somali, Korean or Burmese news headline using any of these words now automatically substitutes the new *globalese* word for peace, friendship and cooking into all its news articles, along with all books, including the quran, shakespeare and the bible. Europe, China and North America have already been starting to gradually roll out, through forerunner initiatives that did not know this was coming globally, a common language, using similar evaluation principles, technology and pace of change controls, and the words they have chosen are automatically entered as front-runners and finalists, but never as the only option, in the global process to pick the one word for each meaning.

23 years in, there are still a lot of localities who have voted not to go along with the change, but eventually, they see sense, allowing all children to learn and use this new language. Those same localities become the places not so many people wish to visit, which affects their tourist and conventions trade heavily, but eventually each of these areas has a change of government, either to a left-centre grouping who understands the benefits of joining this movement, or to a new generation of more globally aware young leaders, who now do all their reading, TV viewing and thinking in the new global language.

By the end of year 35 it is no longer awkward expressing yourself when travelling around the world without multiple language fluency, as, regardless of which border you have crossed, the new global words, given plenty of time to slip into your vocabulary, are now exactly the same (plus or minus some persisting but rather pleasant local pronunciation accents) all over the world.

Whereas, in your reality, many words have two or more very different meanings, which makes confusion more likely at every turn, this new global language is specially assembled to be truly brilliant, allowing all listeners all over the world to know exactly what the person speaking or writing this means, even if irony or ridicule is implied but not obvious, for which a simple "ovek" sentence ending is brought in globally to show that humour was the intention of the spoken sentence.

Further changes are made on a slower pace, after the year 95 full step 380 launch, with only one word every 15 years being replaced with a new one hereafter, often picked from a more old obscure language, or specially invented, just to ensure that further

improvements in the conciseness, clarity, shortness,
pronounceableness, unconfusableness, the systematic and logical
relationship with other words and in the poetic sound of the world
language can occur, and then, after five such 15-year periods, it is
decided to add one more year before each further review, so a 16-
year period of no changes follows, in 2193, and then a 17-year
period, etc.

The world government, made up of a fair balance of representatives
from all of the world's religious, political, old lingual and regional
groups, has many challenges, issues and struggles to consider
making a wise intervention in, or not, and in doing so, it must always
make sure that it does so only to give people and localities more
options, more help, and better-informed options, rather than to
remove options, overrule and prescribe.

Best of all: There are no veto powers, and so the law, the global
human rights charter, the recommendations and the availability of
help for the most vulnerable applies equally all over the world.
Every jurisdiction area initially pays just 0.02% of its GDP to the
UN as tax, rising slightly to a new mutually agreed 4-tier system in
later years, and 57% of the areas qualify for a 30% reduction in this
tax, as these areas offer all migrants and all residents guaranteed
jobs, income and housing as part of the highly successful universal
system of local-area-owned business with an unlimited intake of
labour to share the work between. Of these, 22 areas even qualify for
a 0.0% rate of tax, as these areas contribute satisfactorily and fully
both to the x-offenders super-welcome-scheme and to the world
army recruitment system, while also coming under the poor region
heading in the UN's global anti-poverty initiative that extends tax
decreases to help more money stay in these areas.

Guns and Hunting: Although some forms of pest control, meat
farming, endangered plant helping entrapment, bear, crocodile and
lion tranquilizing and limited ethical and sustainable fishing are still
in use at first, all guns and all big game-, bird-, fox- and rabbit
hunting are completely phased out worldwide, over a three-year
transition programme, with a few exemptions and non-participating
areas to mop up later. It started with a ban on the manufacture and
sale of all firearms. Then it got expanded to a number of cash-paying
trade-in options, and then to full confiscation. Even sharp knives are
no longer publicly accessible, and people now go to special places to
have bread, textile or wood cut up for day-to-day use, which is a
pain for some, but it makes life for our youngest and oldest a lot
safer, a lot.

Completely de-gunning society was never going to be quick or easy
to achieve, and it was always going to encounter a lot of entrenched
resistance, especially in the Americas and in Africa, but it had to be
done, as human society was completely out of control, and organized

criminal gangs were in no way tolerable, subjecting a lot of people to a lot of horrific coercion, and it had to be accompanied with a lot of digging around, as the crafty people then buried and hidden their weapons from trans-west, from the police and from the other degunning, deweaponizing authorities for a long time.

This gave rise to new problems, including a rise in night-time and holiday-time burglary, which required launching a better bedroom alarm button response system in response. Also, rat, rabbit and fox, mouse, raccoon, possum, squirrel, beetle, ant and deer populations were now becoming so big in some areas that people were starting to panic. But there are a number of solutions to each problem, and in most cases a catch, sterilize and release program is enough to bring these populations under control.

On the opposite side, this still did not solve the problem of critters getting run over in traffic ever so often. Well, fortunately, with trans-eur, trans-east, trans-brit, the UN, and other backing, initiatives to construct protective fences, tunnels, netting, perches, hedges and trenches were brought in worldwide, thus saving billions of innocent lives and sparing billions of bird, mammal, turtle, insect, frog, crab and other youngsters from the grief of losing their mummy or daddy or baby.

Many pockets of mass human migration, including Tower Hamlets, St Dennis, Lyon, Queens, Bronx, Manhattan, Dade, Philadelphia, Toronto, Dublin, Bruxelles-Midi, Hamburg, Köln, Berlin, Moscow, Istanbul, Athens, Johannesburg, Guyana, Fiji, Hawaii, Ibiza, Singapore, Mumbai, San Francisco, LA, Detroit, Vancouver, Mexico City, Rio, Stockholm, Vienna, Leicester, Hounslow, Tower Hamlets, Thetford, Yarmouth, Cambridge, Slough, Portsmouth, Birmingham, Burnley and Bradford, Lisbon, Danzig, Sarajevo, Hong Kong, Shanghai, Sydney, Dubai, Lagos, Casablanca, Kuwait, Qatar and Brussels are all placed under a special electoral system that guarantees that its 10 biggest minority groups (defined in terms of being different ethnicities or family beliefs from the surrounding hundred mile areas) get to govern these areas, with the ethnic majority only electing one third of the delegates to their 15-member city-parliaments. Some of these, such as Bradford and Tower Hamlets even go so far as to set up an all-Muslim second legislative chamber with a veto and a rewind option on all changes.

The continuation of mass-expulsions from areas in Africa and in Asia that vote to have a society based on Sharia law leads to each of the above hyper-cosmopolitan areas being overrun with thousands, and sometimes millions of displaced migrants who soon become additional euro-Muslims. The growth of this population in Europe does not go unnoticed, and a number of county shires, departments, provinces, kreise, oblasts, voivodeships, estadoses, local authority areas, districts and boroughs decide to set up a new quota limiting the number of new Muslims allowed to move into the area per year to 5, 10, 20, 50, 100, 200, or 500. While each of these specific quota limits is only brought in in a few places, it does give places that are particularly anxious about the prospect a chance to control the pace of the influx. It also creates a need for special new panels, scoring systems, refences and evaluation entities to be made up in these areas to ensure that the application process remains as fair as can be.

Overall, this scheme is regarded with widespread support, though many experts still argue that whatever the "best way" is, should be applied everywhere, not just in some provinces. There are two instances in the 2030s where areas who are currently experiencing their Muslim population rising from recently still under 45% to now over 50% are met with such a stressed out and hateful response that the interregional sees no alternative but to intervene. In addition to this it also intervenes in 17 places in Asia where tensions between secular and reformation-orthodox Muslims has led to such escalations in tensions that a two-state solution ends up being necessary. The two-state solution is an effective way of giving each individual and each family a safe place to move to, where their way of life is under no threat at all.

Other provinces end up receiving a three-chamber legislative system instead, with one chamber for all, one for the Muslims and one for all the others, where both ethnic group, sectarian, ideology or belief communities are able to block, water-down, modify and to reverse changes that they were against all along, and where each is given a budget to spend and a set of government posts to fill. A third set of solutions we see being occasionally applied is to scrap all barriers to inward migration of non-Muslims, though some of those do find it hard to work out which of the applicants was lying on their application.

ISIS ends up with a homeland granted in the NorthEast corner of what we know as Syria and with a second in Chechnya, a third in Southern Afghanistan and a 4th in Niger, allowing its adherents to live a pure, clean fully Muslim devoted devout sin-free life-style. The decision to grant these is much criticized, but it is done in good faith, as hating any group of people and depriving it of its own specially crafted utopia is not really the true human way. Other right-wing societies, including scientologist, Montana freeman, ultra-libertarian, ultra-orthodox Jewish, aryan evangelical, Amish, branch dravidian, mayan, voodoo, rastafarian, anarchist, pre-Christian druid, falun gong, kuo min dang, mormon, taoist, zoroastrian, and many other fringe groups are also allowed and granted a true homeland where they can build their unique version of utopia.

This does make it harder to bring everyone together when a global problem-solving effort is under way, make no mistake, but in a world where most solutions have to be pragmatically made in a multi-wave timetable way that only includes the willing in each wave, that's how it needs to be, and besides: what's the hurry?

Leicester becomes the first city to put a gathering of Hindu scholars in as its second legislative chamber that also has the power to overrule the verdicts of its judges for up to one year. This leads to a number of other areas putting all-migrant, Jewish, African, Muslim, oriental, indigenous, pro-gay, feminist, vegetarian, x-offender and pagan bodies into their local province government's policy-formulation committees, which leads to a very large number and variety of new schemes and rules being trialled, all over the world.

In Libya, where trans-arab has been keeping an eye on the rise of supporters of change, Qaddafi is made by trans-arab to accept that he can only hang on to one small corner of Libya, and only for his life time plus two years only for a chosen successor. When he sees his movement being toppled in elections everywhere, he reluctantly agrees to retreat into this region, along with all of his loyal forces and bodyguards, and with his nearest and dearest. This one SouthWest Libya area, where only 6% of Libyans live, is where his reign will continue, but within the constraints of a multipart electoral system that gradually gets 25% then 48% then 52% and eventually, 45 years later, 100% of all power in this area over the course of a slow but safe and mutually agreeable multi-stage transition period. There he lives on, freely able to write his books and to speak to the media of the world.

The ayatollah of Persia undergoes a similar "managed retreat". So does Mugabi on SE Zimbabwe and the Castro family in Cuba, who both find themselves voted out and suddenly no longer welcome in the government they worked so long to build, but luckily the inter-regs saw fit to give them the security of a retreat-to, so they could be safe, themselves and not dead or in foreign exile.

The tragedy of the 9/11 disaster in Manhattan in 2001, which was not prevented, sadly, tragically, reveals the need for a tougher system vis-à-vis extremists. It also changes a lot of provinces all around the world into "no more than five Muslims per year are to move here" resistant and standoffish lands. The world has been giving all the most extreme and hostile groupings a place where they can flourish and from where they can dump all their lies onto the internet from. This is further exacerbated by the Charlie Hedbo murders and by a number of rock concert, city bridge, city square and road system bombings, all over Europe, Israel and New Zealand, which the interreg system, the police intelligence system and the media never saw coming and which the entire world reacts to in total shock.

It leads to a lot of soul-searching, a lot of debate and a lot of anger in the big discussions that shape the world's response to these. It strengthens the reactionary and hate-fuelled far right in most elections, while also weaking the centre-left. The wise majority of the planet does eventually realise that is is never right to punish the many for the actions of a few, which means that stripping all locations of some of their electoral options, or of their chosen elected leaders is not an option.

Instead, we see a raft of new laws, criminalising all sorts of complicity, assistance, influence-giving, radicalising and keeping secret from the police a number of relationships to these attacks. Unfortunately, this requires not just local but also international taxes to rise, to fund these actions, which is such a shame, as we are getting a little more like East Germany and Moscow (in reality A 1950-89) by the day. Let's prey it never goes all the way, as it would mean the loss of almost all our rights, freedoms and the loss of trust itself.

After a lot of surveillance work, there are a number of arrests of minor, marginal and major contributors to these terrible attacks. And much progress is made also in making the ingredients for bomb-making much less widely available, much more controlled and measured, and in putting roadblocks in some spots where cars and pedestrians should never overlap. Tough decisions have to be made, and in the long-run, no onslaught to eradicate these groupings completely can really be made. Well, not until such time as when one of those groupings, ISIS, goes completely rogue, vicious, deadly and non-compliant, in 2017. This is when the world leaders unite, with a 473-0 UN vote to support an exceptional move to ban ISIS from all governments, all forms of gun-ownership and from all elections globally for a 10-year period to allow all weapons, all militiamen, all bomb-making tools and items, and all its propaganda to be found and exposed, and to free all those who were being held hostage (or who had their doubts) from having to bear life in those tough locations.

By the year 2009, the last remaining vestiges of residual one-town-only powers for kings, nobility, barons, dukes, popes and for the successors of dictators such as Franco, Lukashenko, Putin, Kim-Yong-Un, She Jinping, Menangagwa, Kabila, Zuma, Castro, Chavez, Morales, Qaddafi and Mussolini finally ends, with locally elected multi-party systems, using many different electoral methods, rising and flourishing everywhere, now that the last of the autocrats has been retired. In the 2170s the world government pledges to let each locality, borough, district and province have a voting system election, to choose the same as now or a different way of holding elections. This gives areas that have fallen under one or two party dominance the chance to open the door to better ways, while also letting the most misfunctioning gridlocked large coalition systems try something else for a limited length of time and then get the chance to switch back if it wishes to.

Many great men such as Kofi Annan, U Thant, Ban Ki Moon and Boutrous Boutrous-Ghali (no relation to me, though I was named after him when I changed my birth name) have served in reality B as UN secretary generals, and these were great men with impeccable morals and with a daring devotion to tackle the difficult and controversial issues of their time in search of a mutually beneficial best for all solution. You and I can only hope that maybe one day some of us can match their wonderful input into the pursuit of world peace and a better dignity for all living beings in the world. We can only hope and aspire to the fate that maybe one day our efforts will be recognized as making a big difference and for our contributions to building a good world government. It probably won't be possible for us, but we can try and by releasing this book I feel I have done something to hopefully help the world out too.

Venezuela's 26 states (much like also those of Brazil, the US, Mexico, Germany and Australia), in reality A, all go very different routes, depending on how the voters respond in the ballot box, thus leading to some areas where nationalisations are comprehensive, some where they never started to happen, some where they are slow cautious and not as far-reaching, and others where they were backed but later reversed. In doing so, they allow a larger number of people who are closer in so many ways to the issues that local people face to make those big decisions that help empower the local people and the dialect-speaking and immigrant ethnic groups to build a far better system that responds better to the lessons it has learned and that offers people more ways to flourish and be free, economically independent and politically influential at the same time.

Syria, Lebanon, Iran, Iraq, Turkey, Russia, Vietnam, China, Mexico, Nicaragua, Venezuela, Korea, the US, France, Britain, Germany, Spain and all sorts of other places never end up existing as one mega-state with winner-takes-all power struggles. This has been said once before, but it is worth repeating. As a result of having so many smaller regions, the potential for confrontation is so much smaller too, and so is the scale. It also allows different groups to fully flourish, rule and put their ideas into action simultaneously, and without spoiling it for the others. It also allows people who have run for office or supported someone who ran for office and did not win to move into a nearby country where the kind of things they believe in are the norm anyway. This makes for a much better world, one where there is not winners and losers, as in reality A after every election, but rather there is winners and the different winners next door, setting up something they can support in their area, while watching how the other way they did not want to be a part of fares from afar.

Pollution: all forms of pollution are a terrible thing, and they cause both immediate and long-term harm, especially when their cumulative scale is allowed to get out of hand. This is why certain filters have to be mandatory world-wide, and this cannot wait for those who opt-in only to take part. Similarly, emissions from all sorts of facilities, industrial plants, chimneys and fires all need to be monitored, not for its own sake but to ensure that as soon as we humans of earth fins a better way, a way that works in a cleaner manner, this way is rolled out worldwide, making the world cleaner.

We cannot have opt-in only systems regulating the fumes that come out of cars and the industrial wate that goes into rivers. It has to be a proper worldwide high standard that prevents all the bad things from happening in the first place, while also making a good standard of living still feasible for all of us, and this, in the end, can only be done with a world government that is big enough, strong enough, well enough informed and tooled up and enabled to get the problem solved in all parts of the planet, and to do so before lots of needless deaths and illnesses can occur, preventatively. This is why we do need a global world order of tax-funded pro-earth actions, and there cannot be any disagreement on this, not unless you are totally evil, suicidal or misinformed.

By 2104 trans-east has given the power of self-determination to over 600 areas in its East-of-the-Mississippi realm, and so there no longer is a United States, or a Confederate States of America or a Canada either. Each area corresponding to a US county (or NY borough, Louisiana parish or Canadian or Alaska local government census area) now has the full power to choose its own leadership, and the voting systems vary from area to area, but only very few of them are stuck in a malfunctional US-style two-party system, where hostile heinous lies about the main opponent are enough to win an election. Instead, each area's issues are given proper detailed suggested fixes in the debates and in the now-binding election manifestos, and whoever ends up being elected is then bound to follow through and make those promises come true, unless the council votes a change down or adds in its own changes.

The Olympic Games and their many continental qualifiers now play host to delegations from over 2,647 countries, including Merseyside, Basque Country, Cornwall, Bretagne, Corsica, Versaille et Loire, Omsk, the Navajo nation, Mohawkland, Quebec, Aboriginal NW & Inner Australia, Brisbane, Gold Coast, Chiapas, Kurdishland, Chechnya, the Pueblo nation, and many, many others. The medals table is topped by teams from Brooklyn, Dade, LA, Cook (Chicago),

South Holland, Kurdishland, Kansai, Queensland, North Island New Zealand, Oslo, Jiangsu, Rheinland, Volgograd, Hertfordshire, St Louis, Wales, London, Sao Paolo, Mexico City, Buda Pest and Central Hungary, Skåne, Ile de France, Quebec, Dnjeprotrovsk, Seoul, Kanto, Buenos Aires, Croatia, Romania, Catalonia, Bavaria, Silesia, Prussia, Glasgow, Jiangsu, Guangdong, Szechuan, Henan and Moscow. Each of these have made the overall summer games medal table top ten in one of the five most recent games, and no one team has topped the table more than twice.

Drug crime and mafias: well, this is a global problem too, transcending borders and continents. We could opt to save money and to let them continue flourishing and ruining people's lives as they currently do in reality A. But why the hell would we choose this course of action? They are a huge problem and we do not need to wait for two thirds of us to have experienced it ourselves before we take concerted international action to solve it.

Company profits: A number of independent provinces and other entities have decided to enact the smart-override system to company profits. This varies by sector, size of company, age of company and economic recessionary climate, but it tends to place a three-way split of all company profits: 82% go into taxes, 04% to the shareholders and 14% into the rainy day, foundation use and better future fund, at least for larger, long-established companies in not overly volatile and recession-affected sectors. Other countries have other systems in use, but I do wish to point out that the smart-override system does allow all of us to suffer less of a tax burden on our day-to-day earnings, shopping, renovation, expansion and licence renewal actions, as most of the tax revenues your society needs can be harvested in this way, rather than letting it all go to people who do not work for the company and who have done nothing to help it or the society at large by buying some company shares.

Ejected serial killers, armed robbers, burglars, paedophiles and rapists often tend to get barred from living in the city they call home, which is all good and well and understandable, but what happens in the next place, the place they end up going to live in next? Well, that's a good question. We don't want a world where the same sort of crime is committed again and again, and this is exactly what would happen if we did not have much sharing of information between the independent authority areas.

Well, trans-eur, trans-pac and trans-east have each pioneered a scheme that places additional tracking, surveillance and bugging into x-offenders devices, even if they now live in a different remit area. This is a great way at stopping them from doing it again, but what happens when they either find a way to fool the tracking device, take it off, hide their true actions from it or move out of the continent to a region that does not operate the same system? Well, there are a hundred answers to these questions. I can't pretend these are simple and easily resolved, but efforts to improve the way these people can be monitored for their actions without impeding their career options, and new forms of transcontinental cooperation and information and advice sharing do all contribute greatly to solving these problems.

Public sector debt: Even in the utopia that is reality A, we still cannot pretend that there is no issue with local, regional and global governments ending up spending way more than what the collected taxes add up to. And so, as the years go by, an ever larger percentage of next year's tax revenues will be needed to pay for the overspend we had years ago, plus the interest that is payable on this debt. So how do we solve this problem? Should each entity be restricted to having no increases in spend until it has the money it will need in the bank? Or is there some clever way that we have not thought of that may make this problem a thing that has finally been solved? Well, I would love to have your input into this if you have the answer (I am reachable on fanofgreatsportingaction@gmail.com).

Trying out the five or six most brilliant ideas, all simultaneously, just to see which one works best may be the best way to solve this problem. Some of the big ideas involve either annulling some of the debt, not paying it back, declaring partial bankruptcy, setting up a second central bank that issues money that pays the debts off, or creating a second currency that is just for owning land, private additional pensions, distant future holidays, special shipments and company shares, in order to have different rates of inflation and different hand-outs to all in one currency that does not affect the other.

A lot of thought is needed to work out which the best front-runner scheme could be, and trial and error is a good way for less genius people like me to work out which way works best. But overall, I would be very surprised if letting the debt keep on growing forevermore turns out to be the best way. Plus interregional or global cooperation may be beneficial here, especially if we are now in a world with one currency and one central bank interest rate only. Maybe it could be better solved by having some of the debt turned into five-year bonds that are funded 90% from newly created money and 10% from tax hikes, or some tweak or augmentation of one of the above ideas, maybe?

In addition to the many different electoral systems that flourish in the world we live in, of which proportional representation is the best way to get a lot of groups to have some of the say each, but round-robin (eg a vs b + a vs c + b vs c) systems are probably the best way of electing one overall leader, budget, plan, solution, governing team, etc. The median numbers vote system has been massively underutilised in helping to set the scale of a new budget, the penalty or age cut-off or other quota on anything involving any sort of number in the decision-making process; jury systems and mini-referendums, including elections through opinion polling would be a terrific way of letting the people choose between the two possible routes to go next; a ransel party, where it main decision-making leaders are all chosen by a lottery is a novel but special way of making sure that the decisions and advocated actions of a party truly reflect what the wider society would have wanted; interselection tournaments among all applicants, of strangers, and among all who turn up are a great way of finding those who people tend to trust and to pick as their prospective leaders in a way that may find a better leadership team than any other way; and the use of intelligence, relevant knowledge and best solution finding exams, quizzes and contests could be a better way of finding those candidates for office who have the brain power to find new and better solutions and who have a better understanding of the problem as it currently stands.

Having made life so much better for all humans, let us return now to the plight of our cattle, pigs and poultry birds'. They too should have certain inalienable rights: Once substantial rights to a decent life are made global, requiring all kept birds and all farm animals to have seventeen rights, from birth to harvest, which make up a good and decent life with space to roam, dignity, clean ground, treats, ample perching places, and a painless death in their sleep, if they have to die prematurely at all. Don't get me wrong, there are still some appalling conditions in use on some farms, in 2023, all over the world, and there is a long way to go, but overall trans-eur, trans-east, trans-pac and all the other bigger bodies, plus the local authorities' actions have already made clear, big, substantial improvements in the lives and deaths of farm animals, and there is never, in recent memory, a decade where further real clear progress was not made, and so the future does look bright for all creatures now, at last, especially when the world government acts to bring best-practice to the places that have not spontaneously opted in, because they wanted to keep their costs lower.

Forests: The UN made every inch of forest land protected from ever being built on, way back in 1918, when it was first founded, and from ever being polluted, plus all hunting is also ended, following a three year transition programme, worldwide; fishing is phased out in most spots, especially in reefs and in rivers and anti-vermin and anti-insect products are made to be subject to a much more considerate, nonlethal, nonpainful and humane list of criteria, which is now being brought out worldwide.

There is still a world population problem, as the number of people on this planet is now dangerously close to 15 billion, which cannot be sustained with all the food, waste-collection and water-supply issues a population of this size requires. This is why some very difficult decisions have had to be made, and the three-child policy, now that it has been rolled out worldwide, along with the birth control options menu, is making a huge difference in this. But what happens when this is not enough, and the population shoots up to 38 billion?

Many a meeting of world leaders and of subject matter experts has grappled long and hard with this difficult subject. In the end, the only way to achieve a slow-down in world population growth is to have one, two, or three child households become the norm and for anything else (having more than three over a lifetime) to become rare. In achieving this, we needed to roll out a number of optional education, birth control and lifestyle option changes, bringing to an end the shaming of those with no children in regions where this was a big problem, by bringing in a system of escalating fines for the insult-slingers.

By making it so that the number of children a person has had now determines the official pension (and other allowance) category status equally as much as the number of contribution years (and the criminal record) does. This then determines the parents' pension amount. All young are given ample access to good education options, so we are not returning to the days of the one child policy, but we do need to keep the numbers under control, and men and women who have had children with more than two partners already are now starting to be given medical intervention to prevent them from having many more after this, until they have spent 15 full years in a perfectly functioning long-term loving partnership of parents first.

In areas with a large death at young age from diseases rate it would be too cruel to impose a two-child policy; but a four child policy, along with a massive upgrade in their healthcare systems may be right for these, while places where death under the age of 70 is extremely rare can be given a two child policy more easily; and the tolerance for people who have ended up having more children needs to remain soft, supportive and human, even when the overall figures are having to be kept a close eye on.

The problems of loneliness, singletons and a lack of desirable males or females in certain areas has also arisen in the UN get-togethers, and here the array of solution ideas is so dazzling that rather than reject all but one at stage one, the best thing to do was to start off by having each local authority area encouraged to try something different out, and to make each one hire 'someone from outside' to help evaluate its success or otherwise. Then the more in-depth evaluations can follow, and the better ones can be identified empirically (like with lab tests).

Solutions in use include some cities and countryside towns trial-legalising the seven husbands on seven days of the week system, which only around 2% of women would ever want to enter into, and even these would only want this for a short period of time before they choose one of them to be their hubby. A bunch of introducing single people to potential suiters who meet the main requirement criteria schemes, some of which involve video dates only at first,

a scheme of allocating dates by age, location and lottery; and the trial partners six-month reducing list size "tournament system", where the last person still to be on the list at the end of these months becomes the finacée, are all new and exciting contenders currently competing with many others on this list.

A whole load of systems of putting potential pairings together from within commonality categories is allowed to flourish, mostly through the private sector, all three of which serve to make sure that all people do find good long-term companions, affection and love. And each of these arms its participants with ample birth control, topic suggestion options, date venue options, and with a 'go away, meddling parents' option that, if used, can make them finable. It also arms them all with a "leave me alone, I said you're off my list" option, to make sure it all stays consensual, with no xs allowed to turn into stalkers or anything like that.

Guaranteed jobs, work, housing and income for all schemes have become rather popular, as the world government has been incentivising the use of them with tax and spend incentives, in order to generate more places people who find themselves displaced can flee to. More and more areas that don't yet have so many migrants living there have made the decision to become special socialist 'welcome here' places, in which all the jobs and all the income are dished out fairly and equally, according to how many people are available, who has signed up for which training, and how much work will need doing in this sector this week.

One in three areas worldwide, areas where all land and all businesses are either state-owned and employee-run, on a gradual transition in this direction programme, or are out on 10-year loans to privateers. One in 15 local authority area worldwide is now designated a 'welcome to all' place, which means that people with heavy criminal records are welcome and supported to get into respectable honest work here.

Global tax rates vary from 0.2% of GDP in 'guaranteed work for all' places, 0.1% tax levels are in place in the 'welcome to all' places, which are fantastic towns for allowing x-convicts who have lost their welcome where they have come from to work their way back into respectable society – the ultra-close monitoring system here, with CCTV cameras inside and outside each and every building help to ensure that none of them are tempted to re-offend; the shortage of younger women in these x-offender towns is resolved with a seven-days-per-week wide-sharing scheme of the single older (mostly widowed and divorced) women, from whom a good reference can go a long way, and who are to be empowered and treated ultra-well at all times.

With the younger women and future wives choosing their husbands very carefully and gradually, and with the older widowed or divorced ones swapping out one of their seven one-day-per week husbands every two years for a new one, things are quite interesting in the lands of Kern, Massapequa, Irkutsk, Uppsala, Cadiz and Naples. But most jurisdiction areas are instead opting for a solution that simply makes everyone choose five (to ten) good sets of friends (who tend to come with a partner) to keep in constant touch with, and it allows them to pick their favourite four of these once a year and to swap out the fifth lot of people for a new pairing that is recommended by a special computer formula system based on what it can be programmed to know about your type of person, the kind you get on best with. A version of this for matching up single people is also in use, and further improvements keep being added to it every year, making it a fairly good and reliable way to meet new people who fit well with you.

The global tax is currently set at 0.3% of GDP in lands where land and businesses are owned by local individuals, rather than by the state, and 0.4% in lands where land and businesses are owned by individuals and companies who do not necessarily live locally.

To be eligible for any of the categories below 0.4% a society must also have a clean outcome when it is examined for birth rates, pollution rates, crime rates, corruption rates, income and wealth inequality rates, good-regulation rates, good mediation schemes, women's empowerment, birth control, victim-help promoting part-time-working, and freedom of expression civil liberties, with the required levels of each rising further for areas applying for the coveted 0.2% and 0.1% tax rates. The ability to pay is also taken into consideration, and temporary adjustments of up to 0.07% upwards or downwards are applied in response to localised times of particular wealth or hardship, with the funds these taxes raise used to benefit the people and nature everywhere in the world.

As there are now, in 2024, over 17,130 completely free and independent countries in the world, it is deemed unnecessary to have one representative from each one sitting at the world government at all times or at any of the trans-regional bodies, and so five overarching neutrals are employed to oversee each trans-reg body's work instead, with the selection process allowing a variety of quotas and regional interests to be applied in the gradual elimination of applicants, until the five are found who best represent the entire world's true interests. Elections are also held, not so much to determine who fills which post, but more to help decide which initiatives need to receive more of the available funding instead.

A new trend of temporary and partial mergers of like-minded local authority areas, boroughs, counties, provinces and districts, such as in rural Kansas and Nebraska, in the New York City area, in the Thames Valley, in Central Finland, in most of Korea and Vietnam, and in Nordrhein Westfalen have made a lot of accelerated progress through a pooling of resources, an increase in specialisation and an increase choice of providers a big win for all. It is a brilliant new form of partnering up and making the best use of common resources, commonly used contracted out services, commonly used computer systems and more a wisely used and targets workforce that achieves more through better specialisation of job roles.

We expect this trend to further accelerate, as there is now nothing stopping two thousand communities, spread over four of five continents from forming one, two or three big centralised, temporary, voluntary service buying alliances on a trial-basis, with a joint leadership to tackle certain problems they all have and will all want handling in a similar and ever-improving way, making the people of the cooperating areas better way off together. After all, it's not like there will still be a language barrier, a plug-types or legislation-based systematic barrier, any residual mistrust or animosity, or a clash of national or trans-island systems.

The only thing preventing it from happening right now is fear of the unknown and a stupid reluctance to try something promising and new out. I notice that places who no longer have political party factions are far more open to try such progressive things out, while those who still have parties are also good at this when the same party finds 'very similar to me' twins elsewhere. As the same sort of grouping tends to be in power in a whole bunch of countries, these then find a way of bagging lots of gains by joining forces. When, a few years later, there is a change in who is in power over the area, a realigning tends to follow, with new international partnerships being brought in or switched over to, under which there is also much to be gained by pooling resources and by procuring the best solutions together, as part of a wider and better resourced management, buying and contracting team.

Covid-19 is a tough blow to the world in 2020, and it takes the world a long while before it develops the most potent of vaccines. But fortunately, those people who require a tighter lockdown in 2020 and those who require a looser one, can both, in our world, in reality A, if they so choose, move away to a differently governed land, not far away, for a while, which nobody can object to and which kind of works better for everyone, much like the way the huge variety of gambling, drugs, censorship, rehabilitation, welfare, and birth control laws seem to actually work much better for the world overall than having just one solution applied to all.

The main down side of the opposite simultaneous solutions approach is that the countries who have brought covid under control through cutting off personal contacts and human to human exposure are left with a huge challenge when trying to keep all goods and people who enter from places that have gone the other way from getting in too easily, before they are properly examined, and declared checked and clean.

Mobsters, now, in 2025 are being caught very soon after any sort of bank robbery, human smuggling, abduction, extortion ring or other robbery. They sure try to evade the track downs system by selling off their stolen goods quickly, or with a long flight to a new identity in another continent, but thanks to some very high-tech face recognition, finger print and DNA recognition software, a newly globalised system of tracked money, interlinked CCTV cameras and a wide use of covert recordings, we are catching them quicker than ever, with better evidence than ever, which is winning wide support, even from those who at first objected to being surveillanced at all.

A bunch of new trade agreements have been struck worldwide, with a World Trade Organisation system ensuring that every kind of trade deal on the table anywhere in the world is made available as an opt-in for a bilateral add-on deal everywhere else too, so this has helped to link up the achievements made by each regional trans-org locally at first, now going global. It means that goods and services are now widely available internationally, with a good list of options on everyone's menu now, along with a good variety of impartial examiners who can warn a person, organisation, council, department or company when they are about to order something that does not work in the reliable way the seller presents it.

The whole of Europe has long had a general right for all non-migrants and non-x-convict EU citizens to roam freely all across all of the continent. This is now being expanded to a nearly global new expanded mega-alliance deal, called the Atlantopacific, under which people who come from areas where the main language used, before the global convergence into globalese, used to be any European, Japanese, Korean, Malaysian, Australian, North American, Slavic, Latin American, Celtic, indigenous, Spanish or British language can now move freely between all of these wonderful vast areas, though there are a few special limit restriction exceptions retained, such as a limit on the number of people moving to North America from Central America and the number of people moving from Urdu and Arabic speaking areas to cities that have suffered from terrorist attacks.

This goes alongside an existing agreement on the free travel of goods, services, finance and labour, from which all these regions have been benefitting for some time, achieving lower food, appliances and building material prices, more choice and far higher standards of living as a result.

Realising they have been left out, the Asian, African, Turkish and Arab regions have struck a massive free trade deal with each other, allowing all kinds of commerce, lending, investing and know-how borrowing to occur right across all these areas. They are also about to bring out a free movement of people agreement, with each area only to limit the number of new arrivals from two of its neighbouring states, and not to anyone else. A mega-link-up between this and the Atlantopacific free trade agreement has just recently been reached, creating a global free trade zone that will help the system of aspiring ambitious and growing companies from warmer and colder countries find many new clients elsewhere in the world, bringing about a much better-served world population overall who has a much-improved choice now when it comes to buying anything it is thinking of buying.

There are still many issues around the African-born visionary ideas of a worldwide free-movement of people deal, as we have fiercely guarded quotas limiting the number of people (other than top doctors, artists, sportsmen, engineers, scientists, school principals, IT experts, architects, TV-show makers, nurses, carers and other listed shortage area members) who may migrate to Europe, Siberia, Oceania, North America, East Asia, wider Turkey, North Africa, South Africa, South America, the Caribbean and West Asia at present, and these rules vary widely from one destination province, state or borough to another.

But all this is under review, and a fairer way is destined to be found soon, under which people will at least be able to visit the area they have always wanted to visit most for a few weeks, and if they still love it as much as they thought they would, they will at least be able to sign up for a temporary guest worker's work permit for this destination, if they have a clean criminal record and the local knowledge, for ten years. Then, if this is not renewed, they can either go somewhere else they have always been interested in next or return to where they lived before until retirement and then return to their top pick place to live permanently.

The rise of Nigel Farage, Boris Johnson, Donald Trump, and some other narrow-minded bozo in Hungary, Turkey, Belarus and elsewhere is not such a big news story in reality A. For a start, they could only ever govern over an area with a population of less than 1 million, the international bodies would never let people like this work in them, and they all have powers that are also limited by a number of rule-enforcement and electoral-promise enforcement bodies. as well as by the wider legislature itself too.

Tighter new immigration restrictions are on the rise, as a result of the few recent and tragic terrorist attacks in Kabul, Bagdad and Paris, but a growing shortage of people to do the dirty and hard jobs is making the most restrictive cities and areas reconsider how many places of origin to keep on the most restricted list. And so most places have recently put a long list of places or origin on the totally unrestricted list for a few years on a trial basis, while also ensuring that the most dangerous people and ideologies can come nowhere near their lovely cities, and that a few top applicants from all other areas are also allowed to come and work in their first preference destination for a ten-year trial period.

Most of the locations who, in the 1990s, 2000s, 2021s and 2020s decided to quit their interregional agreement or just its free trade element, or to quit the UN, have since changed their mind, and the effects of missing out on the security, the shared resources, the extra low tariff trade, the joint working on fighting crime and the many other benefits have made nearly all such areas decide to rejoin the eurotranspacific agreement, to rejoin their trans-reg body, and to rejoin the UN. Some are even rejoining the old Southeast North America Confederacy. In fact, as the UN anti-pollution, anti-gangster, anti recession and disease eradication programmes are only going to work as well as they ought to work if every person and area takes part. It is not unlikely that the UN will soon decide to make unjoining some of its action areas an option that no longer exists.

After all, letting a few rich selfish narrow-minded people, somewhere, who refuse to pay a single penny toward making the whole world so much better for everyone, opt to pay no taxes at all toward keeping the entire planet alive, inhabitable, safe, clean, salvageable, and in order for their families' and for everyone's benefit is not something you could say they don't benefit heavily from.

And making the paying of the low but crucial taxes that make saving the planet happen optional is almost like giving up on making anything good ever happen. Letting the richest opt-out of paying toward making it happen would be the same as abolishing all forms of cooperation, including roads, waste collection and the police overnight. So maybe it's finally time to use the world's biggest army, now firmly in the hands of the UN, to make it clear that you can choose between a lot of courses of action, and between a lot of different policy, appointments, law variations, schemes, partnerships and a to a lot of different solutions to various social issues, but you can not opt to no longer be part of this planet, where the air we breathe and the water in our rain clouds and in our oceans is common to us all.

Just a brief note to say that a lot of team sports and individual sports have scheduled a lot of brilliantly planned and well-presented truly exciting events soon, from rugby to baseball, from chess to handball, from volleyball to basketball, and from golf to tennis (and many others!). Each of them is open to all, and each of them has a number of trophies available to those with fewer resources to throw behind their team too.

The next FIFA world cup will go to either Croatia or to South Holland, in two days' time, which will try its best to be as great a treat for all the viewers of the world as the Sao Paolo versus Wales showdown we had last time around was, or the Lombardy versus Zambia finale in last year's global opportunity cup, or as last week's UEFA Champions Cup final between Atletico Madrid and Manchester City. Regardless of what happens on the night, we just know that it is the millions of spectators all around the world who will win, as the whole thing will be broadcasted on so many channels worldwide that it will be easy to channel hop away from all the adverts.

Going forward, the challenges are many and great:

How do we bring in the lowest carbon emissions form of car engine ever to be invented worldwide, without making the company who had it first and who patented it lose out?

Surely we award it's key people a tax-funded reward and compensation payment that is almost equal to what is stands to lose by us letting hundreds of other companies all over the world simultaneously (and very soon) roll out their own quicker, cheaper and more intelligently and high-quality maintaining mass-produced copies of the best product. This is fair, and it is right. We cannot wait 75 or 150 years for all patents and copyrights to expire before bringing in the best functioning car engine systems with the lowest pollution emission levels worldwide, so this is roughly what to do, and we have to do it in the way the world's smartest people recommend we do it. A similar process is needed also in boiler/furnace production, in loft insulation production, in HVAC production and in the regulation of all forms of industrial fumes and waste, as well as with garden and household waste and recycling initiatives, water purification systems and in all other forms of infrastructure improvement too. Only by rolling out the very best way ever found everywhere in the world do we get everyone the best outcome they deserve.

How do we bring in the cleanest form of electricity production worldwide?

It's not a quick and easy roll-out, but with the guidance of some really smart, devoted, impartial people acting on our behalf, we can get there soon.

How do we improve the rehabilitation of x-offenders who have been committing crimes both before and after prison? This too requires the entire planet getting its most intelligent people to work together in trialling and evaluating the 300+ ways it could be handled and then making sure that the truly most effective, affordable, results-achieving and ethical solutions are gradually identified and rolled out where they are most needed.

How do we bring support for the new world government and for the new world language, army and regulators up to the target levels of 99.99%, or up a little closer to these levels anyway, quickly, before there are riots and uprisings of those who do not understand that this is all for the best for all of them?

This requires tackling disinformation and fake-news stories. Most of the mass-panic we have found is based on people saying things that are not true, which is hard to regulate well. We advise rolling out some very small fines that do not decimate anyone, do not turn us into tyrants and do not leave those who do harm fully unpunished either. Most people don't realise what is true and what is not true, and that's a problem we will struggle ever to fully solve, but it will help to make the right answer more easily found in internet searches and in libraries. We must always encourage people to remain sceptical and to learn they are not being forced to trust anything. In the end, they will only carry on believing a small number of lies and untruths anyway, which does not do us much harm, and which is the human way, the way of a planet full of varieties and of different philosophies, ideologies and hobbies and interests, each of which are to flourish in a perfect world.

How do we help people who are rolling out good new and old products to get the importation, sale and health system coverage process ok'd by the regular of more countries more quickly and easily in a world with thousands of independent jurisdictions and countries? This needs to be facilitated by all the trans-regional bodies, as well as by the voluntary opt-in partnership buying alliances, but it cannot ever be made compulsory for any entity to forego its powers to block something it deems as harmful from getting into its country. Much to the contrary, if something is harmful, high-risk, addictive, dangerous, a bad influence or non-functional, we should let all the other trans-regional bodies know about this too, so they can also take action to protect all their regions full of good people too.

How do we get the best vaccines and the best medicine out to everyone who needs them? This requires a lot of cooperation, collusion, pooling of powers, resources, intelligence and capabilities. It also requires competition and evaluation, and the winners of the competition need to be rewarded well, while we also ensure that all parts of the world who need a form of medicine, a vaccine or a cure or prevention tactic do get given access to it, including the chance to borrow the money to fund the rolling out of the best solution for all programmes, and everything that goes with it.

How do we best democratise the world government, without letting it become a vicious rule by one faction who hates the other factions and refuses to help their main causes kind of system? This is a very good and difficult question, and one that requires some brilliant minds to make some deep evaluative comparisons between a number of particularly good specific nitty-gritty proposals. I would strongly hope to see something built into each of the winning proposals that ensures that the people of each and every country in the world who disagree with the views of the world leader are allowed to try out their other solution ideas instead, for a while.

I also hope to see a system in use that gives maybe 100 political parties and alliances of parties from all over the world some proportional voting power and say in this virtual world legislature, and that gives the candidates for the top head of budget-setting and government posts a round-robin voting system (not one that costs more to run than current systems), under which the ultimate winner has to beat all of his opponents in A or B and A or C type two option head to heads, attaining more 50+% vote wins in head-to head one group against another votes than any other group gets. In the end, we cannot have any one country rule over another, and no one faction may ever become so strong as to harm the others. Instead, we need to make it a world where any truly good new ideas do indeed succeed in winning over the panels of experts who then in turn recommend to the voters of the world to back these bringers of good new ideas, as well as those others who also find a place for the good solution ideas to be tried out in their plans as well.

How do we eradicate the mafias, arms-traders, the espousers of terrorism and the drug cartels? This requires a lot of bullet-proofing and a lot of intelligence. Once we have gathered all the intel, at whatever price it takes and offering all the rewards and sentence reductions we needed to, we can then take them out by converting each participating member of these criminal organisations into a 'good dad and good worker' type person who gets all his income from legal mainstream professions instead. If we find that the only way to ever achieve this is to remove cash worldwide and make all transactions electronically traceable, then this is what we must do. When the battle has been fully won, I hope and believe that it will become clear that it was all worth doing.

In all of these, there are a number of good solutions already, and by trying them all out in a wise way that then learns which are best and rolls them out all over the world, we can achieve the 100% optimal outcome that everyone in the reader's world (B) will keep on promising but will never deliver. Only a world unity cooperation system in which all options are on the table and are examined before we decide which the best solution is can take us to the best possible of worlds.

Exploring each of the 8 main systemic options again and working out what to expect if this is the most commonly chosen way:

A lottery drawing is held to determine which 1% (for QFs) and which 3% of polling stations (for SFs) to activate in each of the preliminary rounds, with the affected voters notified with two weeks' notice to make their decision carefully, plus a lottery drawing also determines each option's opponent and its position in overall the 8-option overall tournament of systemic menu options. The 8 options the voters have in this process (A to H) are basically summarised as: one recent year of the way the nation was set up is chosen and defined as one kind of destination the province could go back to if it chooses to abandon the five-party process and the multiparty democracy idea and to return to the "old way" (G).

Options A and B give the power to choose a different outcome in legal, financial, tax and spend and policy decisions to the towns, villages, workers' councils, communes and districts above the provinces, decentralising the final say on most questions, limiting the national budget to a maximum 6.1% of GDP. These two options, A & B are also different from each other in that A places the power to overrule others and to decide, impose and harmonise in the provincial and in the national centre, while the other, B empowers the locality to make its own decisions. These options are frequent winners in the first century of the 8-option systemic revisions, but when people start realising that one-party majorities are rarely good for the people they serve, modified versions start being picked instead, under which less power is up for grabs and less meddling from corporate lobbyists is possible. That's when things truly improve.

Three of the 8 constitutional ballot options (C, D & E) are three different unique new forms of change and speeds of change toward multiparty democracy, as described in this book: one (C) intends to keep the province in a five party system forever, one (D) intends to allow ten specially created other people's parties (be they a collection of companies, NGOs, individuals chosen by interselection, by lottery or by IQ tests) to function and compete within it too, and a fifth option (E) intends to allow all other independent and oppositional movements to go onto the ballot too, gradually opening the doors to hundreds of possible new challenger parties, groupings, movements and one-man bands who may decide to try and emerge, grow and win, and three of the eight ballot options (F & H) are devoted to three chosen other countries whose system is to be copied as closely as possible. These three countries are chosen by the 35 paid "oversight process delegates" among the 200 nations of the earth now or among any past set-up that any country has ever had or any provinces that have found something good first.

The international advisers have added a recommendation to the 35 organising delegates to please make sure that one of the chosen options (F) should use proportional representation (with or without a qualifying cut-off threshold and with or without regionalised seat compartments) at the legislative level, or to transition from PR over to round-robin. One of the other options should be to use single seat constituencies (G), and one (H) should use round-robin votes (with or without a split into the top few and a qualifying bracket) or a single transferrable vote system. Any one of the 35 delegates may submit a suggested formulation for each of the 8 ballot options, while the full 35 delegate assembly then has a week to study each of the submissions and to choose the best one of the suggested option wordings for each of the 8 ballot options A to H.

Basically it turns out that the voters seem to prefer to keep it simple, at first, but over the years, they realise that one of the more

complex, pluralistic and interselection-based solutions will deliver a way better outcome, and so we end up seeing more and more of

the world adopting a system that uses year-of-birth-based political parties along with some of the 15-seat gatherings of professions ideas

as ways that turn out to work better for them all-round. They also learn the hard way that leaving out restrictions to the powers you give

to the largest party always ends up becoming something you regret, as power is always abused, whenever it is given over to any grouping without attaching a sensible set of restrictions, rules of behaviour, policing and enforcement, and follow-ups to investigate whether what is being delivered

matches what was promised.

Often such systems are abandoned, something else is rolled out after a very charismatic

and convincing leader argues for one of the other systems to be adopted, but 50 years later, the voters usually realise that the best way forward

does involve having interselection-based solutions, ransels, quotas, IQ-selection methods, ballots of ten or more parties competing

for the main positions in a round-robin system of so many simultaneous head-to-heads, while all the smaller movements compete on

ballot section B to become a main section option next time around.

Bringing in a world government too: Due to the threats to the planet, as well as pollution international crime, migration, droughts, people trafficking and military conflict, we ended up agreeing to replace the majority of what has until now been done. While some may always be scared of it, the simple fact it that only a world government can employ the most effective solution to the world's biggest problems in a way that truly solves the problem. No other set-up would truly make use of the full range of tools and approaches the world has to tackle an issue in the wisest and most appropriate way, while also spreading the cost of the action well across the entire world and not just between the three biggest donors, which is not fair on them.

Conclusion: There are many complex pros and cons to having big strong country states, and the world is still a good place, also in our reality, sort-of, and overall, considering the many things that have been but invented, dreamed up, designed, rolled out and built in the world we live in, but overall, on balance, it is the author's view that the world will be a significantly better place if and when the powers of the many big countries are all taken away from them and given out to localities, provinces, towns, continent-wide partnerships for peace, progress and development and to a truly "of the people" global element.

Hatred and hostility, the very substance of the nationalists, is the perfect way to keep on starting new wars, keep on letting international agreements break down, and keep on turning migration into a perceived problem. Much of what nationalists say and think is, on its own, something you and I can agree with, in the reality we currently live in, but the world would be a so much better place if we could remove all the antagonising biases that come with having national languages, national media, national curriculums, national legal systems and national governments.

I strongly hope that by reading this book, and others like it, the world can come to realise what the problem with the current system is, and how to describe the improved way that we could seek to have instead. It won't be easy, and it will take more than one law to be passed to get there, but if there is a rational brain at work inside our leaders' heads, it's not impossible to move in the right direction and to end up, one distant day, in the utopia we would like to choose for ourselves.

Plurality and simultaneously different flourishing utopias and solutions are missing in our world, and so is the convincing big solution to our world's big, big enduring problems. Please, people of our earth, let's bring out a new global united front that can smash our problems to bits, while letting all that is good and manyfold, like our infinitely wide array of hobbies and interests, flourish so much better.

What we did not achieve: There is still poverty, violence, theft, bullying, cheating, pollution, anger, discrimination, misogyny, nationalism and illness in the world. We may be applying better informed responses to all these issues, reducing the severity and the impact of all these, while also offering the victims better support than ever before, but so far no grouping of ballot options has managed to make any of these unfortunate elements of the human condition into complete extinction.

Trolling too, bragging, guilt-trips, show-offs and whinging all still persist. AND there are a lot of people in this world who are NOT allowed to live in the country of their choosing because their applications have been rejected or have not had any reply at all.

Green card lotteries mean that the losing majority is not allowed to pay any tax at all. How crazy is that!!!!

What we did achieve: A far better world that keeps on finding more and more ways to improve yet further and implementing them. That's a truly happy end! Also, the threat of war and of political imprisonment are hugely reduced, as the genuineness of all these new improvements has started to sink in.

Have a good life, dear readers! I love you all!!!!

Best Wishes,

Joseph Oakwood

And Now For the Sequel:

The Great Apocalyse of 2023

Told from No Less than Five Points of View at Once

In the interest of point of view sharing, fairness and equality, we have opted to alternate frequently between them, so we can keep track of all the goings on.

Let us not end with a sad note. Humanity has messed the planet up, behaved terribly, and paid the price. Humanity has also saved a good number of gentle, cute, fury earth species in its ambitious space programs, plus one day, centuries from now, the earth, too, shall bloom again.

And some crazy dreams came true in those last mad days; it was not all bad for all of our characters, especially not for Keith, Greg, Ollie and Sara. They all showed tremendous courage and compassion, a capacity to plan ahead and a determination to do all they could to make the most of their final days. I think we can be proud of all of them. I also commend the way that, in the very end, the women finally found empowerment, and put the males into devotional subordinate positions.

Had it not been for the nuclear strikes, the future would have been bright for all, well, for a few more centuries, before the accumulation of pollution, plastic and emissions wrecks what is left of the planet. And given that none of them were destined to survive the 35-year fallout period, or even to know that this was going to be the minimum length of time they would have to stay away from the surface of the world, we can close somewhat pleased that each one found joy in something very special in their final days.

Ollie has managed to defeat two of the guardians of the royals in a messy and exhausting struggle. But three more of his farmer's militia goons are dead. The jiu jitsu is brutal! And full of desperation! No fancy footwork, just arm chokes, desperate full-force furniture whacks and hard thumps to any body part they could get to, taking their toll on both camps. What a mess! What mayhem! What carnage!

Keith's body was already cold and discarded. They had thrown it onto a massive pile in the back corridor's cell blocks. He was down and out. He died in the belief that he was saving his dream girl and giving her a treat. Greg's much messier and still warm body was now being carried away to the same pile. Well, actually he was on a trolley, pulled along by his femme fatale. It made no difference if he was fully dead or not. Any re-arise-ers would be shot in the routine morning sweep.

The angels of death girls were working long hours and giving it their all, as they knew that only those with the very highest scores were going to be invited into the survival chambers come next week. What they did not know was that by next week a fatal dose of radiation will have built up inside them, not enough to kill them straight away, but enough to mean that 35 years of lurking in a bunker, alive, was not going to happen, unfortunately.

Poor Kate is now in a death-choke hold sleeper grip move that the pretty royal princess herself is administering – her hands are trapped under the side of a piano and of no use – will anyone come to her rescue? Or is this the end of another one of our main characters?

Sara manages to finish her intruder off, and to seal her bunker. She does so with her female friends, a rope, a shoe, a sock, and lot of womanly hands pressing down on their target's mouth, for a long time. "It took 25 minutes of time and a whole lot of energy to finish him off. But he's no longer a threat now, the bastard!" concluded Sara. She looked around for other invaders, saw none, and threw some camouflage and some old junk up to make the area look like just a small patch of trees with nothing worth having under them.

Ollie tries hard to save Kate from the hold she was in, and he would have made it too, had it not been for the gun-fire of the newly arriving militia, now making their move, now that all their opponents were sitting ducks, and Ollie's back was their very first target in the lair. Just as the defeat of the royal family and their entourage was within grasping proximity, the arrival of these gunmen that nobody knew were coming was the death of Ollie, who took several bullets and fell, bleeding to death on the bunker floor. Most of the others, and all the militia men soon followed, as this other militia was now going to be replacing all these residents. They might make an exception for the pretty pregnant princess though, carrying the heir to the throne, as she will have her uses, they thought.

Soon after Ollie, Kate too was sadly shot, and so were the royals. All apart from the pretty princess, who worth keeping. The mysterious late arrivals were in such a hurry to get yet more supplies in, the dead bodies out, and to seal themselves in that they did not take time to get rid of the last two of the bodies. The following day, realising that it was going to be getting very smelly in there very soon, they decided to cook all the dead'uns for supper.

This was ok for protein and carbs, but it raised the CO levels in there, as they were cooking, and it also raised the amount of bone waste that they could not get rid of so easily now that they were sealed in. Then, another day later, they realised that the water supply system was broken or stuck, and so they had to open the hatch again, to try to fix it, while taking in all the deadly radiation they had been sheltering from. Sadly, this incident shortened their life span from years to weeks. They did all they could to nurse the royal princess back to health, and to turn her into their supreme leader, but then they all fell into rapid decline, and those last days were proper depressing like, as none of them had the strength left to nurse the others.

Sara did manage to wave goodbye to the outside world, take a deep breath, and to step inside her new home. The group of four worked together to double-check they had everything and to seal the door. From now on, they knew nothing about what is going on elsewhere. And they were all fully committed to surviving at all costs.

Two days later, Sara got so angry at the one male in there with her that he nearly died, at her unforgiving martial arts prowess-filled hands. He should have learned his lesson then, and turned into a faithful servant, but he didn't learn, and his terrible behaviour was wasting precious supplies at very unsustainable rates of consumption. He had failed to do what was expected of him, and he was of no use, the crappy excuse of a man that he had been! It was time to start keeping him tied up from now on, and to put him on minimum rations. If he struggled, she would have no choice but to KO him or worse.

Sara soon realised that her supplies were only good for a couple of years, and that her bunker might not be fully radiation-proof. So she decided to just make the most of each day she had left. She dived into her fantasy book world, while lying on her tied up man who had to keep really still. She loved these books, the world they were set in, and she analysed each line for hours, before reflecting on how to use this wisdom in raising these young'ens she had in with her. She was convinced she was pregnant, and so it was now ok to straddle squat smother her tied-up male out of existence, which happened at night. She had plans for getting rid of one or two of her other fellow co-residents as a way of making the supplies last longer. But it never came to this.

Not long thereafter, five weeks into her bunker-dwelling time, Sara started getting more and more consumed by the lack of a single living male in her 35-year den. She dreamt of stepping out and finding some fertile, handsome and not particularly strong guy nearby, who was dying like everyone else of the radiation, and of throwing him onto a car and having her way with him right out in the open, without saying a single word.

Sara was in her den for a good number of days, with the two girls who had turned up the previous day, living out their last days in girl chat, book talk, reminiscing, and dishing out as much mutual praise and encouragement as they could. But her lair was attacked several times more, and each time the girls, knowing that their door was by no means unbreakable, had to open the door, whack some half-dead sick zombified blokes into oblivion with shovels and planks of wood, maybe take one in with them if he was cute, submissive and weak enough to tie up, control and instruct (This happened twice!), and they lived out their den days in as much partnership, chatter, massages, good energy and sexual pleasure as they could possibly have, while the radiation was slowly killing them off in their sleep.

It started with these primal cravings and with the fantasies, including a worryingly sick fantasy to 'have some fun' with the face and body of an intruder man that the girls had just bludgeoned to death near the entrance to her cave. And it turned real when one of those who had been locked out of all the safe dens somehow arose from where he had fallen after an earlier invasion attempt and started banging frantically on the door and using a crowbar to rip it open.

This guy, and another one who turned up a week later, had their uses. Sara was lusting "after that male touch in her woman regions," and she failed to resist these urges for more than a day after she realised there were still good-looking boys alive out there, desperate for shelter, and willing and able to give her a good time in between book club chats and reminiscing sessions.

Sara always did it "her way" which involved her tying them up, just in case, with the girls nearby to help her kill them in the event of a struggle, which they knew and understood, and it involved Sara sleeping fully on top of them, both men, full weight, all night long, and then making them pleasure her with more body parts, from nose to mouth, from willy to toe to finger, and in more ways than I care to list. She never turned kind, and she never gave them a break, not even when they were covered all over the face in her juices and she was having a period and had a flatulent spell to boot. To object to whatever she wanted to do to you was to die, they thought, and they much preferred to keep on pleasuring her for now.

Half a year later, Sara and the last of the girls both faded away, all in the same night, in their sleep, in January 2024, with a let's do another book club night tomorrow last thought. They never found out about each other's similar timing. The last of her sex slaves died in the October before, of strangulation after a disagreement, and he even helped Sara get her legs around his throat so she could get rid of him when she had found that the supplies were running short, and that he had been secretly sneaking off with the forbidden snickers bars, and in his mind the women in the den were all preggers by now, and there just wasn't enough food left now so all of them could make it.

The voice that knows: Let us not end with a sad note. Humanity has messed the planet up, behaved terribly, and paid the price. Humanity has also saved a good number of gentle, cute, fury earth species in its ambitious space programs, plus one day, centuries from now, the earth, too, shall bloom again.

And some crazy dreams came true in those last mad days; it was not all bad for all of our characters, especially not for Keith, Greg, Ollie and Sara. They all showed tremendous courage and compassion, a capacity to plan ahead and a determination to do all they could to make the most of their final days. I think we can be proud of all of them. I also commend the way that, in the very end, the women finally found empowerment, and put the males into devotional subordinate positions. Had it not been for the nuclear strikes, the future would have been bright for all. And given that none of them were destined to survive the 35-year fallout period, or even to know that this was going to be the minimum length of time they would have to stay away from the surface of the world, we can close somewhat pleased that each one found joy in something very special in their final days. In a way, they had a better life than they would have had, had they spent 35 years bored to death in a tiny cramped den with terrible air quality and then come out to find nothing much out there that they can use to live on, other than ivy and dandelions.

It was better for them that they had human company and high quality supplies to live on right to the end. And it is better for the planet that it shall, from now on, be home only to plants, flowers, trees, cockroaches, woodlice, worms, squid, crabs, snails, ants, wasps, bats, flies, and coconuts, living happily in a world that does not seek to run them over, spray them with pesticides, squish them, shoot them, trap them, bury them under concrete, drown or electrocute them or expose them to death by dogs, cats or ferrets any more. And while earth, in this new form, flourishes again, so too does Europa, where the last mammals left, from a variety of small cute fur species, sent off on a routine mission that wasn't meant to be the final one, nibble without stress or danger on endless pastures, meadows, forests and wilderness. This is a happy ever after that carries true value, just not for those species who, like humans, did not make it. I hope you are able to see this too.

We are all likely to die in needless wars unless we have a trustworthy world government to sort out the planet. The ideal system will devote 1% of GDP globally to the world government and anything from 9% to 45% is assigned at province or district level, best off if 0% for the nation states (they only ever served one purpose and that was to hate all the others) and these to be scrapped totally / what if we had a world govt that tackles all the global problems from the envt and pollution to unfair play and orgzd crime and taxes are only 2% of GDP going to the world govt, only 0.1% of GDP going to national programmes and a full adjustable range from 9% up to 45% to be decided at local govt district level for all parts of the world, a level that is to be empowered to do all legislation, appointment, planning and budgetary progs for the big 5 areas health, education, justice, infrastructure development and the military, plus a decent very-low-interest lender to all etc the main message of the book is to be that while scenario A can only lead to wars, trade wars, unfair bullying actions, and inevitably nuclear apocalypse, life in B is rather nice for all.

And me, well, I have symbolically inserted my soul into one of the miniature capibara guinea pigs that went on the rocket that has taken us to a whole new world of nibbles and munchies, where there are no predators and no pick-up trucks to run us over. You may cry now if you like. I wonder if they have greengrocers where I'm going? And what sort of den shall we build there, you and I, in our happy new world? The world where all are friends who live in harmony.

Conclusion:

There are many complex pros and cons to having big strong country states, and the world is still a good place, also in our reality (B), sort-of, and overall, considering the many things that have been but invented, dreamed up, designed, rolled out and built in the world we live in, but overall, on balance, it is the author's view that the world will be a significantly better place if and when the powers of the many big countries are all taken away from them and given out to localities, provinces, towns, continent-wide partnerships for peace, progress and development and to a truly "of the people" global element.

Hatred and hostility, the very substance of the nationalists, is the perfect way to keep on starting new wars, keep on letting international agreements break down, and keep on turning migration into a perceived problem. Much of what nationalists say and think is, on its own, something you and I can agree with, in the reality we currently live in, but the world would be a so much better place if we could remove all the antagonising biases that come with having national languages, national media, national curriculums, national legal systems and national governments.

Plurality and simultaneously different flourishing utopias and solutions are missing in our world, and so is the convincing big solution to our world's big, big enduring problems. Please, people of our earth, let's bring out a new global united front that can smash our problems to bits, while letting all that is good and manyfold, like our infinitely wide array of hobbies and interests, flourish so much better.

At the end of the day we only have one life on this earth, and we may as well work together to make it as good as it can be. Why not band together to solve the big problems? It just seems crazy not to go ahead and get it done.